THE EVERYTHING LARGE-PRINT WORD SEARCH BOOK VOLUME 3

Dear Reader,

I go through several stages when solving a word search puzzle. At first glance, the letters appear to be random, but I know they're not. A few obvious words jump out, and then the searching begins. With a little concentration, a whole bunch of words are circled. The "aha" moments come quickly at this point, and it's hard to stop. The last few words usually drive me crazy; they're the ones that are diagonal and backward! Ultimately, I feel a nice sense of accomplishment when all the words are rounded up. The chaos of the grid has been overcome. Order rules!

If you love word search as much as I do, then I think you're going to enjoy this book. I've packed it full of puzzles that are easy on the eyes and fun for the brain. Each grid has a theme, and I cover a wide variety of interesting topics. I hope these puzzles are fun and relaxing for you!

Charles Timmerman

Welcome to the EVERYTHING® Series!

These handy, accessible books give you all you need to tackle a difficult project, gain a new hobby, comprehend a fascinating topic, prepare for an exam, or even brush up on something you learned back in school but have since forgotten.

You can choose to read an Everything® book from cover to cover or just pick out the information you want from our four useful boxes: e-questions, e-facts, e-alerts, and e-ssentials. We give you everything you need to know on the subject, but throw in a lot of fun stuff along the way, too.

We now have more than 400 Everything® books in print, spanning such wide-ranging categories as weddings, pregnancy, cooking, music instruction, foreign language, crafts, pets, New Age, and so much more. When you're done reading them all, you can finally say you know Everything®!

PUBLISHER Karen Cooper

DIRECTOR OF ACQUISITIONS AND INNOVATION Paula Munier

MANAGING EDITOR, EVERYTHING® SERIES Lisa Laing

COPY CHIEF Casey Ebert

ACQUISITIONS EDITOR Lisa Laing

EDITORIAL ASSISTANT Ross Weisman

EVERYTHING® SERIES COVER DESIGNER Erin Alexander

LAYOUT DESIGNERS Colleen Cunningham, Elisabeth Lariviere, Ashley Vierra, Denise Wallace

THE EVERYTHING® LARGE-PRINT WORD SEARCH BOOK

VOLUME 3

150 quick, fun, easy-on-the-eyes puzzles

Charles Timmerman
Founder of Funster.com

Adams Media
New York London Toronto Sydney New Delhi

adamsmedia

Adams Media
An Imprint of Simon & Schuster, Inc.
100 Technology Center Drive
Stoughton, MA 02072

Manufactured in the United States of America

15 2024

ISBN 978-1-4405-2737-1

Dedicated to

Suzanne, Calla, & Meryl

Acknowledgments

I would like to thank each and every one of the more than half a million people who have visited my website, *www.funster.com*, to play word games and puzzles. You have shown me how much fun puzzles can be and how addictive they can become!

It is a pleasure to acknowledge the folks at Adams Media who made this book possible. I particularly want to thank my editor, Lisa Laing, for so skillfully managing the many projects we have worked on together.

Contents

Introduction

The puzzles in this book are in the traditional word search format. Words in the list are hidden in the grid in any direction: up, down, forward, backward, or diagonally. The words are always found in a straight line, and letters are never skipped. Words can overlap. For example, the letters at the end of the word "MAST" could be used as the start of the word "STERN." Only the letters A to Z are used, and any spaces in an entry are removed. For example, "TROPICAL FISH" would be found in the grid as "TROPICALFISH." All punctuation marks, such as apostrophes and hyphens, are also omitted in the puzzles. Draw a circle around each word that you find in the grid. Then, cross the word off the list so that you will always know what words remain to be found.

A favorite strategy is to look for the first letter in a word, then see if the second letter is in any of the eight neighboring letters, and so on until the word is found. Or instead of searching for the first letter in a word, it is sometimes easier to look for letters that standout, like Q, U, X, and Z. Double letters in a word will also stand out and be easier to find in the grid. Another strategy is to simply scan each row, column, and diagonal, looking for any words.

Puzzles

ALTER
BACKSTITCH
BATTING
BINDING
BOBBIN
BUTTONHOLE
CLOTH
CUT
DARNING
DESIGN
EMBROIDERY
EYELET
FABRIC
GATHER
GUSSET
HEM
LINING
MACHINE
MATERIAL
NEEDLEWORK
PATCHWORK
PATTERN
PIN
PLEAT
POCKET
QUILTING
SCISSORS
SEAMSTRESS
SEWING
STITCHES
TACK
TAILOR
TECHNIQUES
THIMBLE
THREAD
TRIM
YARN

Sewing Circle

B	X	O	P	O	C	K	E	T	E	S	S	U	G
K	A	L	A	I	R	E	T	A	M	Y	T	N	N
H	R	C	E	L	B	M	I	H	T	E	I	I	I
D	T	O	K	F	A	B	R	I	C	T	T	B	N
A	R	O	W	S	V	R	A	H	T	P	C	B	I
E	Y	E	L	E	T	O	N	A	A	H	H	O	L
R	J	S	T	C	L	I	B	T	E	G	E	B	G
H	M	R	R	L	Q	D	T	M	L	A	S	P	N
T	A	O	A	U	A	E	E	C	O	T	T	L	I
D	C	S	E	R	R	R	P	E	H	H	A	E	W
E	H	S	N	N	I	Y	A	R	N	E	C	A	E
S	I	I	P	A	T	C	H	W	O	R	K	T	S
I	N	C	I	H	C	G	N	I	T	L	I	U	Q
G	E	S	N	S	E	A	M	S	T	R	E	S	S
N	R	O	L	I	A	T	C	Q	U	U	I	U	U
C	Q	L	G	N	I	D	N	I	B	B	C	M	A

Solution on Page 304

ALUMINUM
BANK
BRASS
BRONZE
CHANGE
COINAGE
COLLECTOR
COPPER
CURRENCY
DATE
HEADS
HISTORY
INFLATION
JAR
LIBERTY
LINCOLN
MEMORIAL
METAL
MINT
MONEY
ONE CENT
PRESIDENT
PROFILE
ROUND
SAVE
SERIES
SHIELD
SMALL
SPEND
STEEL
TAILS
TREASURY
USA
VALUE
WHEAT
YEAR
ZINC

Penny

T	J	Z	E	Q	Y	B	Q	E	U	L	A	V	Y
N	P	T	M	T	S	T	L	S	A	D	S	S	Z
E	Y	R	U	S	A	E	R	T	L	M	U	B	S
D	M	E	N	U	B	D	E	E	I	A	R	E	L
I	O	L	I	C	R	M	I	N	B	O	R	Y	I
S	N	H	M	O	A	H	T	M	N	I	N	A	A
E	E	F	U	I	S	H	N	Z	E	L	L	U	T
R	Y	U	L	N	S	F	E	S	B	L	O	Z	A
P	Q	Y	A	A	G	M	C	A	O	A	C	Q	E
J	P	R	H	G	T	R	E	N	D	M	N	R	H
A	R	O	R	E	A	I	N	M	I	S	I	K	W
R	O	T	C	E	L	L	O	C	O	Z	L	V	G
X	F	S	Y	V	P	Y	C	N	E	R	R	U	C
D	I	I	J	A	S	P	E	N	D	J	I	F	I
C	L	H	R	S	X	R	O	U	N	D	P	A	H
Q	E	G	N	A	H	C	F	C	S	T	E	E	L

Solution on Page 304

AGED
ANIMAL
BARN
BUCKET
BUTTERMILK
CALCIUM
CASEIN
CATTLE
CHEESE
CHURN
COWS
CURDS
FACTORY
FARMERS
FOOD
GOATS
GRASS
HARVESTING
HEALTHY
HEIFER
ICE CREAM
INDUSTRY
LACTOSE
LOW FAT
MANURE
MILKING
PASTURE
POWDER
PROCESSING
PRODUCTS
SKIMMED
UDDER
WHEY
WHOLE
YOGURT

Dairy

P	P	K	W	Y	V	U	E	U	V	F	H	X	R
W	O	P	M	X	O	I	F	D	D	O	O	F	E
H	W	M	I	L	K	I	N	G	E	C	C	O	D
O	D	H	E	A	L	T	H	Y	H	G	Q	C	D
L	E	I	G	N	I	T	S	E	V	R	A	H	U
E	R	U	N	A	M	A	E	R	C	E	C	I	C
F	A	R	M	E	R	S	C	Y	E	H	W	P	H
G	N	I	S	S	E	C	O	R	P	G	R	A	S
C	L	V	F	R	T	X	A	T	C	O	W	S	W
A	S	A	A	E	T	M	L	S	D	H	A	T	B
T	T	A	M	F	U	N	A	U	E	R	U	U	A
T	A	N	V	I	B	M	C	D	G	I	C	R	R
L	O	F	C	E	N	T	T	N	N	K	N	E	N
E	G	L	W	H	S	A	O	I	E	L	S	B	L
F	A	C	T	O	R	Y	S	T	R	U	G	O	Y
C	U	R	D	S	L	D	E	M	M	I	K	S	E

Solution on Page 304

ALBUM
ATHLETE
BASEBALL
BOXING
BUBBLE GUM
CARTOONS
COLLECTOR
COMIC BOOK
CONDITION
EBAY
FLEER
FOIL
FOOTBALL
GAMES
GOLF
HOBBY
HOCKEY
IMAGE
MINT
PACK
PAPERBOARD
PERSON
PICTURE
PLAYERS
PRISTINE
RACING
RARE
ROOKIE
SCARCITY
SELL
SETS
SPORTS
STATISTICS
TELEVISION
TOPPS
TRADING
UPPER DECK
VALUABLE
WRAPPER

Trading Cards

K	D	R	F	O	I	L	E	I	K	O	O	R	S
C	S	C	O	N	D	I	T	I	O	N	R	C	G
A	T	A	O	T	E	L	E	V	I	S	I	O	N
P	R	T	T	R	C	S	P	P	O	T	L	R	I
Y	O	H	B	A	S	E	L	L	S	F	L	A	X
E	P	L	A	D	P	D	L	I	K	D	A	C	O
K	S	E	L	I	I	R	T	L	O	G	B	I	B
C	C	T	L	N	C	A	M	Y	O	U	E	N	L
O	A	E	E	G	T	O	U	B	B	C	S	G	A
H	R	L	D	S	U	B	B	B	C	A	A	W	S
P	C	B	A	R	R	R	L	O	I	R	B	R	R
E	I	A	Z	E	E	E	A	H	M	T	M	A	E
R	T	U	R	E	G	P	E	D	O	O	I	P	Y
S	Y	L	B	U	E	A	P	L	C	O	N	P	A
O	G	A	M	E	S	P	M	U	F	N	T	E	L
N	Y	V	R	A	R	E	N	I	T	S	I	R	P

Solution on Page 304

ASSET
BANKS
BONDS
BUSINESS
CAPITAL
COMMODITY
DEPOSIT
DIVIDENDS
DOW
ECONOMY
FINANCIAL
FUNDS
FUTURES
GAINS
GOLD
INCOME
INTEREST
LAND
LOAN
LOSS
MARGIN
MARKET
MONEY
OPTIONS
PENSION
PERCENTAGE
PRINCIPAL
PROFIT
PROPERTY
PURCHASE
RETURNS
RISK
SAVINGS
SECURITY
SELL
SILVER
STOCK
TIME
TRADE
VALUE

Financial Investment

S	N	I	A	G	K	Q	Z	L	S	D	N	O	B
S	E	I	C	P	Q	C	A	P	I	T	A	L	S
G	D	L	G	E	U	P	O	V	P	I	T	F	I
N	A	O	L	R	I	R	I	T	L	F	T	U	L
I	T	S	W	C	A	D	C	A	S	O	I	T	V
V	Z	S	N	E	E	M	I	H	B	R	S	U	E
A	D	I	Y	N	P	C	O	U	A	P	O	R	R
S	R	L	D	T	N	E	S	N	F	S	P	E	E
P	E	S	O	A	I	I	N	T	E	R	E	S	T
E	B	C	N	G	N	D	I	S	I	Y	D	K	U
U	L	I	U	E	R	N	O	S	I	M	Z	N	R
L	F	A	S	R	C	W	K	M	A	O	E	A	N
A	U	S	N	O	I	T	P	O	M	N	N	B	S
V	N	S	M	D	Y	T	R	E	P	O	R	P	W
F	D	E	D	A	R	T	Y	P	Q	C	C	H	B
Z	S	T	T	J	K	M	A	R	K	E	T	G	S

Solution on Page 305

AIRWAVES
ANTENNA
AUDIENCE
BAND
BBC
BROADCAST
CABLE FM
CHANNEL
DIAL
FCC
FREQUENCY
INTERNET
LISTENER
MICROPHONE
MODULATION
MUSIC
NETWORKS
NPR
ON AIR
PROGRAM
PUBLIC
RADIO
RECEIVER
RECEPTION
SATELLITE
SHORTWAVE
SIGNAL
SIMULCAST
SIRIUS
STATIONS
TALK
TOWER
TRANSMIT
TUNER

Radio Broadcasting

I	M	R	T	R	A	N	S	M	I	T	A	L	K
S	R	U	A	S	T	A	T	I	O	N	S	Q	P
H	E	F	S	I	M	U	L	C	A	S	T	N	Q
O	N	S	R	I	N	T	E	R	N	E	T	S	B
R	E	I	L	E	C	A	E	O	T	D	N	A	B
T	T	G	R	A	Q	V	S	P	E	P	A	T	C
W	S	N	R	U	I	U	H	H	N	U	U	E	N
A	I	A	V	E	I	D	E	O	N	R	D	L	E
V	L	L	C	R	F	P	I	N	A	C	I	L	T
E	O	E	I	D	E	T	J	E	C	Q	E	I	W
S	R	S	E	V	A	W	R	I	A	Y	N	T	O
R	O	U	E	L	N	O	I	T	P	E	C	E	R
Q	A	N	U	Z	V	V	R	T	O	W	E	R	K
A	P	D	A	M	F	E	L	B	A	C	C	F	S
R	O	Y	I	I	C	H	A	N	N	E	L	I	C
M	A	R	G	O	R	P	U	B	L	I	C	Z	L

Solution on Page 305

BRAND
BROTH
CANS
CASSEROLE
CHICKEN
CHUNKY
CONDENSED
COOK
CRACKERS
CREAM
EAT
FOOD
HEALTHY
HOME
KIDS
KITCHEN
LABELS
MEAL
MMM GOOD
MUSHROOM
NOODLE
POP ART
PRODUCTS
RED
RICE
SALT
SODIUM
SOUP
STOCK
TOMATO
VARIETY
VEGETABLE
WARHOL
WHITE

Campbell's Soup

D	B	W	V	D	M	Y	C	U	N	H	D	H	C
R	S	U	V	I	K	S	Y	Y	R	E	D	D	R
M	S	O	D	N	O	O	D	L	E	I	M	M	L
S	A	D	U	D	V	P	R	O	D	U	C	T	S
H	J	H	I	P	M	E	A	L	S	X	R	E	D
N	C	U	K	K	L	E	G	H	D	W	E	N	H
E	M	A	T	L	A	S	R	E	K	C	A	R	C
H	N	L	S	T	D	O	S	F	T	R	M	V	O
C	E	E	E	S	O	N	O	U	B	A	C	N	O
T	K	A	J	M	E	X	H	T	O	R	B	J	K
I	C	F	L	D	P	R	L	L	A	B	E	L	S
K	I	O	N	T	D	O	O	G	M	M	M	X	E
K	H	O	M	E	H	J	P	L	K	C	O	T	S
T	C	D	Y	R	V	Y	T	A	E	D	E	T	I
D	S	N	A	C	U	C	V	A	R	I	E	T	Y
I	G	W	V	X	Z	J	W	H	I	T	E	N	Y

Solution on Page 305

ANATOMY
ANCIENT
ANIMALS
BIOLOGY
BIRDS
BONES
DATING
DINOSAURS
DISCOVERY
DNA
EARTH
ECOSYSTEM
EROSION
EVOLUTION
EXPERIMENT
EXTINCTION
FISH
FOSSILS
FUNGI
GEOLOGY
HUMAN
JURASSIC
LAB
LIFE
MESOZOIC
MUSEUM
OCEAN
ORGANISMS
PALEOZOIC
REPTILES
RESEARCH
ROCKS
SCIENTIST
SITE
STUDY
TAXONOMY
TRIASSIC

Paleontology

C	B	I	O	L	O	G	Y	D	U	T	S	A	B
I	M	U	S	E	U	M	S	L	A	M	I	N	A
O	N	O	I	S	O	R	E	S	E	A	R	C	H
Z	J	F	L	T	G	P	E	N	S	D	R	I	B
O	U	U	A	Q	L	H	A	P	H	N	W	E	S
E	R	N	B	R	T	M	N	T	T	O	S	N	S
L	A	G	S	R	U	A	S	O	N	I	D	T	L
A	S	I	A	H	G	I	T	O	E	T	L	G	I
P	S	E	N	N	T	R	I	C	M	U	S	E	S
C	I	E	I	N	I	T	O	E	I	L	K	O	S
A	C	T	E	A	C	S	F	A	R	O	C	L	O
N	A	I	S	N	Y	I	M	N	E	V	O	O	F
D	C	S	I	S	L	Y	Y	S	P	E	R	G	I
S	I	T	T	Y	M	O	N	O	X	A	T	Y	S
C	X	E	D	I	S	C	O	V	E	R	Y	T	H
E	M	E	S	O	Z	O	I	C	S	E	N	O	B

Solution on Page 305

BAR
BEAN BAG
BEDROOM
BENCHES
BOOKCASE
CABINET
COFFEE TABLE
COUCH
CREDENZA
CUPBOARDS
DAVENPORT
DRAWERS
DRAWING BOARD
DRESSERS
END TABLE
FOOTSTOOL
HEADBOARD
HOPE CHEST
HUTCH
LIVING ROOM
LOVE SEAT
METAL
NIGHTSTAND
OTTOMAN
PLASTIC
RECLINER
SEATING
SIDEBOARD
SOFA
TABLES
WARDROBE
WICKER
WOODEN

Furniture Types

B	T	N	W	Y	F	O	M	F	L	A	T	E	M
E	E	A	S	D	R	A	O	B	P	U	C	G	O
N	N	M	Q	A	W	O	O	D	E	N	D	T	O
C	I	O	B	H	T	O	R	S	A	R	A	P	R
H	B	T	U	S	K	A	G	Z	A	E	L	E	D
E	A	T	T	C	O	S	N	W	S	A	K	T	E
S	C	O	A	B	R	E	I	E	S	C	R	S	B
H	O	S	D	E	D	N	V	T	I	S	E	E	O
L	E	A	W	E	G	O	I	W	B	E	N	H	R
F	E	A	R	B	L	C	L	Z	E	L	I	C	D
H	R	C	O	F	F	E	E	T	A	B	L	E	R
D	N	A	T	S	T	H	G	I	N	A	C	P	A
T	R	O	P	N	E	V	A	D	B	T	E	O	W
D	R	E	S	S	E	R	S	K	A	D	R	H	W
A	F	O	S	E	A	T	I	N	G	N	J	E	N
C	O	U	C	H	D	R	A	O	B	E	D	I	S

Solution on Page 306

ARCHITECT
BIDDING
BRICK
BUILDINGS
BULLDOZER
CARPENTER
CONTRACTOR
CRANES
DELAYS
DESIGN
ENGINEER
EQUIPMENT
ERECT
EXECUTION
FOUNDATION
FRAME
HOUSES
JOB
LABORER
LAND
LOGISTICS
MANAGER
MATERIALS
PLANNING
PROJECT
PROPERTY
SAFETY
SITE
SKYSCRAPER
STEEL
STONE
STRUCTURE
TRADE
WOOD
WORKERS

Construction

C	A	R	P	E	N	T	E	R	S	U	N	C	G
F	R	A	M	E	P	S	P	R	G	S	G	N	E
S	C	W	M	S	R	K	K	E	N	E	I	E	R
R	H	O	V	C	O	Y	C	E	I	D	S	M	E
E	I	O	N	I	P	S	I	N	D	A	E	A	G
K	T	D	A	T	E	C	R	I	L	R	D	T	A
R	E	T	N	S	R	R	B	G	I	T	J	E	N
O	C	N	O	I	T	A	D	N	U	O	F	R	A
W	T	E	I	G	Y	P	C	E	B	C	E	I	M
H	C	M	T	O	T	E	L	T	R	Z	R	A	S
O	E	P	U	L	E	R	D	A	O	I	E	L	Y
U	J	I	C	B	F	N	N	D	N	R	C	S	A
S	O	U	E	K	A	E	L	S	L	N	T	T	L
E	R	Q	X	L	S	L	E	E	T	S	I	O	E
S	P	E	E	R	U	T	C	U	R	T	S	N	D
W	Z	L	A	B	O	R	E	R	S	I	T	E	G

Solution on Page 306

ADDRESS
BLOG
BROWSER
BUSINESS
CLICK
COMPUTER
CONTENT
DESIGN
DOCUMENT
DOMAIN
EBAY
EMAIL
FACEBOOK
FORUM
GAMES
GOOGLE
HOMEPAGE
HOST
HTML
HTTP
HYPERLINK
IMAGES
INTERNET
LINKS
NETWORK
NEWS
ONLINE
PLAIN TEXT
SEARCH
SERVER
SITE
SOCIAL
URL
VIDEOS
VISIT
WEB PAGES
WWW

On the Web

W	D	G	U	B	R	T	H	F	Z	X	N	Q	E
D	E	Z	O	L	Y	H	E	T	P	E	Z	G	Y
H	T	M	C	O	N	T	E	N	T	X	A	A	V
S	E	M	A	G	G	M	N	W	R	P	B	U	I
M	S	O	C	I	A	L	O	I	E	E	L	Y	S
U	S	K	N	I	L	R	E	M	A	R	T	R	I
R	E	K	S	M	K	D	O	C	U	M	E	N	T
O	G	N	S	G	S	H	S	P	L	T	O	F	I
F	A	C	E	B	O	O	K	S	U	I	U	D	O
H	M	K	N	I	L	R	E	P	Y	H	C	N	Q
C	I	R	I	U	D	G	M	D	S	K	L	K	D
R	D	E	S	A	A	O	H	S	I	I	W	E	P
A	K	V	U	P	C	A	O	W	N	V	S	W	S
E	F	R	B	R	O	W	S	E	R	I	W	I	G
S	S	E	R	D	D	A	T	N	G	W	T	G	Y
J	W	S	S	P	L	A	I	N	T	E	X	T	E

Solution on Page 306

AMERICA
BUSINESS
BUYING
CAPITALIST
CONSUMER
COST
CREDIT
DEMAND
DESIRE
ECONOMY
GOODS
INDUSTRY
MALL
MARKETING
MONEY
PACKAGING
PEOPLE
PRODUCTS
PROFIT
PURCHASING
RETAIL
RIGHTS
SELL
SERVICES
SHOPPING
SOCIETY
SPEND
STATUS
STORE
SUPPLY
TRADE
WANT
WASTE
WEALTH

Consumerism

Y	M	J	G	N	I	S	A	H	C	R	U	P	G
P	L	Z	R	P	A	C	K	A	G	I	N	G	X
Z	B	P	S	H	O	P	P	I	N	G	T	P	G
T	U	J	P	G	N	I	Y	U	B	D	Q	A	O
S	S	Y	K	U	T	U	N	N	Z	D	Q	U	O
G	I	T	W	A	S	T	E	D	E	M	A	N	D
H	N	E	L	D	N	E	P	S	U	T	A	T	S
R	E	I	S	E	R	V	I	C	E	S	Y	U	E
E	S	C	T	L	J	R	L	C	I	M	T	P	L
T	S	O	S	E	E	A	T	O	O	Z	P	R	L
A	J	S	X	C	K	M	O	N	E	Y	R	O	Y
I	S	T	H	G	I	R	O	S	A	W	O	D	R
L	T	Z	W	V	T	C	A	U	N	W	F	U	M
P	E	O	P	L	E	V	A	M	E	R	I	C	A
H	T	L	A	E	W	C	R	E	D	I	T	T	L
C	O	S	T	R	A	D	E	R	O	T	S	S	L

Solution on Page 306

ATOMS
CALCULUS
CONCEPTS
EINSTEIN
ELECTRON
ENERGY
EXPERIMENT
FORMULA
GAS
GRAVITY
LAWS
LIGHT
MAGNETISM
MASS
MATTER
MECHANICS
MOMENTUM
MOTION
NATURE
NEWTON
NUCLEAR
PARTICLES
PHENOMENA
PHYSICAL
QUANTUM
QUARKS
RELATIVITY
RESEARCH
SCIENTIST
SPEED
STUDY
TECHNOLOGY
THEORY
UNIVERSE
VELOCITY

Physics Class

E	S	R	E	V	I	N	U	C	L	E	A	R	W	
M	U	D	C	X	T	H	E	O	R	Y	M	D	R	
A	L	I	G	H	T	Y	T	I	C	O	L	E	V	
S	U	X	P	A	R	T	I	C	L	E	S	E	S	
S	C	I	E	N	T	I	S	T	U	D	Y	P	K	
N	L	P	Y	T	I	V	A	R	G	A	S	S	R	
O	A	H	G	S	C	I	N	A	H	C	E	M	A	
T	C	E	M	A	T	T	E	R	U	T	A	N	U	
W	I	N	H	C	R	A	E	S	E	R	K	S	Q	
E	S	O	Y	G	O	L	O	N	H	C	E	T	U	
N	Y	M	S	I	T	E	N	G	A	M	I	P	A	
E	H	E	X	P	E	R	I	M	E	N	T	E	N	
R	P	N	I	E	T	S	N	I	E	S	R	C	T	
G	L	A	W	S	E	L	E	C	T	R	O	N	U	
Y	N	O	I	T	O	M	U	T	N	E	M	O	M	
S	M	O	T	A	F	O	R	M	U	L	A	C	E	

Solution on Page 307

AUTOMATION
BLENDER
CAMCORDER
CAMERAS
CLEANING
CLOCKS
COMPACTOR
COOKING
DEVICES
DISHWASHER
DOMESTIC
DRYER
ELECTRICAL
FREEZER
HEATER
HOUSEHOLD
IRON
KITCHEN
LOAD
MACHINES
MAJOR
MECHANICAL
MICROWAVE
MIXER
OVENS
RANGE
REPAIR
SERVICE
SMALL
STOVE
TECHNOLOGY
TELEPHONE
TOASTER
WASHING

Home Appliance

S	D	A	O	L	A	C	I	N	A	H	C	E	M
S	K	C	O	L	C	S	T	O	V	E	N	S	G
G	N	I	N	A	E	L	C	I	H	D	Y	Y	N
N	N	E	H	C	T	I	K	T	R	L	G	R	I
I	R	E	X	I	M	U	M	A	J	O	R	E	K
H	F	X	R	R	R	S	N	M	L	H	U	T	O
S	R	B	E	T	E	G	Z	O	L	E	E	A	O
A	E	M	T	C	E	H	N	T	A	S	C	E	C
W	E	I	S	E	A	H	S	U	M	U	I	H	I
R	Z	C	A	L	C	M	S	A	S	O	V	D	T
E	E	R	O	E	J	K	C	E	W	H	R	N	S
P	R	O	T	C	A	P	M	O	C	H	E	O	E
A	N	W	B	L	E	N	D	E	R	I	S	R	M
I	S	A	R	E	M	A	C	F	P	D	V	I	O
R	Q	V	T	E	L	E	P	H	O	N	E	E	D
X	S	E	N	I	H	C	A	M	R	E	Y	R	D

Solution on Page 307

ALL TRADES
BUILD
CALL
CARPENTRY
CONSTRUCT
CONTRACTOR
DRILL
DRYWALL
ELECTRICAL
EXTERIOR
FIXING
FLOOR
HAMMER
HANDY
HELPFUL
HOME
HOUSEHOLD
INTERIOR
LEAKS
LICENSED
LIGHT BULB
NAILS
NEIGHBOR
ODD JOBS
PAINTING
PIPES
PLUMBING
PROJECTS
REMODELING
REPAIRS
SERVICE
SKILLED
USEFUL
VAN
WOOD
WORK

Handyman

C	Y	D	N	A	H	I	N	T	E	R	I	O	R
A	X	P	O	P	R	O	J	E	C	T	S	O	E
R	N	L	I	O	A	S	G	N	I	X	I	F	P
P	E	U	D	P	W	I	B	R	A	R	U	O	A
E	I	M	L	A	E	L	N	O	E	I	Z	O	I
N	G	B	O	E	L	S	I	T	J	M	L	C	R
T	H	I	H	D	L	L	X	C	I	D	O	S	S
R	B	N	E	R	E	E	T	A	E	N	D	H	B
Y	O	G	S	Y	Z	L	C	R	S	N	G	O	U
R	R	R	U	W	P	H	I	T	A	K	S	R	I
E	U	O	O	A	E	Z	R	N	R	D	A	E	L
M	S	O	H	L	L	U	A	O	G	I	E	E	D
M	E	L	P	L	C	V	W	C	G	F	C	S	L
A	F	F	A	T	E	C	I	V	R	E	S	A	W
H	U	C	F	H	B	L	U	B	T	H	G	I	L
L	L	I	R	D	E	L	L	I	K	S	O	T	W

Solution on Page 307

BIRTH
BOND
BROTHER
CHILDHOOD
CHILDREN
CLOSE
ETYMOLOGY
FAMILY
FATHER
FIGHTING
FOSTER
FRIEND
FULL
GENETICS
GIRL
HALF
HOME
JEALOUSY
KINSHIP
LOVE
MIDDLE
MOTHER
OLDER
PARENTS
RELATIVE
RIVALRY
SHARE
SISTER
STEP
TOGETHER
TWINS
YOUNGEST

Siblings

A	N	P	A	R	Y	S	U	O	L	A	E	J	I
E	T	I	N	M	U	Z	C	L	O	S	E	K	Q
R	M	O	F	R	J	G	P	I	H	S	N	I	K
A	Z	O	L	Q	C	R	E	H	T	O	M	H	E
H	V	U	H	F	R	I	E	N	D	E	G	K	R
S	N	I	W	T	P	J	V	O	X	I	N	R	T
T	I	X	Y	G	O	L	O	M	Y	T	E	E	O
N	S	G	I	A	B	H	L	F	S	L	R	H	G
E	U	N	M	I	D	D	L	E	A	L	D	T	E
R	G	I	R	L	X	A	G	T	B	S	L	A	T
A	E	T	I	F	H	N	I	Y	O	I	I	F	H
P	H	H	J	K	U	V	J	L	N	S	H	S	E
N	C	G	T	O	E	L	D	I	D	T	C	A	R
O	U	I	Y	O	U	E	L	M	P	E	T	S	A
N	E	F	A	U	R	I	V	A	L	R	Y	D	H
U	F	P	T	G	A	B	K	F	O	S	T	E	R

Solution on Page 307

ART
BATHROOM
CEILING
CEMENT
CERAMIC
COLOR
DECORATIVE
DESIGNER
FLAT
FLOORING
GLAZED
GLUE
GRANITE
GROUT
HARD
KITCHEN
LAY
LIMESTONE
MARBLE
METAL
MORTAR
MOSAICS
PATTERNS
PLASTIC
PORCELAIN
QUARRY
ROOFS
SAW
SHOWERS
SLATE
SQUARE
WALLS
WATER
WHITE
WOOD

Tiles

W	I	M	O	R	T	A	R	O	L	O	C	A	Y
K	R	O	O	F	S	E	G	F	L	A	T	W	H
U	L	K	O	S	S	R	E	W	O	H	S	E	A
Q	O	D	Q	U	A	R	R	Y	W	A	T	E	R
K	G	R	E	N	G	I	S	E	D	A	T	F	D
J	I	U	I	C	D	G	C	S	L	I	C	G	M
B	A	T	H	R	O	O	M	S	H	H	E	L	Q
S	E	N	C	P	F	R	O	W	A	N	R	A	P
Q	C	T	I	H	L	P	A	W	O	W	A	Z	S
U	G	T	R	A	E	A	A	T	N	E	M	E	C
A	M	E	T	A	L	N	S	T	I	L	I	D	R
R	G	N	I	L	I	E	C	T	T	V	C	J	X
E	L	B	R	A	M	J	C	F	I	E	E	F	Z
J	U	L	F	I	T	U	O	R	G	C	R	O	T
W	A	L	L	S	C	F	L	O	O	R	I	N	G
Y	N	F	G	S	L	J	C	N	F	P	B	Y	S

Solution on Page 308

ACTIVITY
AEROBATICS
AMATEUR
ARCHERY
ATHLETIC
BASEBALL
BASKETBALL
BOWLING
BOXING
CRICKET
CURLING
EQUIPMENT
ETHICS
FOOTBALL
GAME
GOLF
GYMNASTICS
LACROSSE
MEDICINE
NUTRITION
PHYSICAL
PLAYERS
POLITICS
RECREATION
RUGBY
RULES
RUNNING
SCORE
SOFTBALL
SWIMMING
TEAM SPORT
TENNIS
TRAINING

Sporting Chance

A	T	H	L	E	T	I	C	U	R	L	I	N	G
S	C	O	R	E	Q	S	O	F	T	B	A	L	L
R	A	M	A	T	E	U	R	U	N	N	I	N	G
E	Z	Y	N	O	I	T	I	R	T	U	N	O	G
Y	B	G	U	R	B	N	G	P	E	M	A	G	N
A	L	N	Y	T	R	O	P	S	M	A	E	T	I
L	T	I	T	M	L	I	Y	L	P	E	G	L	L
P	E	N	E	F	N	T	L	L	O	T	N	H	W
H	K	I	N	E	I	A	M	A	L	H	I	T	O
Y	C	A	N	V	B	E	S	B	I	I	M	Y	B
S	I	R	I	E	D	R	X	T	T	C	M	R	O
I	R	T	S	I	R	C	V	E	I	S	I	E	X
C	C	A	C	U	V	E	X	K	C	C	W	H	I
A	B	I	L	A	C	R	O	S	S	E	S	C	N
L	N	E	F	O	O	T	B	A	L	L	L	R	G
E	S	N	S	C	I	T	A	B	O	R	E	A	T

Solution on Page 308

ALUMINUM
BOWLS
BUNDT PAN
CAKE PAN
CASSEROLE
CAST IRON
CERAMIC
COPPER
DUTCH OVEN
FOOD
FRYING PAN
GLASS
GRIDDLES
KITCHEN
LADLE
LOAF PAN
METAL
NONSTICK
PIE PAN
POTS
PYREX
ROASTING
SAUCEPANS
SILICONE
SKILLET
STOCK POT
STONEWARE
TEFLON
UTENSILS
WOK

Cookware

L	K	C	I	T	S	N	O	N	Q	R	Z	S	A
A	A	F	E	N	O	C	I	L	I	S	S	L	Q
T	P	D	P	I	E	P	A	N	C	A	U	I	C
E	P	C	L	X	R	O	K	H	U	M	X	S	I
M	C	A	K	E	P	A	N	C	I	Q	S	N	M
J	V	S	E	R	A	W	E	N	O	T	S	E	A
Z	N	S	Q	Y	X	P	U	A	O	T	Q	T	R
Y	A	E	C	P	A	M	E	P	S	E	S	U	E
H	P	R	V	N	Z	K	B	F	S	F	E	B	C
T	G	O	S	O	O	I	U	A	A	L	L	B	O
T	N	L	K	R	H	T	N	O	L	O	D	O	P
W	I	E	I	I	R	C	D	L	G	N	D	W	P
K	Y	F	L	T	F	H	T	O	B	W	I	L	E
A	R	R	L	S	M	E	P	U	O	M	R	S	R
T	F	K	E	A	F	N	A	K	D	F	G	D	T
P	P	S	T	C	K	G	N	I	T	S	A	O	R

Solution on Page 308

ANALYSIS
ANCESTRY
BAPTISM
BIRTH
BLOODLINE
BORN
BROTHER
CENSUS
CHILDREN
COUSIN
DATA
DNA
FAMILIES
FATHER
HERALDRY
HISTORICAL
KINSHIP
LIBRARY
LINEAGES
LOCATION
MARRIAGES
MOTHER
NAMES
PARENTS
PAST
PEDIGREES
PEOPLE
RECORDS
RELATIVES
RESEARCH
SIBLINGS
SOCIETY
SOFTWARE
SURNAME
TRADITIONS
TREE

Family Tree

S	E	G	A	E	N	I	L	D	O	O	L	B	P
U	U	T	P	K	S	O	F	T	W	A	R	E	R
P	A	S	T	N	O	I	T	A	C	O	L	T	E
D	D	N	N	R	O	B	E	I	M	B	F	Y	L
H	C	R	A	E	S	E	R	E	A	R	A	R	A
B	Y	T	E	I	C	O	S	N	R	O	M	D	T
A	S	N	O	I	T	I	D	A	R	T	I	L	I
P	Y	R	T	S	E	C	N	A	I	H	L	A	V
T	R	S	I	S	Y	L	A	N	A	E	I	R	E
I	A	H	F	J	P	E	D	I	G	R	E	E	S
S	R	N	C	H	I	L	D	R	E	N	S	H	T
M	B	S	G	N	I	L	B	I	S	E	M	A	N
N	I	S	U	O	C	P	S	U	R	N	A	M	E
E	L	P	O	E	P	P	S	D	R	O	C	E	R
K	X	R	E	H	T	A	F	B	I	R	T	H	A
M	O	T	H	E	R	K	I	N	S	H	I	P	P

Solution on Page 308

ACTIVIST
ACTRESS
AWARDS
BLACK
BROADWAY
CELEBRITY
COMEDIENNE
EMMY AWARD
FEMALE
FILM
GHOST
GRAMMY
GUINAN
LION KING
MOTHER
MOVIES
NUN
OSCAR
PRODUCER
SINGER
SISTER ACT
SOAPDISH
SONGWRITER
STAND UP
STAR TREK
SUCCESSFUL
TALENTED
TELEVISION
THE VIEW
TONY
VOICE

Whoopi Goldberg

T	A	L	E	N	T	E	D	S	I	N	G	E	R
D	B	S	M	S	O	N	G	W	R	I	T	E	R
C	R	T	N	O	S	N	B	Y	M	M	A	R	G
T	O	A	C	N	V	E	T	H	E	V	I	E	W
D	S	K	W	A	F	I	L	M	L	S	S	L	B
P	N	I	I	A	R	D	E	V	I	U	L	L	G
D	U	I	V	B	Y	E	U	S	O	C	A	V	H
D	N	D	E	I	T	M	T	W	N	C	N	K	O
R	I	L	N	Y	T	O	M	S	K	E	F	E	S
A	E	A	M	A	V	C	N	E	I	S	E	R	T
C	M	W	I	W	T	W	A	Y	N	S	M	T	V
S	O	A	P	D	I	S	H	G	G	F	A	R	O
O	T	R	N	A	N	I	U	G	A	U	L	A	I
G	H	D	N	O	I	S	I	V	E	L	E	T	C
S	E	S	J	R	E	C	U	D	O	R	P	S	E
O	R	I	Q	B	S	A	C	T	R	E	S	S	N

Solution on Page 309

ALLOY
ASSAY
BASE METAL
BRASS
BRONZE
BULLION
CAMEO
CARAT
CENT
CIRCULATED
COINS
COLLECTION
CONDITION
COPPER
CURRENCY
DATE
DESIGN
DIME
EAGLE
ENGRAVER
ERROR
EURO
FACE VALUE
GOLD
GRADING
LUSTER
MEDALLIONS
MINT
MONEY
MOTTO
NICKEL
OBVERSE
PATINA
PAYMENT
PROOF
QUARTER
RARE
SILVER
TOKENS
TRADE

Numismatics

F	R	A	L	A	T	E	M	E	S	A	B	G	S
R	E	T	R	A	U	Q	D	E	S	I	G	N	C
E	V	N	O	I	T	I	D	N	O	C	O	U	L
V	C	O	P	P	E	R	A	R	O	I	R	E	Y
L	A	I	R	E	T	S	U	L	L	R	K	E	E
I	M	L	E	M	F	E	L	L	E	C	E	L	N
S	E	L	T	I	A	E	A	N	I	U	S	G	O
D	O	U	A	N	C	D	C	N	G	L	R	A	M
B	J	B	D	T	E	Y	E	O	P	A	E	E	O
R	R	N	I	M	V	M	L	M	D	T	V	R	T
A	S	O	I	T	A	D	Y	I	E	E	B	R	T
S	N	D	N	S	L	C	N	A	T	D	O	O	O
S	E	I	N	Z	U	G	A	I	P	N	A	R	Z
A	K	I	T	R	E	V	A	R	G	N	E	R	B
Y	O	W	Z	A	L	L	O	Y	A	X	K	C	T
C	T	S	H	E	P	R	O	O	F	T	W	W	I

Solution on Page 309

ARTICLES
AUDIENCE
BLOG
BROADCAST
COLUMNIST
COPY
EDITING
EDITORS
EVENTS
FACTS
INFORM
INTERVIEW
ISSUES
JOURNALIST
LEAD
MAGAZINE
MASS MEDIA
NEWSPAPERS
ONLINE
OPINION
PRESS
PRINT
RADIO
REPORTING
RESEARCH
SCHOOL
SOURCE
STORY
TELEVISION
TRENDS
TRUTH
WAR
WRITING

Journalism

P	S	O	U	R	C	E	D	I	T	I	N	G	Z
R	T	R	E	N	D	S	A	S	R	I	D	N	C
E	V	E	N	T	S	I	I	A	N	A	W	I	L
S	N	D	L	C	E	L	D	T	E	N	D	T	B
S	C	I	H	E	A	C	E	L	E	F	K	I	L
M	T	O	Z	N	V	R	M	W	C	A	Q	R	O
V	O	O	R	A	V	I	S	P	I	C	H	W	G
L	G	U	R	I	G	P	S	R	N	T	A	D	E
B	O	N	E	Y	A	A	A	I	F	S	U	U	X
J	S	W	I	P	P	R	M	N	O	I	D	E	I
Q	E	Z	E	T	A	O	T	T	R	N	I	D	M
H	U	R	M	W	R	B	C	I	M	M	E	I	T
T	S	A	C	D	A	O	R	B	C	U	N	T	G
U	S	N	O	I	N	I	P	O	N	L	C	O	R
R	I	O	O	N	L	I	N	E	H	O	E	R	Y
T	W	H	M	R	E	S	E	A	R	C	H	S	V

Solution on Page 309

ANATOMY
ANIMALS
BACTERIA
BOTANY
CELLULAR
CHEMISTRY
CLASS
DARWIN
DNA
ECOLOGY
EVOLUTION
FUNCTION
GENETICS
GROWTH
HEREDITY
HUMAN
KINGDOM
LABORATORY
LIFE
MEDICINE
MICROSCOPE
MOLECULES
NUCLEUS
ORGANISMS
PHYSIOLOGY
PROTEIN
RESEARCH
SCIENCE
SPECIES
STRUCTURE
STUDY
TAXONOMY
TISSUES

Biology

C	E	L	L	U	L	A	R	D	A	R	W	I	N
A	N	D	A	H	G	N	I	E	T	O	R	P	A
Z	I	S	Z	B	N	O	I	T	C	N	U	F	M
S	C	E	Y	G	O	L	O	I	S	Y	H	P	U
P	I	U	T	I	I	R	E	S	E	A	R	C	H
E	D	S	I	E	T	B	A	N	I	M	A	L	S
C	E	S	D	E	U	A	N	T	L	I	F	E	A
I	M	I	E	R	L	C	A	S	O	C	L	C	O
E	O	T	R	U	O	T	T	U	H	R	P	N	R
S	D	A	E	T	V	E	O	E	Y	O	Y	E	G
Y	G	X	H	C	E	R	M	L	G	S	D	I	A
N	N	O	T	U	U	I	Y	C	O	C	U	C	N
A	I	N	W	R	S	A	L	U	L	O	T	S	I
T	K	O	O	T	N	A	N	N	O	P	S	M	S
O	G	M	R	S	S	E	L	U	C	E	L	O	M
B	F	Y	G	S	K	G	E	N	E	T	I	C	S

Solution on Page 309

ANCESTOR
ANIMALS
BIOLOGY
CARE
CHANGE
DEATH
DINOSAURS
DISAPPEAR
DISEASE
DODO
ECOLOGY
ENDANGERED
EVOLUTION
FOSSILS
GENE POOL
GENETICS
GONE
HABITAT
HISTORY
HUMAN
HUNTING
LOST
MAMMOTH
ORGANISM
PAST
PLANTS
POLLUTION
PRESERVE
RAIN FOREST
RARE
SCIENCE
SPECIES
STUDY
SURVIVE
THREATENED

Extinction

P	A	S	T	S	R	U	A	S	O	N	I	D	N
A	N	E	H	A	B	I	T	A	T	E	E	O	A
M	O	C	S	D	E	A	T	H	R	R	E	D	M
B	I	O	L	O	G	Y	R	A	E	A	S	O	U
P	T	L	E	N	M	E	R	G	I	C	A	U	H
L	U	O	V	R	A	I	N	F	O	R	E	S	T
A	L	G	R	T	R	A	E	P	P	A	S	I	D
N	O	Y	E	Y	D	U	T	S	O	L	I	M	H
T	V	N	S	N	N	U	G	R	L	S	D	S	U
S	E	G	E	N	E	P	O	O	L	L	C	I	N
D	S	U	R	V	I	V	E	T	U	I	H	N	T
L	X	S	P	E	C	I	E	S	T	S	A	A	I
V	H	I	S	T	O	R	Y	E	I	S	N	G	N
H	T	O	M	M	A	M	N	C	O	O	G	R	G
S	C	I	E	N	C	E	V	N	N	F	E	O	Y
K	D	E	N	O	G	S	L	A	M	I	N	A	B

Solution on Page 310

ALUMINUM
BATTERIES
BINS
BOTTLES
CANS
CARDBOARD
CENTER
COLLECTION
COMPOST
CONSUMER
CONTAINER
EARTH
ECOLOGY
ENERGY
GARBAGE
GLASS
GREEN
LANDFILL
MATERIALS
METALS
MONEY
NEWSPAPER
PACKAGING
PLANET
PLASTICS
POLLUTION
RECYCLE
REDUCE
RENEW
RESOURCES
REUSE
SALVAGE
SAVING
SORTING
STEEL
TEXTILES
TRASH

Recyclable

R	M	S	A	V	I	N	G	P	V	S	N	I	B
E	R	E	M	U	S	N	O	C	A	N	S	O	G
U	C	D	T	S	E	L	I	T	X	E	T	N	N
S	C	O	S	A	L	V	A	G	E	T	I	E	Y
E	O	N	L	U	L	P	S	I	L	T	E	G	V
R	M	Y	T	L	L	S	H	E	R	R	R	N	X
L	P	I	G	A	E	S	S	O	G	E	S	I	A
A	O	R	N	O	A	C	S	S	N	N	T	G	L
N	S	E	E	R	L	E	T	E	F	I	E	A	U
D	T	S	T	T	G	O	W	I	M	A	E	K	M
F	H	O	A	A	N	S	C	R	O	T	L	C	I
I	T	U	B	L	P	E	E	E	N	N	C	A	N
L	R	R	X	A	G	D	C	T	E	O	Y	P	U
L	A	C	P	Q	U	Z	U	T	Y	C	C	I	M
G	E	E	S	C	I	T	S	A	L	P	E	R	T
R	R	S	E	C	A	R	D	B	O	A	R	D	S

Solution on Page 310

ACTOR
ALBUM
ARMY
ARTIST
BLUE SUEDE
COLONEL
CONCERT
COUNTRY
DANCE
FAMOUS
GOSPEL
GRACELAND
GRAMMYS
GUITAR
HAIR
HAWAII
HIPS
HOUND DOG
ICON
IDOL
JUMPSUIT
LAS VEGAS
LEATHER
LISA MARIE
MEMPHIS
MOVIES
MUSICIAN
PERFORMER
POPULAR
PRISCILLA
RECORDS
ROCK
SIDEBURNS
SINGER
SONGS
STAR
TENNESSEE
THE KING
TOUR
TUPELO

Elvis

G	Y	N	O	C	I	J	P	G	U	I	T	A	R
S	M	M	Y	R	T	N	U	O	C	R	I	L	C
Y	R	E	C	O	R	D	S	M	P	N	D	B	O
M	A	M	B	A	C	T	O	R	P	U	O	U	N
M	P	P	L	A	S	V	E	G	A	S	L	M	C
A	E	H	U	H	I	P	S	G	A	T	U	A	E
R	R	I	E	E	K	C	O	R	R	C	S	I	R
G	F	S	S	I	B	I	R	A	T	O	O	N	T
O	O	I	U	P	R	I	S	C	I	L	L	A	H
S	R	D	E	O	A	A	K	E	S	O	E	I	E
P	M	E	D	H	M	W	M	L	T	N	P	C	K
E	E	B	E	N	K	A	W	A	D	E	U	I	I
L	R	U	O	T	U	H	F	N	S	L	T	S	N
M	L	R	S	G	N	O	S	D	N	I	T	U	G
S	I	N	G	E	R	E	H	T	A	E	L	M	B
E	E	S	S	E	N	N	E	T	D	A	N	C	E

Solution on Page 310

AMATEUR
AMBLE
ARABIAN
ARENA
BOLTING
BRIDLE
BUCKING
CANTER
COAT
COLT
CROP
ENGLISH
EQUINE
FILLY
FOAL
FURLONG
GAIT
GALLOP
GELDING
HALTER
HARNESS
HOOF
JOCKEY
JUMPING
MANE
MARE
PONY
POSTING
RACE
REINS
RIDING
RODEO
SADDLE
STALLION
STIRRUPS
STRIDE
TACK
TROT
WESTERN
WHINNY

Speaking of Horses

A	Y	D	S	M	X	Z	W	R	O	D	E	O	G
E	N	A	M	K	X	H	O	Y	E	K	C	O	J
E	G	E	G	R	I	D	I	N	G	I	A	G	R
B	R	H	R	N	W	E	S	T	E	R	N	K	R
R	F	A	N	A	B	A	G	E	L	X	T	S	T
I	I	Y	M	G	O	M	A	N	D	R	E	O	F
D	L	B	P	N	L	A	S	I	I	E	R	O	N
L	L	T	E	O	T	T	T	U	N	T	A	K	Y
E	Y	I	D	L	I	E	A	Q	G	L	S	P	N
N	J	Q	I	R	N	U	L	E	N	A	A	O	O
G	U	H	R	U	G	R	L	A	I	H	D	L	P
L	M	U	T	F	Y	J	I	X	K	H	D	L	K
I	P	P	S	L	C	B	O	O	C	O	L	A	C
S	I	N	O	O	A	E	N	W	U	O	E	G	A
H	N	H	A	R	N	E	S	S	B	F	L	J	T
G	G	T	A	E	C	A	R	J	G	A	I	T	Y

Solution on Page 310

BACKYARD
BARN
BIKES
BUILDING
DOORS
EQUIPMENT
FARM
GARAGE
GARDENING
HOBBIES
HOOKS
HOUSE
KEEP
LAWN MOWER
LOCKED
METAL
OUTSIDE
PAINT
PLASTIC
POTTING
ROOF
SHELTER
SHELVES
SMALL
SPACE
STEEL
STORAGE
STRUCTURE
SUPPLIES
TOOLS
VINYL
WALLS
WOODEN
WORKSHOP

Shed

X	W	G	M	S	T	O	R	A	G	E	L	O	P
S	P	A	C	E	S	R	F	A	N	X	L	L	N
E	P	A	I	N	T	B	R	N	I	V	A	O	Y
D	R	A	Y	K	C	A	B	G	T	S	M	C	S
I	E	E	L	Q	G	R	L	N	T	N	S	K	L
S	T	R	W	E	G	N	U	I	O	M	S	E	L
T	L	U	O	O	E	N	C	N	P	H	E	D	A
U	E	T	R	M	M	T	I	E	O	O	I	K	W
O	H	C	K	J	R	N	S	D	U	B	L	H	T
Y	S	U	S	E	A	E	W	R	L	B	P	U	O
M	K	R	H	S	F	M	O	A	V	I	P	K	O
T	O	T	O	U	Y	P	O	G	L	E	U	I	L
E	O	S	P	O	I	I	D	K	C	S	S	B	S
G	H	C	E	H	D	U	E	V	I	N	Y	L	P
L	J	P	E	P	H	Q	N	F	O	O	R	T	E
B	B	I	K	E	S	E	V	L	E	H	S	L	M

Solution on Page 311

ANALYZE
BIOLOGY
CHEMISTRY
CONCLUSION
CONTROL
DATA
EMPIRICAL
EXPERIMENT
HYPOTHESIS
INQUIRY
KNOWLEDGE
LAB
LOGIC
MEASURABLE
METHOD
MODEL
OBJECTIVE
OBSERVE
PHENOMENA
PREDICTION
PROCEDURE
QUESTION
REACTION
REASONING
RESEARCH
RESULTS
RETEST
SCIENTISTS
STEPS
TECHNIQUES
THEORIES

The Scientific Method

S	T	L	U	S	E	R	E	S	E	A	R	C	H
E	V	I	T	C	E	J	B	O	P	T	U	H	T
G	N	I	N	O	S	A	E	R	H	A	S	E	I
D	P	R	O	C	E	D	U	R	E	D	C	M	N
E	M	P	I	R	I	C	A	L	N	N	I	I	Q
L	O	R	T	N	O	C	R	S	O	M	E	S	U
W	S	E	E	X	P	E	R	I	M	E	N	T	I
O	E	D	J	R	T	Q	S	S	E	A	T	R	R
N	U	I	L	E	L	U	L	E	N	S	I	Y	Y
K	Q	C	S	A	L	E	A	H	A	U	S	G	E
D	I	T	B	C	O	S	N	T	L	R	T	O	V
O	N	I	N	T	G	T	A	O	E	A	S	L	R
H	H	O	W	I	I	I	L	P	D	B	T	O	E
T	C	N	P	O	C	O	Y	Y	O	L	E	I	S
E	E	B	S	N	X	N	Z	H	M	E	P	B	B
M	T	H	E	O	R	I	E	S	J	F	S	Y	O

Solution on Page 311

AGING
BABY OIL
BEAUTY
BIKINI
BOOTHS
BRONZER
COLOR
COPPERTONE
DARK
EXPOSURE
FRECKLES
HEALTH
HOT
LOTION
PALE
PROTECT
RELAXING
RESORT
SALON
SPF
SUMMER
SUNBATHING
SUNBURN
SUNGLASSES
SUNLIGHT
SUNSCREEN
SWIMMING
UV RAYS
VITAMIN D
WRINKLE

Get Some Sun

C	G	N	I	M	M	I	W	S	A	L	O	N	H
O	G	N	P	T	A	H	T	B	O	O	T	H	S
P	O	V	I	T	A	M	I	N	D	T	C	U	T
P	H	K	K	H	E	A	L	T	H	L	E	V	B
E	S	H	N	O	T	O	Y	G	S	E	T	R	I
R	K	R	E	T	M	A	I	T	S	S	O	A	K
T	T	O	E	G	K	L	B	T	U	N	R	Y	I
O	R	L	R	B	N	A	O	N	Z	A	P	S	N
N	E	O	C	U	G	B	G	E	U	R	E	B	I
E	M	C	S	I	O	L	R	X	Q	S	R	B	P
L	M	U	N	E	A	R	I	P	A	L	E	K	W
K	U	G	U	S	R	A	N	O	I	T	O	L	P
N	S	I	S	P	F	J	S	S	Y	C	K	L	K
I	N	E	N	R	U	B	N	U	S	B	W	R	F
R	S	S	E	L	K	C	E	R	F	Q	A	U	P
W	L	G	N	I	X	A	L	E	R	D	R	B	S

Solution on Page 311

BAKING
BISCUIT
BROWNIES
BUTTER
CHEF
CHIPS
CHOCOLATE
CUTTER
DESSERT
DOUGH
DROP
EGGS
FAT
FLAT
FLOUR
FRUITS
GINGER
GIRL SCOUT
ICING
JAR
MILK
MONSTER
NUTS
OATMEAL
OREO
OVEN
PRESSED
RAISIN
RECIPE
ROUND
SHORTBREAD
SNACK
SOFT
SPICES
SUGAR
SWEET
TREAT
VANILLA

Cookies

R	H	G	U	O	D	N	U	O	R	L	F	E	Y
U	E	K	E	G	I	R	L	S	C	O	U	T	Q
O	K	C	H	I	P	S	C	H	E	F	H	S	X
L	C	W	I	C	H	O	C	O	L	A	T	E	L
F	R	U	T	P	E	E	P	R	J	E	I	I	Z
Q	B	U	T	T	E	R	B	T	Y	G	U	N	N
S	W	E	E	T	E	O	R	B	N	G	C	W	X
O	P	M	X	S	E	E	V	R	H	S	S	O	U
F	O	F	S	A	S	R	J	E	T	P	I	R	S
R	R	E	T	S	N	O	M	A	N	I	B	B	U
C	D	A	E	R	S	A	F	D	R	C	A	S	G
A	L	D	E	T	I	T	F	O	S	E	K	N	A
F	K	M	L	C	R	M	I	N	I	S	I	A	R
Q	T	G	I	N	G	E	R	U	T	J	N	C	H
V	A	N	I	L	L	A	A	U	R	L	G	K	O
B	G	T	H	H	K	L	N	T	C	F	B	X	A

Solution on Page 311

ALGORITHMS
BASIC
COBOL
CODE
COMMANDS
COMPILER
COMPUTERS
DATA
DEBUG
DESIGN
ENGINEER
EXECUTE
EXPRESSION
FORTRAN
FUNCTIONAL
HTML
INPUT
JAVASCRIPT
LINES
LOGIC
MACHINE
MICROSOFT
NUMBER
OBJECT
PASCAL
PERL
PROGRAMS
PYTHON
RUBY
SCIENCE
SEMANTICS
SOFTWARE
SQL
SYMBOLS
SYNTAX
TECHNOLOGY
TYPE

Programming Languages

O	T	L	N	G	I	S	E	D	O	C	T	T	C
B	Y	P	R	E	E	N	I	G	N	E	F	S	N
J	P	A	V	E	I	N	F	C	C	O	B	O	L
E	E	S	U	H	P	O	O	H	S	A	H	F	Y
C	H	C	C	U	R	M	N	O	S	T	C	T	H
T	T	A	T	T	M	O	R	M	Y	A	O	W	C
P	M	L	R	A	L	C	H	P	I	D	M	A	I
I	L	A	N	O	I	T	C	N	U	F	P	R	S
R	N	D	G	M	I	G	U	B	E	D	U	E	A
C	S	Y	P	R	O	G	R	A	M	S	T	T	B
S	A	N	O	I	S	S	E	R	P	X	E	U	R
A	Q	G	B	C	O	M	P	I	L	E	R	C	U
V	L	L	S	E	M	A	N	T	I	C	S	E	B
A	S	Y	M	B	O	L	S	E	N	I	L	X	Y
J	X	A	T	N	Y	S	C	I	E	N	C	E	I
L	O	G	I	C	W	D	N	U	M	B	E	R	G

Solution on Page 312

AYURVEDA
BODY WORK
CHINESE
CURE
DIET
DISEASE
DOCTOR
ENERGY
FASTING
HEALING
HERBALISM
HERBOLOGY
HOLISTIC
HOMEOPATHY
HYPNOSIS
LIFESTYLE
MASSAGE
MEDITATION
MIND
NATUROPATH
OSTEOPATHY
PLANTS
REIKI
REMEDIES
SHIATSU
SPIRITUAL
SUPPLEMENT
TEA
THERAPY
TREATMENT
VEGAN
WATER
WELLNESS
YOGA

Alternative Medicine

O	G	L	Y	P	A	R	E	H	T	E	I	D	R
R	Y	C	A	H	E	R	B	A	L	I	S	M	O
D	G	G	H	U	T	N	E	M	T	A	E	R	T
S	R	N	O	I	T	A	T	I	D	E	M	G	C
S	E	I	A	L	N	I	P	K	K	Y	H	N	O
E	N	T	R	G	O	E	R	O	N	I	T	I	D
N	E	S	E	N	E	B	S	I	E	E	A	L	F
L	C	A	M	T	W	V	R	E	P	M	P	A	K
L	I	F	E	S	T	Y	L	E	T	S	O	E	R
E	T	A	D	U	S	T	A	I	H	S	R	H	O
W	S	D	I	S	E	A	S	E	E	R	U	C	W
A	I	N	E	O	S	T	E	O	P	A	T	H	Y
T	L	I	S	A	D	E	V	R	U	Y	A	R	D
E	O	M	S	U	P	P	L	E	M	E	N	T	O
R	H	Y	P	N	O	S	I	S	Y	O	G	A	B
V	M	A	S	S	A	G	E	P	L	A	N	T	S

Solution on Page 312

ABSINTHE
ALCOHOL
BARLEY
BEER
BOOZE
BOTTLE
BOURBON
BRANDY
CHAMPAGNE
COGNAC
DRINKING
ETHANOL
GIN
GLASS
HOPS
LAGER
LIQUOR
MEAD
MIXED
PARTY
PORT
PROOF
PUB
RUM
SCHNAPPS
SCOTCH
SHERRY
SHOTS
SPIRITS
TEQUILA
VERMOUTH
VODKA
WHISKEY
WINE

Intoxicating

M	A	W	N	J	N	L	R	J	B	Q	Q	G	P
U	K	S	H	R	B	O	T	T	L	E	E	W	Z
E	D	H	P	I	V	H	B	T	D	E	X	I	M
F	O	O	R	P	S	P	I	R	I	T	S	S	U
P	V	P	Z	E	A	K	I	Y	U	J	C	W	R
H	U	S	E	A	E	N	E	F	D	O	I	Z	G
H	C	V	H	T	K	B	H	Y	T	N	B	L	Y
T	B	A	T	I	H	Y	R	C	E	J	A	R	P
U	J	B	N	L	O	A	H	A	S	S	R	R	U
O	Y	G	I	G	O	L	N	K	S	E	L	O	B
M	V	I	S	T	O	H	S	O	H	M	E	U	O
R	L	N	B	P	E	C	O	S	L	B	Y	Q	O
E	N	G	A	P	M	A	H	C	A	H	Q	I	Z
V	R	R	O	T	E	Q	U	I	L	A	D	L	E
Q	T	R	O	P	A	O	R	E	G	A	L	U	A
Y	T	Y	D	B	D	J	X	A	M	J	Q	D	Z

Solution on Page 312

AIR
ANIMALS
ATMOSPHERE
BIOLOGY
BIOSPHERE
CHEMISTRY
CHRONOLOGY
CLIMATE
CORE
CRUST
EARTHQUAKE
ECOLOGY
ENERGY
GEOGRAPHY
GEOLOGY
GEOPHYSICS
GEOSCIENCE
GEOSPHERE
GLACIOLOGY
HYDROLOGY
LAVA
LIFE
MAGMA
MANTLE
MOUNTAIN
NATURE
OCEANS
PLANET
PLATES
ROCKS
SOIL
SPHERES
STUDY
TECTONIC
VOLCANOES
WEATHER

Earth Science

Y	D	U	T	S	W	E	A	T	H	E	R	O	C
T	H	N	A	T	U	R	E	C	O	L	O	G	Y
E	N	E	R	G	Y	X	Y	G	O	L	O	E	G
T	E	N	A	L	P	L	A	T	E	S	J	F	O
A	G	E	O	S	P	H	E	R	E	S	O	I	L
M	E	S	E	K	A	U	Q	H	T	R	A	E	O
I	O	C	H	R	O	N	O	L	O	G	Y	N	I
L	G	I	N	Y	E	R	E	H	P	S	O	I	B
C	R	S	T	E	D	H	E	F	I	L	M	A	A
I	A	Y	S	A	I	R	P	L	A	V	A	T	N
N	P	H	U	C	H	C	O	S	T	Q	G	N	I
O	H	P	R	O	C	K	S	L	O	N	M	U	M
T	Y	O	C	E	A	N	S	O	O	M	A	O	A
C	H	E	M	I	S	T	R	Y	E	G	T	M	L
E	Y	G	O	L	O	I	C	A	L	G	Y	A	S
T	Q	B	B	V	O	L	C	A	N	O	E	S	G

Solution on Page 312

ACCOUNTS
ATMS
BALANCE
BILLS
BONDS
BRANCH
BUSINESS
CAPITAL
CASH
CHANGE
CHECKING
COINS
CREDIT
CURRENCY
CUSTOMERS
DEBT
DEPOSITS
DRAFT
ECONOMY
FEES
FINANCIAL
INTEREST
INVESTMENT
LENDING
LINES
MANAGER
MONEY
MORTGAGE
NATIONAL
OVERDRAWN
PAYMENT
RATE
ROBBERY
SECURITY
TELLER
VAULT
WITHDRAWAL

Bank Terms

F	E	E	S	R	E	L	L	E	T	H	E	H	D
M	O	R	T	G	A	G	E	H	R	C	Y	S	R
N	Z	G	N	I	K	C	E	H	C	N	C	W	A
A	Y	T	U	W	L	A	I	C	N	A	N	I	F
T	M	L	O	I	A	I	N	T	E	R	E	S	T
I	O	U	C	L	W	R	C	L	O	B	R	E	N
O	N	A	C	I	A	C	D	A	S	O	R	C	E
N	O	V	A	N	R	U	E	R	S	Y	U	U	M
A	C	S	E	E	D	S	G	C	E	H	C	R	Y
L	E	N	D	S	H	T	T	N	N	V	K	I	A
A	E	I	E	L	T	O	O	I	I	A	O	T	P
T	T	O	B	L	I	M	F	K	S	D	L	Y	L
I	A	C	T	I	W	E	E	U	U	O	N	A	U
P	R	O	B	B	E	R	Y	N	B	I	P	E	B
A	A	B	O	N	D	S	C	A	T	M	S	E	L
C	H	A	N	G	E	R	E	G	A	N	A	M	D

Solution on Page 313

ASTRONOMY
CHURCH
COMPASS
DISCOVERY
EARTH
EXPERIMENT
GALILEO
GENIUS
GEOCENTRIC
GEOMETRY
HERETIC
HISTORY
ITALIAN
JUPITER
KINEMATICS
MATH
MOON
ORBIT
PENDULUM
PHILOSOPHY
PHYSICS
PISA
PLANETS
REVOLUTION
ROMAN
SCIENTIST
SKY
STARS
SUNSPOTS
TELESCOPE
THEORIES

Galileo Galilei

T	G	E	N	I	U	S	T	E	N	A	L	P	T
M	A	T	H	S	R	A	T	S	I	S	K	Y	R
U	G	G	E	O	C	E	N	T	R	I	C	L	O
L	H	M	C	X	P	J	M	W	H	P	C	Z	R
U	N	B	Y	H	P	O	S	O	L	I	H	P	B
D	I	S	C	O	V	E	R	Y	O	Z	U	Y	I
N	G	E	O	M	E	T	R	Y	Q	N	R	M	T
E	K	I	N	E	M	A	T	I	C	S	C	O	E
P	S	S	C	I	S	Y	H	P	M	Y	H	N	L
C	E	N	O	I	T	U	L	O	V	E	R	O	E
I	I	E	M	H	I	S	T	O	R	Y	N	R	S
T	R	A	P	S	C	I	E	N	T	I	S	T	C
E	O	R	A	F	S	U	N	S	P	O	T	S	O
R	E	T	S	N	A	I	L	A	T	I	K	A	P
E	H	H	S	C	O	E	L	I	L	A	G	R	E
H	T	B	J	U	P	I	T	E	R	O	M	A	N

Solution on Page 313

ALPHABET
ANCIENT
BIBLE
CATHOLIC
CHURCH
CLASSICAL
CLERGY
CULTURE
DEAD
FORMAL
FRENCH
GRAMMAR
GREEK
HISTORICAL
INFLECTED
ITALY
LANGUAGE
LATIUM
LEGAL
LITERATURE
MASS
MEDICINE
MEDIEVAL
MUSIC
PIG
ROMANCE
ROOTS
SCHOOLS
SCIENTIFIC
SPANISH
SPOKEN
VATICAN
VOCABULARY
WRITTEN

Latin

F	R	E	N	C	H	V	A	T	I	C	A	N	Z
S	X	L	K	Q	E	R	U	T	L	U	C	E	N
C	V	O	C	A	B	U	L	A	R	Y	H	K	E
B	H	E	M	I	M	U	S	I	C	G	H	O	T
T	I	U	R	U	F	S	X	Y	I	R	I	P	T
E	E	B	R	U	I	I	J	P	N	E	S	S	I
C	R	B	L	C	T	T	T	P	F	L	T	C	R
N	I	E	A	E	H	A	A	N	L	C	O	H	W
A	R	L	F	H	N	G	R	L	E	G	R	O	L
M	I	A	O	S	P	I	T	E	C	I	I	O	E
O	R	N	M	H	P	L	C	N	T	D	C	L	G
R	O	G	M	M	T	A	A	I	E	A	A	S	A
V	O	U	M	E	A	A	N	M	D	I	L	E	L
I	T	A	L	Y	C	R	C	I	R	E	C	D	D
Y	S	G	R	E	E	K	G	Y	S	O	M	N	O
S	M	E	D	I	E	V	A	L	E	H	F	F	A

Solution on Page 313

AGED
ALCOHOL
AROMA
BARREL
BODY
BOTTLE
BOUQUET
BREATHING
BURGUNDY
CABERNET
CASK
CELLAR
CHAMPAGNE
CORKSCREW
DECANTING
DRY
FINISH
FRANCE
FRENCH
FRUIT
GLASS
GRAPES
ITALY
MERLOT
NOSE
OAK
PORT
RESERVE
SANGRIA
SHERRY
SPARKLING
SWEET
TASTING
VARIETAL
VINEYARD
VINTAGE
WHITE
WINERY
YEAR
YIELD

Speaking of Wine

E	E	L	T	T	O	B	X	Y	L	A	T	I	A
S	Y	D	N	U	G	R	U	B	R	G	V	P	M
O	R	V	A	R	I	E	T	A	L	E	I	W	O
N	R	S	M	B	J	A	V	S	F	D	N	H	R
Y	E	P	E	A	J	T	L	R	E	R	T	I	A
V	H	A	R	V	K	H	U	C	E	Y	A	T	W
W	S	R	L	A	I	I	A	E	O	S	G	E	H
E	R	K	O	Y	T	N	N	L	B	H	E	T	C
R	A	L	T	S	T	G	E	O	P	A	O	R	N
C	L	I	G	I	A	R	U	Y	I	J	T	L	E
S	L	N	N	P	R	Q	P	R	A	A	W	C	R
K	E	G	M	A	U	O	G	Y	S	R	N	T	F
R	C	A	B	E	R	N	E	T	E	A	D	E	J
O	H	O	T	T	A	X	I	G	R	A	P	E	S
C	D	G	H	S	I	N	I	F	W	C	R	W	V
Y	I	E	L	D	G	L	A	S	S	C	A	S	K

Solution on Page 313

ALPACA
BUFFALO
CAMEL
CANARY
CATS
CHICKENS
COCKATIEL
DONKEYS
DOVE
DUCK
ELEPHANT
FERRET
FINCH
GEESE
GOATS
GOLDFISH
GOOSE
GUINEA PIG
HAMSTER
HONEY BEE
HORSE
LLAMA
MOUSE
PET
PIGEON
RABBIT
REINDEER
SHEEP
SWAN
TURKEY
YAK

Domesticated Animals

W	D	M	T	L	C	K	V	Q	I	D	F	B	Z
Y	X	C	A	U	G	O	O	S	E	C	M	L	P
J	J	N	H	S	I	F	D	L	O	G	T	S	O
I	G	X	D	T	A	F	Q	C	A	D	B	T	Q
G	C	E	E	O	N	F	K	H	A	F	U	A	H
U	L	A	E	D	N	A	I	A	S	N	F	C	Q
I	Z	C	B	S	T	K	H	N	Y	X	A	U	K
N	K	A	Y	I	E	S	E	P	C	M	F	R	B
E	B	P	E	D	G	K	S	Y	E	H	N	F	Y
A	T	L	N	Y	C	R	Y	L	S	L	O	E	E
P	L	A	O	I	R	E	E	D	N	I	E	R	K
I	J	S	H	T	U	A	S	T	A	O	G	R	R
G	W	C	O	I	I	M	B	U	S	D	I	E	U
I	Z	R	R	S	W	A	N	B	O	M	P	T	T
G	E	T	S	T	B	L	O	V	I	M	A	T	O
S	H	E	E	P	E	L	E	P	E	T	X	H	N

Solution on Page 314

ANGER
ANXIETY
AWE
BORED
CONTENT
DESIRE
DESPAIR
DISGUST
ELATION
EMPATHY
ENVY
FEAR
FEELING
FRIGHT
GLAD
GLEE
GRIEF
GUILT
HATRED
HOPE
HORROR
HURT
JOY
LONGING
LOVE
LUST
NERVOUS
OPTIMISM
PANIC
PITY
PLEASURE
PRIDE
RAGE
RELIEF
SADNESS
SHAME
SORROW
SYMPATHY
TRUST
ZEST

Emotional

C	R	G	B	A	H	A	T	R	E	D	F	S	S
A	W	E	L	T	I	X	Q	R	O	T	O	W	X
B	T	P	L	E	F	W	I	D	E	R	O	B	L
H	S	I	D	I	E	S	B	Y	R	U	R	U	J
G	U	T	E	A	E	E	V	O	L	S	S	O	S
G	L	Y	V	D	L	F	W	J	Y	T	U	S	H
F	Z	D	P	U	I	G	Y	H	J	W	O	S	A
N	M	I	A	T	N	E	T	N	O	C	V	E	M
O	E	S	N	V	G	A	E	X	N	F	R	N	E
I	T	G	I	P	P	R	I	A	P	S	E	D	G
T	H	U	C	M	P	F	X	R	E	G	N	A	A
A	G	S	E	E	I	J	N	Y	E	G	X	S	R
L	I	T	K	Y	H	T	A	P	M	Y	S	Y	H
E	R	U	S	A	E	L	P	R	I	D	E	V	F
J	F	E	I	R	G	V	L	O	N	G	I	N	G
P	A	C	Z	E	S	T	R	U	H	O	P	E	H

Solution on Page 314

ACOUSTIC
BANJO
BOWED
CELLO
CHORD
DULCIMER
ELECTRIC
FIDDLE
GUITAR
HARP
INSTRUMENT
KACAPI
KOTO
LUTES
LYRE
MANDOLIN
MUSICAL
OCTOBASS
PANDURA
PIANO
PLUCKED
REBAB
SITAR
TAMBURA
TANBUR
UKULELE
VIOLIN
ZITHER

String Instruments

A	H	K	R	S	A	R	U	B	M	A	T	J	L
N	N	P	E	A	N	I	L	O	D	N	A	M	Q
M	H	R	E	H	T	I	Z	E	E	R	R	V	G
Z	R	C	S	S	O	I	K	M	N	U	U	G	G
S	A	E	I	M	F	C	U	A	W	B	D	B	V
Q	T	L	M	R	U	R	T	G	C	N	N	V	D
A	I	L	C	I	T	S	U	O	C	A	A	N	C
W	S	O	F	S	C	C	I	N	B	T	P	G	N
J	V	E	N	H	U	L	E	C	Q	A	T	I	J
S	P	I	O	K	B	D	U	L	A	P	S	U	D
Y	L	R	O	N	A	I	P	D	E	L	K	S	C
A	D	T	A	L	R	V	E	B	Y	U	T	E	N
I	O	S	J	H	I	W	A	R	L	C	F	T	K
V	V	R	O	R	O	N	E	E	M	K	E	U	G
R	E	B	A	B	J	Z	L	R	Z	E	B	L	Q
Y	S	N	G	O	I	E	E	L	D	D	I	F	I

Solution on Page 314

ACTIVITY
AMUSEMENT
BOOKS
BOWLING
CARD GAME
CARTOONS
CINEMA
CIRCUS
CLOWNS
COMEDY
COMICS
CONCERT
DANCE
DIVERSION
ENJOYMENT
FILM
FUN
GAMBLING
HOBBIES
HUMOR
LAUGHTER
LEISURE
MEDIA
MONOPOLY
MOVIE
MUSICAL
OPERA
PEOPLE
PLAYS
PUPPETS
RADIO
READING
RECREATION
RELAX
SINGER
SPORTS
STORY
THEATRE
VIDEO

Entertainment

H	O	B	B	I	E	S	Y	A	L	P	B	X	Y
R	E	L	A	X	M	O	N	O	P	O	L	Y	T
V	A	P	E	O	P	L	E	O	W	R	S	H	R
Y	I	M	U	S	I	C	A	L	O	E	U	Y	E
S	D	D	Z	P	Y	T	I	V	I	T	C	A	C
C	E	E	E	B	P	N	Q	L	D	H	R	G	N
I	M	L	M	O	G	E	S	H	I	G	I	A	O
M	S	E	A	O	R	M	T	A	V	U	C	M	C
O	I	I	G	K	C	E	U	S	E	A	L	B	I
C	N	S	D	S	R	S	A	N	R	L	O	L	N
S	G	U	R	T	H	U	F	D	S	F	W	I	E
P	E	R	A	R	O	M	U	H	I	U	N	N	M
O	R	E	C	R	E	A	T	I	O	N	S	G	A
R	H	E	N	J	O	Y	M	E	N	T	G	B	Q
T	D	A	N	C	E	I	V	O	M	L	I	F	M
S	T	O	R	Y	A	R	E	P	O	I	D	A	R

Solution on Page 314

AUTISM
AUTONOMY
BABY
BEHAVIOR
BIRTH
BRAIN
CHANGES
CHILDHOOD
CHILDREN
COGNITIVE
EDUCATION
EMOTIONAL
GENETICS
GROWTH
INFANT
LANGUAGE
LEARNING
LOVE
MENTAL
NEWBORN
NURTURE
NUTRITION
PARENTS
PHYSICAL
PLAYING
PRESCHOOL
PSYCHOLOGY
PUBERTY
SKILLS
STUDY
TEACHING
TEETHING
THEORIES
TODDLER

Child Development

G	H	H	T	R	I	B	C	H	A	N	G	E	S
E	L	N	B	P	R	E	S	C	H	O	O	L	T
N	E	R	D	L	I	H	C	P	N	I	E	E	U
E	A	O	L	A	T	A	T	H	U	T	V	M	D
T	R	B	A	Y	P	V	N	Y	R	I	N	O	Y
I	N	W	T	I	S	I	A	S	T	R	I	T	T
C	I	E	N	N	Y	O	F	I	U	T	A	I	R
S	N	N	E	G	C	R	N	C	R	U	R	O	E
P	G	S	M	J	H	G	I	A	E	N	B	N	B
A	N	K	D	O	O	H	D	L	I	H	C	A	U
R	I	I	Y	C	L	M	S	I	T	U	A	L	P
E	H	L	B	N	O	I	T	A	C	U	D	E	S
N	C	L	A	N	G	U	A	G	E	V	O	L	K
T	A	S	B	C	Y	M	O	N	O	T	U	A	D
S	E	I	R	O	E	H	T	O	D	D	L	E	R
N	T	E	E	T	H	I	N	G	R	O	W	T	H

Solution on Page 315

APPETIZER
ASPARAGUS
BEANS
BREADS
BROCCOLI
CABBAGE
CARROTS
CHIPS
COLESLAW
CORN
COURSE
COUSCOUS
CUISINE
DESSERT
DINNER
DRESSING
FOOD
FRIES
GREENS
LUNCH
MEAL
MUSHROOMS
PASTAS
PEAS
PLATE
PORTION
POTATOES
RESTAURANT
RICE
ROLLS
SALADS
SAUCE
SERVING
SMALL BOWL
SOUPS
SQUASH
STARCH
STUFFING
VEGETABLES

Side Dish

E	H	C	N	U	L	N	O	I	T	R	O	P	X
T	C	U	A	S	T	A	R	C	H	C	D	V	H
B	S	I	K	P	C	L	C	A	R	R	O	T	S
R	N	S	R	O	P	O	T	A	T	O	E	S	E
E	E	I	R	R	L	E	B	D	I	N	N	E	R
A	E	N	V	E	G	E	T	A	B	L	E	S	V
D	R	E	S	S	I	N	G	I	W	Y	E	M	I
S	G	L	T	T	S	C	D	O	Z	G	E	O	N
L	A	E	M	A	O	C	B	O	A	E	B	O	G
W	S	U	E	U	L	L	O	B	O	S	R	R	N
S	N	P	R	R	L	P	B	U	A	F	O	H	I
O	A	S	P	A	R	A	G	U	S	L	C	S	F
U	E	T	M	N	C	S	C	N	L	C	C	U	F
P	B	S	S	T	R	E	S	S	E	D	O	M	U
S	D	A	L	A	S	Q	U	A	S	H	L	U	T
O	O	S	I	S	P	I	H	C	F	R	I	E	S

Solution on Page 315

ADDRESS
ADHESIVE
AIRMAIL
BOOKLET
COLLECTOR
COST
COUNTRY
DELIVERY
DESIGNS
ENVELOPE
FOREVER
GOVERNMENT
HOBBY
LETTERS
LICK
MAILING
METER
PACKAGE
PAPER
PERFORATED
PHILATELY
PICTURE
POST CARDS
POSTMARK
PRICE
ROLL
SEND
SHEETS
SMALL
STICK
USPS

Stamp It

A	R	S	K	E	C	I	R	P	M	U	X	F	R
P	I	C	T	U	R	E	A	S	E	P	I	I	C
O	D	R	O	L	L	C	P	S	T	E	E	H	S
S	T	E	M	Y	K	E	O	N	E	R	B	X	T
T	E	A	L	A	L	P	S	G	R	F	G	U	I
M	L	S	G	I	I	O	T	I	J	O	N	S	C
A	K	E	C	I	V	L	C	S	V	R	I	P	K
R	O	K	X	C	Q	E	A	E	G	A	L	S	C
K	O	E	Y	C	A	V	R	D	U	T	I	M	C
O	B	T	V	S	E	N	D	Y	F	E	A	A	Q
T	S	O	C	I	M	E	S	O	Z	D	M	L	J
A	D	D	R	E	S	S	R	E	T	T	E	L	P
H	D	K	N	Y	L	E	T	A	L	I	H	P	I
R	T	T	B	G	V	L	H	O	B	B	Y	F	Q
M	P	A	P	E	R	D	O	D	X	N	L	V	C
U	T	Y	R	T	N	U	O	C	A	I	V	Y	A

Solution on Page 315

APPS
AUDIO
BATTERY
BUSINESS
COMPUTER
DESIGN
DEVICE
DISPLAY
EBOOKS
ELECTRONIC
GADGET
GAMES
INNOVATION
INTERNET
IPHONE
IPOD
ITUNES
JAILBREAK
LAPTOP
MAC
MEDIA
MOBILE
MOVIES
MULTITOUCH
MUSIC
PHOTOS
POPULAR
PORTABLE
SAFARI
SCREEN
SOFTWARE
STEVE JOBS
TABLET
TECHNOLOGY
VIDEO
WEB
WIFI
WIRELESS

iPad

S	M	H	M	J	W	I	R	E	L	E	S	S	Z
C	P	O	C	K	A	E	R	B	L	I	A	J	T
R	R	P	B	U	I	N	T	E	R	N	E	T	E
E	E	Y	A	I	O	S	C	P	O	T	P	A	L
E	T	A	S	Y	L	T	Y	R	E	T	T	A	B
N	U	L	I	G	R	E	I	E	O	I	D	U	A
O	P	P	N	O	A	V	P	T	C	M	S	P	T
E	M	S	N	L	L	E	O	M	L	I	V	A	R
D	O	I	O	O	U	J	D	W	N	U	V	T	O
I	C	D	V	N	P	O	B	E	I	S	M	E	P
V	I	M	A	H	O	B	S	B	R	K	D	G	D
I	S	O	T	C	P	S	C	Z	A	O	E	D	G
F	U	V	I	E	R	A	W	T	F	O	S	A	A
I	M	I	O	T	M	E	D	I	A	B	I	G	M
W	A	E	N	O	H	P	I	C	S	E	G	O	E
B	M	S	O	T	O	H	P	I	T	U	N	E	S

Solution on Page 315

ANIMAL
AQUARIUMS
AURELIA
BEACH
BLOOMS
CLEAR
COLORFUL
CUBOZOA
CURRENTS
DEADLY
DEEP SEA
FIRST AID
FISH
FLOATING
FOOD
FRESHWATER
GELATINOUS
JELLIES
MEDUSOZOA
NATURE
OCEAN
ORGANISM
PAINFUL
POISON
RED
SCYPHOZOA
SMALL
SOFT
STAUROZOA
STINGING
SWARMS
SWIMMING
TENTACLES
TOXIC
UMBRELLA
VINEGAR

Jellyfish

T	O	X	I	C	F	L	O	A	T	I	N	G	T
G	A	D	U	M	B	R	E	L	L	A	M	S	F
O	B	L	O	O	M	S	I	N	A	G	R	O	O
D	E	R	F	O	P	G	N	I	M	M	I	W	S
S	A	I	R	E	F	S	F	N	A	T	U	R	E
W	C	G	E	L	A	T	I	N	O	U	S	C	I
A	H	D	S	M	U	I	R	A	U	Q	A	U	L
R	P	E	H	C	R	N	S	O	R	A	O	B	L
M	A	A	W	L	E	G	T	Z	A	N	Z	O	E
S	I	D	A	E	L	I	A	O	G	I	O	Z	J
G	N	L	T	A	I	N	I	H	E	M	S	O	N
O	F	Y	E	R	A	G	D	P	N	A	U	A	O
C	U	R	R	E	N	T	S	Y	I	L	D	H	S
E	L	U	F	R	O	L	O	C	V	A	E	S	I
A	O	Z	O	R	U	A	T	S	A	F	M	I	O
N	X	S	E	L	C	A	T	N	E	T	S	F	P

Solution on Page 316

ADOBE
ALGORITHMS
APPLE
BUSINESS
CODE
COMPUTER
DATA
DISK
DOWNLOAD
DRIVERS
FIRMWARE
FREEWARE
FUNCTION
GAMES
HARDWARE
INSTALL
INTERFACE
JAVA
LANGUAGE
LINUX
MAC
MEMORY
MICROSOFT
MIDDLEWARE
OFFICE
PHOTOSHOP
PROCEDURES
PROGRAMS
SHAREWARE
SYNTAX
SYSTEM
TOOLS
USER
WINDOWS
WORD

Computer Software

I	P	U	T	O	O	L	S	Y	S	T	E	M	E
N	F	R	E	E	W	A	R	E	M	L	I	S	C
S	S	C	O	M	P	U	T	E	R	D	E	W	I
T	J	E	C	C	W	P	M	A	D	M	I	T	F
A	F	B	C	O	E	O	V	L	A	N	U	U	F
L	I	O	R	A	R	D	E	G	D	S	N	E	O
L	R	D	S	Y	F	W	U	O	E	C	D	R	T
W	M	A	S	O	A	R	W	R	T	D	A	A	J
V	W	P	S	R	R	S	E	I	E	I	O	W	A
D	A	R	E	D	O	C	O	T	N	S	L	E	V
R	R	O	N	G	A	N	I	H	N	K	N	R	A
I	E	G	I	P	P	C	A	M	G	I	W	A	P
V	J	R	S	M	P	O	H	S	O	T	O	H	P
E	G	A	U	G	N	A	L	A	T	A	D	S	L
R	D	M	B	H	A	R	D	W	A	R	E	M	E
S	U	S	Y	N	T	A	X	U	N	I	L	Q	L

Solution on Page 316

BRAN
CHEERIOS
CLUSTERS
CORN POPS
CORNFLAKES
CRISPIX
CRUNCHY
FIBER ONE
FRUITY
GRANOLA
HONEY NUT
HONEYCOMB
KASHI
KELLOGG'S
KIX
LIFE
MUESLI
OATMEAL
PEBBLES
POST
RICE CHEX
SPECIAL K
SUGAR POPS
TOTAL
TRIX
WHEAT CHEX
WHEATIES

Breakfast Cereals

Y	T	G	E	H	W	J	S	B	X	P	Z	M	G
T	U	N	I	O	A	T	M	E	A	L	F	D	I
I	X	A	K	G	S	O	I	R	E	E	H	C	E
U	C	R	U	N	C	H	Y	K	I	X	E	F	M
R	W	B	L	Y	P	C	N	X	E	C	I	G	C
F	I	B	E	R	O	N	E	H	X	L	R	R	S
V	D	N	S	Q	X	H	C	I	T	U	I	E	L
N	O	I	U	M	C	E	R	U	S	S	I	S	A
H	K	L	G	T	C	T	N	E	P	T	P	P	T
I	A	S	A	I	S	Y	L	I	A	E	U	O	O
E	S	E	R	O	E	B	X	E	C	R	M	P	T
O	H	U	P	N	B	K	H	I	V	S	K	N	I
W	I	M	O	E	J	W	A	L	O	N	A	R	G
Q	M	H	P	K	E	L	L	O	G	G	S	O	P
Z	E	X	S	E	K	A	L	F	N	R	O	C	X
P	N	B	C	G	U	K	W	R	Q	U	P	S	I

Solution on Page 316

APPLIANCES
ASSOCIATES
BLUE
BUSINESS
CAMERAS
CELL PHONE
COMPUTERS
CONSUMER
CUSTOMERS
DRYERS
DVD PLAYER
ELECTRONIC
EXPENSIVE
GADGETS
GAMES
GEEK SQUAD
MEDIA
MOVIE
MUSIC
ONLINE
PHONES
RETAILER
SALES
SERVICE
SHOPPING
SOFTWARE
STEREO
STORE
TECHNOLOGY
TELEVISION
TVS
WARRANTY
YELLOW TAG

Best Buy

C	S	R	Y	T	N	A	R	R	A	W	S	B	E
S	E	E	N	I	L	N	O	P	S	A	T	L	V
O	N	M	T	S	Q	R	P	R	L	O	E	U	I
F	O	U	A	A	E	L	E	E	H	C	C	E	S
T	H	S	B	O	I	M	S	T	T	D	H	C	N
W	P	N	P	A	O	C	A	R	A	Z	N	C	E
A	L	O	N	T	Z	A	O	G	J	I	O	A	P
R	L	C	S	S	E	N	I	S	U	B	L	M	X
E	E	U	E	C	I	V	R	E	S	S	O	E	E
S	C	Y	E	C	S	T	E	G	D	A	G	R	R
F	X	D	A	U	Q	S	K	E	E	G	Y	A	O
Y	Y	E	L	L	O	W	T	A	G	T	V	S	E
S	R	E	T	U	P	M	O	C	I	S	U	M	R
E	I	V	O	M	E	D	I	A	S	T	O	R	E
F	I	N	O	I	S	I	V	E	L	E	T	S	T
S	H	O	P	P	I	N	G	D	R	Y	E	R	S

Solution on Page 316

AESTHETIC
BASEBALL
BERMUDA
CARE
CUT
DIRT
EDGE
FERTILIZER
FLOWERS
FOOTBALL
GARDENS
GOLF
GRASSES
GREEN
GROW
HOME
HOUSE
INSECTS
IRRIGATE
LANDSCAPE
LAWN MOWER
MOWING
PARKS
PESTICIDE
PLANTING
SEEDS
SERVICE
SHRUBS
SOIL
SPRINKLER
SUMMER
TENNIS
TREES
TRIM
TURF
WATERING
WEED
YARD

Lawns

Y	H	L	Y	S	G	Z	B	T	H	B	F	K	Y
U	G	O	L	V	R	A	G	R	O	W	L	E	O
P	W	R	M	A	S	E	R	I	U	Y	O	B	N
H	E	I	A	E	B	S	W	D	S	S	W	E	T
H	D	S	B	S	T	T	E	O	E	F	E	R	F
K	P	A	T	C	S	H	O	E	M	N	R	M	E
Y	L	Q	E	I	V	E	R	O	D	N	S	U	R
L	A	S	Q	N	C	T	S	D	F	S	W	D	T
I	N	R	S	P	R	I	N	K	L	E	R	A	I
I	T	S	D	O	L	C	D	W	O	R	S	C	L
G	I	R	R	I	G	A	T	E	G	V	K	U	I
G	N	I	R	E	T	A	W	I	M	I	R	T	Z
R	G	I	R	H	L	A	N	D	S	C	A	P	E
E	G	A	W	S	H	R	U	B	S	E	P	D	R
E	C	L	I	O	S	I	N	N	E	T	G	Q	L
N	C	S	U	M	M	E	R	W	E	E	D	K	A

Solution on Page 317

APPETIZER
BACON BITS
BOWL
CAESAR
CARROTS
CHEESE
CHICKEN
COBB
CROUTONS
CUCUMBERS
DRESSING
EGGS
FRESH
FRUIT
GREENS
HAM
HEALTHY
ITALIAN
LETTUCE
MEAT
NUTS
OLIVES
ONIONS
PASTA
PEPPERS
PLATE
POTATO
RADISH
RANCH
ROMAINE
SAUCE
SEAFOOD
SIDE DISH
SPINACH
TOMATOES
TOSSED
TUNA
VEGETABLES
VINEGAR

Toss a Salad

E	C	U	A	S	W	D	H	J	P	S	Y	A	S
R	I	H	O	N	I	O	N	S	O	H	T	S	P
G	R	E	E	N	S	O	N	U	T	S	N	G	E
V	A	T	G	E	K	F	B	L	A	O	P	C	P
I	D	A	G	H	S	A	A	P	T	T	U	A	P
N	I	L	S	S	G	E	C	U	O	C	P	S	E
E	S	P	R	I	H	S	O	J	U	P	E	E	R
G	H	T	A	D	Z	R	N	M	E	L	D	O	S
A	E	I	S	E	C	C	B	T	B	R	L	T	N
R	C	U	E	D	H	E	I	A	E	I	O	A	C
O	U	R	A	I	R	Z	T	S	V	R	I	M	O
M	T	F	C	S	E	E	S	E	R	L	W	O	B
A	T	K	R	R	G	I	S	A	A	N	U	T	B
I	E	Y	M	E	N	K	C	T	O	S	S	E	D
N	L	K	V	G	S	P	I	N	A	C	H	A	M
E	U	R	A	N	C	H	M	E	A	T	U	N	C

Solution on Page 317

AGATE
AGGIE
ALLEY
BALL
CAT'S EYE
CHILDREN
CIRCLE
CLAY
COLLECTING
COLORS
DESIGN
DIRT
FLICK
FOR KEEPS
GAMES
GLASS
HIT
KEEPSIES
LOSE
NOSTALGIA
PLAY
POCKET
QUITSIES
RINGER
ROLLING
ROUND
SHOOTER
SIZE
SMALL
SPHERICAL
STEEL
STONE
SWIRL
TAKE
TARGET
THUMB
TOYS
TRADE
WIN

Marbles

N	G	I	S	E	D	N	U	O	R	T	U	U	Y
T	P	T	E	K	C	O	P	E	I	G	G	A	P
O	N	R	I	S	I	R	S	H	N	G	G	L	Z
Y	H	I	S	L	M	E	T	A	G	A	A	L	X
S	A	D	P	P	R	A	L	L	E	Y	E	E	X
E	Q	S	E	C	H	I	L	D	R	E	N	X	E
M	P	E	E	N	L	E	W	L	T	G	S	H	W
A	I	I	K	Y	O	A	R	S	N	Q	T	E	I
G	Q	S	I	Z	E	S	Y	I	R	O	O	K	C
L	N	T	P	T	J	S	T	E	C	T	N	A	S
A	I	I	H	E	R	C	T	A	R	A	E	T	G
S	W	U	L	O	E	O	F	A	L	L	L	E	H
S	M	Q	L	L	O	K	D	R	C	G	S	G	S
B	A	O	L	H	O	E	R	R	E	O	I	R	F
M	C	O	S	V	K	R	I	O	L	L	L	A	B
Q	C	R	F	L	I	C	K	J	F	O	X	T	U

Solution on Page 317

ACTIVITIES
ADDITION
ART
BLOCKS
BOOKS
BUS
CENTERS
CHILDHOOD
CHILDREN
CLASSROOM
DRAWING
EDUCATION
ELEMENTARY
FUN
INTERACT
KIDS
LANGUAGE
LEARNING
LINE
MATH
MUSIC
NUMBERS
PARENT
PLAY
PRESCHOOL
PRINCIPAL
READING
SINGING
SKILLS
SOCIAL
SONGS
STORY
STUDENTS
TEACHERS
VOCABULARY
WRITING
YOUNG

Kindergarten

I	N	T	E	R	A	C	T	M	S	O	N	G	S
G	C	H	I	L	D	H	O	O	D	F	T	G	Y
N	H	N	O	M	E	O	G	N	I	T	I	R	W
I	S	O	A	U	R	M	S	L	L	I	K	S	A
G	K	I	W	S	T	N	E	D	U	T	S	J	C
N	C	T	S	I	U	L	A	N	G	U	A	G	E
I	O	A	A	C	T	I	V	I	T	I	E	S	N
S	L	C	V	O	C	A	B	U	L	A	R	Y	T
C	B	U	Y	O	U	N	G	O	G	M	R	K	E
H	A	D	D	I	T	I	O	N	P	J	A	Y	R
I	Q	E	N	I	L	H	I	K	I	D	S	T	S
L	L	A	P	I	C	N	I	R	P	W	A	N	H
D	Y	A	Z	S	R	E	B	M	U	N	A	E	P
R	A	T	E	A	C	H	E	R	S	T	O	R	Y
E	L	R	E	A	D	I	N	G	F	U	N	A	D
N	P	L	A	I	C	O	S	K	O	O	B	P	F

Solution on Page 317

AGE
ART FORM
ARTISTIC
BARK
CARE
CHINESE
DWARFING
FORMS
GARDEN
GRAFTING
GREEN
GROWTH
HISTORY
HOBBY
INDOOR
JAPANESE
JUNIPER
LEAVES
MINIATURE
NATURE
NURSERY
OLD
OUTDOOR
PENJING
PERENNIAL
PINE
PLANTING
POTTED
PRUNING
SAMURAI
SHAPING
SHRUB
SOIL
STYLES
TOOLS
TREES
TRIMMING
WATER
WIRING
ZEN

Bonsai

S	M	C	H	I	N	E	S	E	N	A	P	A	J
E	Y	G	M	T	R	E	E	S	U	E	O	H	M
L	R	G	N	I	N	U	R	P	R	B	Z	J	K
Y	O	U	A	I	D	L	O	E	S	G	J	U	G
T	T	B	T	B	J	W	N	E	E	R	G	N	N
S	S	A	U	A	O	N	A	E	R	A	C	I	I
C	I	R	R	P	I	N	E	R	Y	F	C	P	T
I	H	K	E	A	C	N	D	P	F	T	M	E	N
S	T	S	L	S	R	C	I	T	S	I	T	R	A
L	W	L	N	A	Z	T	G	M	R	N	N	A	L
E	O	O	S	M	R	O	F	O	K	G	T	G	P
A	R	O	O	U	T	D	O	O	R	Z	E	E	O
V	G	T	I	R	Y	D	G	A	R	D	E	N	T
E	S	N	L	A	N	G	N	I	M	M	I	R	T
S	H	A	P	I	N	G	N	I	R	I	W	M	E
W	A	T	E	R	H	O	B	B	Y	J	Z	M	D

Solution on Page 318

APPLIANCES
AUTOMOTIVE
BEDDING
BUSINESS
CATALOG
CHAIN
CHICAGO
CLOTHING
CRAFTSMAN
CREDIT
DEPARTMENT
FURNITURE
HARDWARE
HOUSEWARES
JEWELRY
KENMORE
KMART
LAWN MOWER
MAIL ORDER
MALLS
MOWERS
OLD
PAINT
REPAIR
RETAILER
ROEBUCK
SALES
SERVICE
SHOPPING
STORES
SUPPLIES
TOOLS
TOWER
TOYS
WISHBOOK

Sears

T	R	A	M	K	E	R	U	T	I	N	R	U	F
N	T	J	C	O	R	E	L	I	A	T	E	R	R
B	O	S	H	O	P	P	I	N	G	S	D	R	O
G	Y	S	I	B	S	G	T	I	D	E	R	C	E
O	S	E	C	H	R	N	S	F	P	H	O	T	B
L	E	N	A	S	E	I	E	A	E	O	L	O	U
A	C	I	G	I	W	H	R	P	C	U	I	W	C
T	N	S	O	W	O	T	O	A	I	S	A	E	K
A	A	U	T	O	M	O	T	I	V	E	M	R	B
C	I	B	L	E	N	L	S	N	R	W	A	A	E
H	L	D	N	F	W	C	U	T	E	A	L	W	D
A	P	T	R	I	A	P	E	R	S	R	L	D	D
I	P	S	E	I	L	P	P	U	S	E	S	R	I
N	A	S	O	H	C	R	A	F	T	S	M	A	N
J	E	W	E	L	R	Y	S	A	L	E	S	H	G
S	L	O	O	T	E	R	O	M	N	E	K	D	N

Solution on Page 318

AEROSPACE
ANALYSIS
BRIDGES
BUILDING
CHEMICAL
COLLEGE
COMPUTERS
CONSTRUCT
EDUCATION
INDUSTRIAL
INGENUITY
JOB
KNOWLEDGE
MATERIALS
MECHANICS
PHYSICS
PLAN
PROBLEMS
PRODUCTION
PROFESSION
REGULATION
RESEARCH
SAFETY
SOFTWARE
STRUCTURES
SYSTEMS
TECHNICAL
TECHNOLOGY
TRAIN
UNIVERSITY
WORK

Engineering

S	B	S	L	Y	G	O	L	O	N	H	C	E	T
A	U	E	A	U	M	P	R	O	B	L	E	M	S
F	I	G	I	S	L	A	I	R	E	T	A	M	W
E	L	D	R	N	S	T	B	O	J	N	Q	A	O
T	D	I	T	A	A	H	C	R	A	E	S	E	R
Y	I	R	S	L	C	O	L	L	E	G	E	R	K
T	N	B	U	P	P	H	Y	S	I	C	S	O	T
I	G	G	D	S	Y	S	T	E	M	S	T	S	K
S	E	S	N	O	I	T	C	U	D	O	R	P	N
R	N	O	I	S	S	E	F	O	R	P	U	A	O
E	U	F	O	L	A	C	I	M	E	H	C	C	W
V	I	T	C	O	N	S	T	R	U	C	T	E	L
I	T	W	C	I	N	O	I	T	A	C	U	D	E
N	Y	A	A	C	O	M	P	U	T	E	R	S	D
U	T	R	C	L	A	C	I	N	H	C	E	T	G
I	T	E	M	E	C	H	A	N	I	C	S	O	E

Solution on Page 318

AGE
ANIMAL
AQUATIC
BEACH
BOX TURTLE
CARAPACE
CLAWS
CRAWL
EGGS
ENDANGERED
FLIPPERS
GREEN
HARE
HIDE
LAND
MARINE
NATURE
NECK
OCEAN
OLD
PETS
REPTILES
SEA TURTLE
SHELLS
SHIELD
SLOW
SNAPPING
SOUP
SPECIES
SWIMMING
TAIL
TERRAPIN
TORTOISE
WATER
ZOO

Turtle Life

C	P	C	D	F	S	E	I	C	E	P	S	Y	N
O	J	Y	E	N	M	G	C	I	T	A	U	Q	A
R	B	D	E	R	E	G	N	A	D	N	E	C	T
L	I	L	L	E	L	E	E	I	P	N	O	M	U
H	O	O	T	S	T	I	R	C	M	A	A	T	R
N	H	O	R	I	R	T	A	G	P	M	R	L	E
P	A	Z	U	O	U	E	H	T	T	M	I	A	X
P	F	V	T	T	T	E	P	U	R	G	D	W	C
Q	E	M	A	R	X	R	E	P	T	I	L	E	S
J	W	T	E	O	O	D	L	E	I	H	S	L	N
L	S	A	S	T	B	A	H	E	N	L	L	T	A
R	O	C	T	H	G	F	N	C	G	E	F	R	P
G	U	C	R	E	C	I	L	I	H	G	C	W	P
W	P	H	E	A	R	A	B	S	M	W	S	K	I
F	U	K	E	A	W	T	E	R	R	A	P	I	N
E	T	P	M	S	N	L	C	B	W	O	L	S	G

Solution on Page 318

ASPHALT
BUILDING
CHIMNEY
COLLAPSE
COVERING
DRAINAGE
DURABILITY
DWELLING
EAVES
FELT
FLAT
GABLE
GUTTERS
HOUSE
INSULATION
MATERIAL
METAL
NAILS
PEAKED
PITCH
PROTECTS
REPAIR
REPLACE
ROOFER
SHINGLES
SLATE
SLOPE
SNOW
SOLAR
STRAW
TAR
THATCHING
TILES
TOP
WEATHER
WOOD

Roofs

T	A	L	F	G	D	T	B	A	L	W	O	O	D
I	T	F	O	Y	E	N	M	I	H	C	G	B	E
L	L	A	I	R	E	T	A	M	O	N	W	U	K
E	A	V	E	S	G	R	O	V	I	O	M	I	A
S	H	V	Y	N	A	S	E	H	G	A	B	L	E
W	P	S	C	T	N	R	C	W	J	J	E	D	P
A	S	H	N	O	I	T	A	L	U	S	N	I	I
R	A	I	W	N	A	L	N	L	P	Q	L	N	T
T	O	N	G	H	R	J	I	A	O	J	L	G	C
S	C	G	T	L	D	W	L	B	I	S	N	C	H
L	R	L	P	T	E	L	E	C	A	L	P	E	R
A	L	E	O	A	O	P	R	Z	L	R	S	E	E
T	A	S	T	C	E	T	O	R	P	T	U	P	P
E	T	H	R	T	G	N	I	L	L	E	W	D	A
U	E	A	H	O	U	S	E	E	S	S	H	S	I
R	M	Q	S	V	C	G	F	R	O	O	F	E	R

Solution on Page 319

- ATTACK
- BISHOPS
- BLACK
- BOARD GAME
- CAPTURE
- CASTLING
- CHAMPION
- CHECKERED
- CHECKMATE
- CHESSBOARD
- CLUB
- COMPUTER
- FORK
- FUN
- GAMBIT
- KINGS
- KNIGHTS
- MASTERS
- MOVES
- OPPONENT
- PAWNS
- PIECES
- QUEEN
- ROOKS
- RULES
- SKILL
- SQUARES
- STALEMATE
- STRATEGY
- TACTICS
- THINKING
- TURN
- WHITE
- WIN

The Game of Kings

B	O	A	R	D	G	A	M	E	R	P	N	T	O
C	A	P	T	U	R	E	E	I	W	I	N	A	O
F	B	L	N	E	T	A	M	K	C	E	H	C	A
P	A	W	N	S	E	V	O	M	C	C	E	T	J
X	S	S	P	O	H	S	I	B	A	E	T	I	D
A	C	M	A	S	T	E	R	S	S	S	A	C	E
T	E	T	I	H	W	C	K	S	T	S	M	S	R
T	K	V	G	K	R	O	F	K	L	E	E	H	E
A	I	I	V	U	O	M	R	O	I	R	L	H	K
C	N	C	H	A	M	P	I	O	N	A	A	K	C
K	G	B	H	N	J	U	P	R	G	U	T	G	E
Z	S	S	L	Q	E	T	E	O	J	Q	S	A	H
N	S	T	R	A	T	E	G	Y	N	S	R	M	C
R	U	L	E	S	C	R	U	H	N	E	E	B	L
U	R	Z	L	L	I	K	S	Q	F	U	N	I	U
T	U	S	C	U	G	N	I	K	N	I	H	T	B

Solution on Page 319

ACCENT
ARTIFICIAL
BRIGHT
BULBS
CANDLES
CEILING
DARK
DAYLIGHT
DIM
ELECTRICAL
FILAMENT
FIXTURE
FLOODLIGHT
FLOOR LAMP
GLOW
HALOGEN
ILLUMINATE
INDOOR
LAMPS
LANTERN
LED
LIGHT BULB
NATURAL
NEON
NIGHT
OUTDOOR
RECESSED
SCONCE
SEE
SHADOW
SHOW
SOLAR
SPOTLIGHT
STAGE
SUN
SWITCH
TRACK
VIEW
WATT
WIRING

Lighting

E	C	N	O	C	S	H	A	D	O	W	L	L	S
W	R	S	F	C	A	N	D	L	E	S	Z	A	B
O	E	U	P	L	V	I	E	W	P	L	G	R	L
L	T	H	T	M	O	R	O	O	D	N	I	U	U
G	A	Z	C	X	A	O	T	D	I	M	N	T	B
L	N	T	L	T	I	L	D	R	E	B	O	A	J
P	I	E	H	A	I	F	I	L	A	M	E	N	T
O	M	G	G	G	I	W	E	E	I	D	N	N	H
K	U	A	H	A	I	C	S	G	T	G	T	R	A
C	L	T	L	T	T	R	I	Y	H	D	H	E	L
A	L	N	D	R	B	S	B	F	G	Y	G	T	O
R	I	E	I	O	O	U	C	E	I	L	I	N	G
T	C	C	N	K	O	O	L	C	L	T	N	A	E
K	A	C	R	U	D	R	L	B	Y	U	R	L	N
L	R	A	L	O	S	E	E	F	A	T	T	A	W
U	D	R	E	C	E	S	S	E	D	W	O	H	S

Solution on Page 319

BALD
BARBER
BLACK
BLOND
BODY
BROWN
BUN
CLIP
COMB
CONDITION
CURLY
CUTTING
DERMIS
DYE
EYELASHES
FINE
FOLLICLES
GEL
GRAY
GROWTH
HAIRCUT
HEAD
KERATIN
LENGTH
LONG
PERMANENT
RED
ROOT
SCALP
SCISSORS
SET
SHAVING
SHORT
SOFT
STRAIGHT
STYLE
TEXTURE
WASH
WAVY
WIGS

Hair

B	H	I	H	L	H	C	G	X	M	S	L	Y	G
W	A	V	Y	S	U	U	N	L	Z	O	E	C	R
I	P	L	A	C	S	H	A	V	I	N	G	T	O
G	G	W	D	K	E	R	A	T	I	N	F	H	W
S	V	K	Z	X	D	E	O	C	N	O	T	G	T
G	S	Z	C	A	N	B	U	S	S	W	N	I	H
N	H	J	E	A	O	R	G	N	S	I	O	A	V
O	O	H	L	D	L	A	U	E	T	I	I	R	P
L	R	I	Y	Y	B	B	H	T	L	R	C	T	B
C	T	E	T	A	N	S	U	T	C	O	O	S	D
F	H	S	S	I	A	C	E	U	G	A	M	T	D
Q	T	L	I	L	D	X	T	Q	R	A	B	E	B
E	G	O	E	M	T	N	E	N	A	M	R	E	P
X	N	Y	O	U	R	Y	O	D	Y	E	K	I	Y
P	E	I	R	R	S	E	L	C	I	L	L	O	F
D	L	E	F	L	B	U	D	M	A	C	T	Q	U

Solution on Page 319

- ALIENS
- AMBUSH
- ARCADE
- ASTEROIDS
- ATARI
- BATMAN
- BATTLEZONE
- CENTIPEDE
- COMMANDO
- CONTRA
- CRAZY TAXI
- DEFENDER
- DIG DUG
- DUCK HUNT
- FROGGER
- GALAXIAN
- GAUNTLET
- JOUST
- MAPPY
- MARIO BROS.
- METAL SLUG
- PACMAN
- PINBALL
- PLAY
- PONG
- QIX
- SIMPSONS
- STAR WARS
- TEKKEN
- TETRIS
- TRON

Classic Arcade Games

N	E	L	S	O	R	B	O	I	R	A	M	J	A
W	T	E	K	K	E	N	G	X	I	Q	G	P	Z
H	N	A	M	C	A	P	U	A	M	B	U	S	H
L	U	E	N	O	Z	E	L	T	T	A	B	S	D
R	H	T	E	T	R	I	S	Y	C	F	D	R	I
E	K	A	S	O	I	J	L	Z	Y	I	I	A	X
D	C	L	I	I	R	X	A	A	O	P	P	W	L
N	U	I	M	I	A	R	T	R	D	I	P	R	I
E	D	E	P	I	T	N	E	C	N	G	W	A	D
F	J	N	S	N	A	T	M	B	A	A	R	T	M
E	P	S	O	M	S	P	A	L	M	U	E	S	E
D	O	C	N	A	P	L	A	Y	M	N	D	U	V
Q	N	N	S	Y	L	X	W	M	O	T	A	O	D
R	G	U	D	G	I	D	B	Y	C	L	C	J	K
A	C	S	G	A	F	R	O	G	G	E	R	I	Q
T	R	O	N	A	M	T	A	B	C	T	A	M	G

Solution on Page 320

HICCUPS
HICKEYS
HICKORY
HIDINGS
HIGH ROAD
HIGHEST
HIGHLIFE
HIGHNESS
HIGHTAIL
HIGHWAYS
HIKING
HILARITY
HILLERS
HILLIEST
HILLSIDE
HILLTOPS
HILTING
HIMSELF
HINDMOST
HINTING
HIPBONES
HIPLINES
HIPSHOT
HIPSTERS
HIRABLE
HIRELING
HIRING
HISSINGS
HITCHING
HITHERTO
HIVELESS

Starts with HI

S	R	E	L	L	I	H	I	M	S	E	L	F	C
T	S	E	I	L	L	I	H	I	C	K	O	R	Y
S	H	L	Y	T	I	R	A	L	I	H	J	D	P
S	I	B	S	U	A	T	S	E	H	G	I	H	S
E	P	A	Y	T	T	S	O	M	D	N	I	H	T
L	S	R	A	G	H	I	L	L	T	O	P	S	X
E	T	I	W	S	G	N	I	S	S	I	H	E	H
V	E	H	H	H	I	P	B	O	N	E	S	N	I
I	R	F	G	Q	H	I	C	C	U	P	S	I	T
H	S	T	I	H	I	T	H	E	R	T	O	L	C
I	Y	O	H	L	G	N	I	T	L	I	H	P	H
D	E	H	I	G	H	N	E	S	S	O	F	I	I
I	K	S	K	K	R	G	N	I	T	N	I	H	N
N	C	P	I	E	O	H	I	R	E	L	I	N	G
G	I	I	N	F	A	S	C	H	I	R	I	N	G
S	H	H	G	E	D	I	S	L	L	I	H	N	V

Solution on Page 320

ACROBATICS
APPLES
AUDIENCE
BALLS
BEANBAGS
CATCHING
CHAINSAWS
CIRCUS
CLOWN
CLUBS
FESTIVAL
FIRE
HANDS
HOBBY
JESTER
JUGGLERS
KNIVES
MOTION
OBJECTS
PERFORMER
PROP
RHYTHM
RINGS
SHOW
SKILL
SPORTS
THROWING
TORCHES
TOSS
TRICKS

Juggling

Y	N	R	S	C	I	T	A	B	O	R	C	A	G
P	N	X	S	G	H	R	A	S	E	V	I	N	K
R	P	C	E	H	U	A	B	W	S	K	I	L	L
L	E	F	H	O	O	C	I	Q	X	W	M	L	M
P	I	M	C	P	G	W	I	N	O	N	P	A	Z
H	Y	O	R	C	M	N	X	R	S	I	X	V	D
V	A	O	O	O	A	J	H	I	C	A	G	I	S
B	P	P	T	A	F	T	F	V	Z	U	W	T	T
R	U	I	P	J	C	R	C	I	I	D	S	S	C
I	O	O	Q	L	U	R	E	H	R	I	A	E	E
N	G	K	O	S	E	G	D	P	I	E	F	F	J
G	X	W	L	T	M	S	G	A	B	N	A	E	B
S	N	L	S	R	S	B	U	L	C	C	G	U	O
X	A	E	H	O	B	B	Y	X	E	E	R	P	Q
B	J	I	T	P	M	H	T	Y	H	R	R	T	D
H	A	N	D	S	V	T	R	I	C	K	S	A	T

Solution on Page 320

ASSONANCE
BALLAD
BEAUTIFUL
BOOKS
CLASSIC
COLLECTION
COUPLET
DRAMA
EPIC
FEELINGS
FREE VERSE
HAIKU
IAMBIC
LANGUAGE
LIMERICK
LINES
LITERATURE
LOVE
LYRICS
MEANING
METER
ODES
POETS
PROSE
READING
RHYMING
RHYTHM
ROMANCE
SIMILE
SONNET
STANZAS
STORY
TEXT
THOUGHTS
TONE
VERSES
WHITMAN
WORDS
WRITING

Poetic

H	R	E	E	S	O	R	P	O	E	T	S	N	E
S	E	N	I	L	I	M	E	R	I	C	K	U	P
P	T	O	S	E	C	N	A	M	O	R	W	W	I
W	E	T	C	O	B	A	L	L	A	D	R	R	C
F	M	E	I	F	D	E	L	I	M	I	S	I	S
S	E	S	R	E	V	E	E	R	F	S	B	T	T
P	A	E	Y	U	C	E	S	S	T	M	E	I	O
R	S	S	L	T	T	G	T	H	A	C	A	N	R
W	S	K	I	I	E	A	G	I	S	L	U	G	Y
R	O	O	M	K	N	U	R	O	F	A	T	N	L
H	N	O	T	Z	O	G	N	E	E	S	I	I	D
Y	A	B	A	H	U	N	S	V	T	S	F	M	R
T	N	S	T	K	E	A	O	V	J	I	U	Y	A
H	C	X	I	T	E	L	P	U	O	C	L	H	M
M	E	A	N	I	N	G	N	I	D	A	E	R	A
T	H	S	D	R	O	W	H	I	T	M	A	N	E

Solution on Page 320

BAGELS
BOLOGNA
BREAD
CAVIAR
CHEESES
CHICKEN
COFFEE
COLD CUTS
COOKIES
COUNTER
DELICIOUS
DIPS
DRINKS
FINE FOODS
GERMAN
GROCERY
HAM
JEWISH
KOSHER
LUNCH
MEATS
MILK
NEW YORK
NUMBER
OLIVES
ORDER
PASTRAMI
PICKLE
SALAMI
SANDWICHES
SAUSAGE
SHOP
STORE
TEA
TUNA
TURKEY
WINE

Delicatessen

S	Y	T	G	L	I	M	A	R	T	S	A	P	O
K	O	S	H	E	R	K	S	N	U	M	B	E	R
C	O	O	K	I	E	S	P	O	G	C	K	N	D
Q	U	F	R	N	B	Y	I	S	D	O	W	I	E
F	P	T	O	D	I	C	D	A	H	F	L	W	R
T	I	U	Y	K	I	R	E	N	A	F	S	O	J
D	C	N	W	L	E	R	D	D	M	E	N	E	B
H	K	A	E	T	B	N	S	W	V	E	W	R	P
G	L	D	N	F	C	T	Z	I	K	I	A	V	O
R	E	U	X	A	O	K	L	C	S	E	E	T	H
O	O	N	V	R	L	O	I	H	T	G	S	N	S
C	U	I	E	I	D	H	D	E	A	L	A	N	H
E	A	Z	M	D	C	S	E	S	E	E	H	C	C
R	Y	E	K	R	U	T	U	G	E	R	M	A	N
Y	B	B	U	G	T	A	A	W	F	U	K	E	U
I	M	A	L	A	S	B	K	C	B	E	H	M	L

Solution on Page 321

APERTURE
ASPECT
CAMERA
CANON
CAPTURE
CARD
COMPUTERS
CROPPING
DELETE
DOWNLOAD
EASY
EDITING
EXPOSURE
FILTER
FLASH
FOCUS
IMAGING
INTERNET
KODAK
LANDSCAPE
LENS
LIGHT
MEGAPIXEL
MEMORY
OLYMPUS
PICTURES
PIXELS
PRINTING
RAW
SCANNING
SENSOR
SHARE
SIZING
SLR
SOFTWARE
SONY
STORAGE
UPLOAD
VIEW
ZOOM

Digital Photography

Y	N	O	S	F	T	E	N	R	E	T	N	I	R
Q	S	F	I	L	T	E	R	X	L	E	N	S	O
W	S	A	M	A	R	D	P	A	F	O	C	U	S
C	C	W	E	S	M	O	O	Z	W	E	I	V	N
R	A	W	M	H	S	W	C	A	P	T	U	R	E
W	N	J	O	U	I	N	G	C	C	T	F	P	S
P	N	H	R	C	K	L	R	S	C	A	N	O	N
G	I	E	Y	O	B	O	O	L	Y	M	P	U	S
W	N	C	D	M	P	A	P	E	R	T	U	R	E
I	G	A	T	P	P	D	E	X	G	E	S	G	E
T	K	A	I	U	P	P	R	I	N	T	I	N	G
H	C	N	R	T	R	W	A	P	I	E	Z	I	A
G	G	E	D	E	U	E	H	A	T	L	I	G	R
I	W	R	P	R	M	H	S	G	I	E	N	A	O
L	A	N	D	S	C	A	P	E	D	D	G	M	T
C	U	P	L	O	A	D	C	M	E	I	Y	I	S

Solution on Page 321

ACTION
AUDIO
BACKUP
BLANK
BLU-RAY
BURN
CASE
COMPACT
COMPUTER
DATA
DIGITAL
DISK
DRIVE
DVD PLAYER
FILM
FORMAT
HOME
LASER
MEDIUM
MOVIES
MUSIC
NETFLIX
OPTICAL
PAUSE
PHILIPS
PLASTIC
RECORDABLE
RENTAL
ROUND
SCRATCH
SHOW
SONY
SPEED
STORAGE
TECHNOLOGY
TELEVISION
TOSHIBA
VHS
VIDEO
WATCH

DVD

X	T	O	S	H	I	B	A	K	S	I	D	J	M
C	Z	E	G	A	R	O	T	S	E	E	Q	H	L
O	X	H	C	T	A	R	C	S	E	S	M	C	I
M	I	G	P	H	I	L	I	P	S	R	U	T	F
P	L	H	S	O	N	Y	S	R	U	Z	S	A	V
A	F	T	A	M	R	O	F	E	C	K	I	W	P
C	T	P	R	E	S	A	L	C	C	I	C	C	S
T	E	L	E	V	I	S	I	O	N	S	R	A	D
K	N	A	L	B	S	L	M	R	G	E	C	S	B
M	U	A	C	N	D	P	Y	D	Y	Y	I	E	M
E	V	E	C	R	U	L	L	A	C	I	T	P	O
D	I	G	I	T	A	L	L	B	R	A	S	N	V
I	D	V	E	T	I	P	W	L	O	U	A	R	I
U	E	R	N	O	D	O	Y	E	U	D	L	U	E
M	O	E	Z	V	H	S	N	F	N	I	P	B	S
S	R	N	D	S	P	A	T	A	D	O	Z	O	D

Solution on Page 321

AZTECS
BIOFUEL
CEREAL
COOK
CORNMEAL
CROP
CULTIVATE
EARS
ETHANOL
FARMING
FIELDS
FOOD
GENETICS
GRAIN
GRITS
GROUND
HARVEST
HOMINY
HUSK
INDIAN
KERNELS
MAYANS
MEXICO
MILL
OIL
PLANT
POPCORN
SEASON
SEEDS
STAPLE
STARCH
SWEET CORN
TASSEL
TORTILLA
TRADE
VARIETIES
VEGETABLE
YELLOW

Maize

T	N	A	I	D	N	I	H	U	S	K	N	C	T
R	T	S	L	H	C	R	A	T	S	T	I	R	G
A	L	A	E	M	N	R	O	C	X	A	D	O	Z
D	I	V	S	E	S	N	U	C	L	F	K	P	E
E	O	E	S	K	D	L	A	L	P	E	F	M	V
B	N	G	A	S	T	S	I	Z	R	O	L	A	Y
I	R	E	T	I	C	T	E	N	T	F	P	Y	E
O	O	T	V	A	R	I	E	T	I	E	S	A	L
F	C	A	P	O	R	I	T	E	H	A	C	N	L
U	T	B	T	C	S	F	L	E	G	A	R	S	O
E	E	L	S	I	C	D	Y	L	N	Z	N	G	W
L	E	E	E	X	S	N	D	T	I	E	A	O	J
P	W	R	A	E	I	U	S	N	M	M	G	C	L
A	S	T	S	M	A	O	H	A	R	V	E	S	T
T	A	K	O	O	C	R	L	L	A	E	R	E	C
S	F	H	N	V	R	G	S	P	F	O	O	D	N

Solution on Page 321

ACTIVITIES
ADVERTISE
BEBO
BLOG
CHAT
CLASSMATES
COMMENTS
COMMUNITY
COMPUTER
CONNECTION
CONTACT
DATING
E-MAIL
EVENTS
FACEBOOK
FRIENDSTER
INTERACT
INTERESTS
INTERNET
LIKE
LINKEDIN
MYSPACE
NETWORKING
ONLINE
PEOPLE
PICTURES
PLATFORM
PRIVACY
SHARING
TECHNOLOGY
TWITTER
WALL
WEBSITE

Social Networks

L	G	B	C	O	N	T	A	C	T	E	K	I	L
L	C	L	Y	K	S	T	S	E	R	E	T	N	I
A	H	O	A	D	V	E	R	T	I	S	E	I	N
W	A	G	M	R	E	T	U	P	M	O	C	E	K
R	T	D	P	M	J	G	N	I	R	A	H	S	E
M	E	Y	I	W	E	B	S	I	T	E	N	O	D
Y	R	T	C	O	N	N	E	C	T	I	O	N	I
S	E	I	T	I	V	I	T	C	A	N	L	E	N
P	T	N	U	I	H	I	A	S	D	T	O	T	P
A	S	U	R	E	W	N	M	T	A	E	G	W	R
C	D	M	E	N	O	T	S	N	T	R	Y	O	I
E	N	M	S	I	B	E	S	E	I	A	L	R	V
P	E	O	P	L	E	R	A	V	N	C	I	K	A
Q	I	C	K	N	B	N	L	E	G	T	A	I	C
C	R	K	O	O	B	E	C	A	F	D	M	N	Y
Y	F	M	R	O	F	T	A	L	P	J	E	G	K

Solution on Page 322

BRIDGES
BRUSHING
CAVITIES
CHAIR
CLEANING
CROWNS
DECAY
DENTIST
DENTURES
DIAGNOSIS
DISEASES
DOCTOR
DRILLS
EXTRACTION
FEAR
FILLINGS
FLOSSING
FLUORIDE
GINGIVITIS
GUM
HEALTH
HYGIENISTS
MEDICINE
MOLAR
ORAL
PAIN
PATIENT
PLAQUE
PREVENTION
ROOT CANAL
SEDATION
SPIT
SURGERY
TOOTHACHE
TREATMENT

Dentistry

T	H	T	L	A	E	H	R	M	Y	A	C	E	D
S	U	R	G	E	R	Y	O	U	T	L	Y	D	I
I	S	L	S	O	M	G	O	G	R	P	A	I	N
T	N	S	T	N	O	I	T	N	E	V	E	R	P
N	W	C	P	D	P	E	C	I	A	S	H	O	O
E	O	A	L	I	A	N	A	S	T	E	C	U	O
D	R	V	A	S	T	I	N	S	M	R	A	L	I
C	C	I	Q	E	I	S	A	O	E	U	H	F	W
N	H	T	U	A	E	T	L	L	N	T	T	D	C
O	A	I	E	S	N	S	I	F	T	N	O	R	L
I	I	E	Z	E	T	Z	J	V	J	E	O	I	E
T	R	S	I	S	O	N	G	A	I	D	T	L	A
A	R	A	E	F	I	L	L	I	N	G	S	L	N
D	F	E	X	T	R	A	C	T	I	O	N	S	I
E	N	I	C	I	D	E	M	O	L	A	R	I	N
S	E	G	D	I	R	B	R	U	S	H	I	N	G

Solution on Page 322

BAR
BICYCLE
CLOSED
CYLINDER
DEADBOLT
DEVICE
DOOR LOCKS
ELECTRONIC
ENTRY
FASTENING
GUARD
KEYCARD
KEYCODE
LOCKSMITH
LUGGAGE
MAGNETIC
MASTER
MECHANICAL
METAL
OPEN
PADLOCK
PASSWORD
PICKING
PIN LOCK
PREVENT
PRIVACY
PROTECT
RFID
SAFETY
SECRET
SECURITY
STEEL
THIEF
TUMBLER
TURN
VAULT
YALE

Lock Up

L	E	E	T	S	Y	V	E	M	A	S	T	E	R
Q	N	C	C	P	A	D	L	O	C	K	C	I	F
D	T	M	A	G	N	E	T	I	C	E	E	R	I
O	R	R	E	D	N	I	L	Y	C	Y	T	E	D
O	Y	C	L	H	T	I	M	S	K	C	O	L	K
R	C	G	K	C	O	L	N	I	P	A	R	B	E
L	A	C	I	N	A	H	C	E	M	R	P	M	Y
O	V	G	U	D	Y	N	R	U	T	D	D	U	C
C	I	N	O	R	T	C	E	L	E	S	R	T	O
K	R	I	T	O	I	T	L	O	B	D	A	E	D
S	P	K	E	W	R	N	C	U	P	E	U	F	E
A	V	C	R	S	U	E	Y	X	G	E	G	K	S
F	A	I	C	S	C	V	C	B	R	G	N	Y	O
E	U	P	E	A	E	E	I	M	E	T	A	L	L
T	L	M	S	P	S	R	B	A	R	L	U	G	C
Y	T	H	I	E	F	P	E	D	E	V	I	C	E

Solution on Page 322

- AGES
- AMERICAN
- ANCIENT
- ART
- BOOKS
- CIVIL WAR
- CLASS
- COUNTRIES
- CULTURE
- ERA
- EVENTS
- GOVERNMENT
- HISTORIANS
- KINGS
- KNOWLEDGE
- LEARNING
- LESSONS
- MILITARY
- MODERN
- MUSEUM
- NARRATIVE
- NATIONAL
- OLD
- PAST
- PEOPLE
- PERIODS
- POLITICS
- PREHISTORY
- RECORD
- RELIGION
- REVOLUTION
- SCHOOL
- STORIES
- STUDY
- TIME
- WARS
- WESTERN
- WORLD

History

P	E	O	P	L	E	L	A	N	O	I	T	A	N
B	R	S	T	G	O	L	D	R	O	C	E	R	A
O	U	N	C	N	O	I	T	U	L	O	V	E	R
O	T	O	T	I	E	V	E	N	T	S	J	L	R
K	L	S	N	N	T	M	U	E	S	U	M	I	A
S	U	S	E	R	A	I	N	Y	P	O	H	G	T
G	C	E	I	A	W	G	L	R	D	Q	I	I	I
N	I	L	C	E	D	M	E	O	E	U	S	O	V
I	V	N	N	I	P	H	Y	S	P	V	T	N	E
K	I	N	A	C	I	R	E	M	A	P	O	S	W
C	L	A	S	S	A	S	M	Y	S	E	R	G	E
I	W	R	T	T	C	O	U	N	T	R	I	E	S
N	A	O	I	H	D	T	I	M	E	I	A	R	T
W	R	L	O	E	G	D	E	L	W	O	N	K	E
Y	I	O	R	J	G	W	O	R	L	D	S	R	R
M	L	N	X	S	T	O	R	I	E	S	A	G	N

Solution on Page 322

ADDICTION
ALERTNESS
ALKALOID
AWAKE
BEANS
BITTER
BUZZ
CAPPUCCINO
CHEMICAL
CHOCOLATE
COCA COLA
COFFEE
CUP
DECAF
DIURETIC
DRINKS
DRUG
ENERGY
ESPRESSO
FRUIT
HEADACHE
HEART RATE
HYPER
JITTERS
JOLT
KOLA NUT
LATTE
LEAVES
MOLECULE
PILLS
PLANT
POP
RED BULL
SLEEP
SODA
SOFT DRINK
STIMULANT
TEA
WITHDRAWAL

Caffeine

I	C	O	N	I	C	C	U	P	P	A	C	A	V
Z	I	S	L	L	I	P	L	A	N	T	L	O	J
Z	T	R	E	T	T	I	B	E	N	E	R	G	Y
U	E	E	T	E	S	S	E	N	T	R	E	L	A
B	R	T	N	S	N	O	I	T	C	I	D	D	A
K	U	T	A	P	D	F	D	Q	L	M	B	R	S
W	I	I	L	R	E	T	E	A	A	O	U	I	L
U	D	J	U	E	T	D	B	J	W	L	L	N	E
H	E	G	M	S	A	R	E	C	A	E	L	K	E
E	C	A	I	S	L	I	A	H	R	C	E	S	P
A	A	W	T	O	O	N	N	E	D	U	A	V	L
D	F	A	S	P	C	K	S	M	H	L	V	F	A
A	L	K	A	L	O	I	D	I	T	E	E	R	T
C	R	E	P	Y	H	P	G	C	I	H	S	U	T
H	C	O	C	A	C	O	L	A	W	Q	G	I	E
E	E	F	F	O	C	K	O	L	A	N	U	T	P

Solution on Page 323

ARTIFACTS
BASEBALL
CAPITALIST
CHRISTIAN
CLASSICAL
CULTURES
DEMOCRACY
EDUCATION
EQUALITY
EUROPEAN
EXPRESSION
FOOTBALL
GLOBALISM
GREEKS
HERITAGE
HOLLYWOOD
LIFE
LITERATURE
MEDIEVAL
MODERN
MUSIC
PEOPLE
PHILOSOPHY
POWER
ROMANS
TECHNOLOGY
TELEVISION
TRADITION

Western Culture

L	A	V	E	I	D	E	M	N	R	E	D	O	M
I	N	C	E	N	A	E	P	O	R	U	E	A	E
L	O	U	X	T	R	A	D	I	T	I	O	N	M
L	I	L	P	H	I	L	O	S	O	P	H	Y	S
A	T	T	R	E	Z	A	I	I	Y	A	Y	F	I
C	A	U	E	M	O	L	I	V	C	S	T	E	L
I	C	R	S	R	A	P	K	E	A	T	I	B	A
S	U	E	S	T	A	I	L	L	R	C	L	A	B
S	D	S	I	X	K	T	N	E	C	A	A	S	O
A	E	P	O	W	E	R	U	T	O	F	U	E	L
L	A	S	N	A	M	O	R	R	M	I	Q	B	G
C	Y	G	O	L	O	N	H	C	E	T	E	A	R
I	H	O	L	L	Y	W	O	O	D	R	Q	L	E
S	C	B	C	H	R	I	S	T	I	A	N	L	E
U	H	E	R	I	T	A	G	E	F	I	L	N	K
M	L	C	Q	L	L	A	B	T	O	O	F	N	S

Solution on Page 323

AIRCRAFT
AIRPLANE
ASSEMBLY
BALSA WOOD
BUILDING
CHILDREN
CONSTRUCT
CONTROL
ELECTRIC
ENGINE
EXPENSIVE
FIBERGLASS
FLIGHT
FOAM
FUSELAGE
GLIDER
HELICOPTER
HOBBY
JETS
KITS
MILITARY
MINIATURE
MODELS
MOTOR
NONFLYING
PAINT
PARTS
PILOT
PLASTIC
PROPELLERS
ROCKET
SCALE
TAIL
TOYS
WINGS

Model Aircraft

X	J	N	O	N	F	L	Y	I	N	G	B	O	F
T	S	R	E	L	L	E	P	O	R	P	K	D	E
G	E	Y	E	N	E	N	A	L	P	R	I	A	L
Q	L	V	O	T	G	T	E	K	C	O	R	I	E
B	W	I	I	T	P	I	R	O	T	O	M	R	C
A	P	I	D	S	C	O	N	S	T	R	U	C	T
L	A	I	N	E	N	T	C	E	R	M	Y	R	R
S	S	A	L	G	R	E	B	I	F	O	B	A	I
A	S	A	V	O	S	N	P	T	L	D	B	F	C
W	E	I	L	O	T	E	E	X	I	E	O	T	A
O	M	I	N	I	A	T	U	R	E	L	H	V	T
O	B	U	I	L	D	I	N	G	D	S	T	E	J
D	L	I	A	T	O	F	U	S	E	L	A	G	E
Z	Y	R	A	T	I	L	I	M	T	N	I	A	P
S	C	A	L	E	M	A	O	F	L	I	G	H	T
K	I	T	S	T	R	A	P	L	A	S	T	I	C

Solution on Page 323

BAKEWARE
BOWL
BRUSH
CLEANING
CLEAVER
COLANDER
COOKBOOK
COOKING
COPPER
CUTLERY
DRAWER
EATING
FLATWARE
FOOD
FORKS
FRYING PAN
GLASSWARE
GRATER
HOLDER
IRON
KNIVES
MORTAR
OVEN
PANS
PEELER
PLATE
POTS
PRESS
SIEVE
SILVERWARE
SKEWER
SPATULA
SPOONS
STOVE
STRAINER
TOOLS
WASH

Kitchen Utensils

D	I	U	E	V	E	I	S	E	V	I	N	K	K
D	R	E	D	E	E	T	M	N	X	N	E	V	O
O	O	A	S	O	R	E	D	N	A	L	O	C	O
O	N	T	W	A	A	A	R	A	T	R	O	M	B
F	O	I	I	E	W	Q	W	E	V	O	T	S	K
P	R	N	B	A	R	E	W	E	K	S	P	E	O
Y	E	G	S	S	E	R	P	I	K	A	T	C	O
R	T	H	B	P	V	G	N	I	N	A	E	L	C
E	A	B	O	W	L	G	I	S	L	R	B	E	S
L	R	F	R	Y	I	N	G	P	A	N	C	A	K
T	G	H	T	U	S	K	G	W	H	O	T	V	R
U	A	L	U	T	A	P	S	S	P	C	P	E	O
C	K	T	O	O	L	S	U	P	J	V	D	R	F
F	L	A	T	W	A	R	E	R	E	L	E	E	P
R	M	W	C	L	B	R	S	P	O	O	N	S	N
A	S	F	G	M	B	U	T	H	U	K	M	X	U

Solution on Page 323

ACROBATS
AIR
ATHLETE
BOUNCING
CIRCUS
COILED
DANGEROUS
DIVING
ELASTICITY
EXERCISE
FABRIC
FALLING
FLIGHT
FRAME
FREE
GRAVITY
GYMNASTICS
HIGH
INJURY
JUMPING
MAT
PADS
PLAY
REBOUND
RECREATION
ROUND
SAFETY NET
SCHOOL
SIT
SOMERSAULT
SPORTS
SPRINGS
STEEL
STRETCH
TAUT
TRAINING
TRAPEZE
TUMBLING
TWIST

Trampolines

E	M	S	C	O	I	L	E	D	D	R	T	P	L
T	A	P	F	R	E	E	N	A	D	W	H	A	O
R	C	O	R	B	O	U	N	C	I	N	G	D	O
A	R	R	A	C	O	G	H	S	Y	T	I	S	H
P	O	T	M	B	E	I	T	T	A	U	L	O	C
E	B	S	E	R	G	N	I	L	L	A	F	M	S
Z	A	R	O	H	H	C	T	E	R	T	S	E	Y
E	T	U	N	O	I	T	A	E	R	C	E	R	R
S	S	C	I	T	S	A	N	M	Y	G	V	S	U
I	Y	I	S	A	F	E	T	Y	N	E	T	A	J
C	A	A	T	U	M	B	L	I	N	G	T	U	N
R	L	A	S	P	R	I	N	G	S	H	M	L	I
E	P	G	R	A	V	I	T	Y	L	P	A	T	E
X	C	I	R	B	A	F	O	E	I	N	T	I	C
E	S	U	C	R	I	C	T	N	D	N	U	O	R
L	E	E	T	S	X	E	G	N	I	V	I	D	Q

Solution on Page 324

ACTIVITY
BENEFITS
BODY
BRAIN
CARE
CHILDREN
CLINIC
DIET
DISEASE
EDUCATION
EXERCISE
FITNESS
FLU
FOOD
GENETICS
HEALTHY
HYGIENE
ILLNESS
LEAN
LIFESTYLE
LIVING
LONGEVITY
MEDICATION
MENTAL
NUTRITION
ORAL
PHARMACY
PHYSICAL
REST
RISK
SLEEP
SMOKING
STRESS
TREATMENT
WATER
WEIGHT
WELLNESS

Health

G	N	I	K	O	M	S	N	I	A	R	B	Y	X
P	P	U	Q	I	L	L	N	E	S	S	O	Y	N
H	L	A	T	N	E	M	U	E	S	S	D	H	O
Y	C	A	M	R	A	H	P	C	I	E	Y	E	I
S	H	I	E	C	I	N	I	L	C	N	M	A	T
I	I	F	T	A	C	T	I	V	I	T	Y	L	A
C	L	O	N	G	E	V	I	T	Y	I	B	T	C
A	D	W	Y	N	I	L	B	O	E	F	R	H	I
L	R	A	E	N	F	E	Y	S	N	E	M	Y	D
E	E	G	G	L	N	O	I	T	A	C	U	D	E
S	N	N	A	E	L	C	O	T	S	P	A	S	M
T	W	E	F	R	R	N	M	D	T	E	A	R	R
R	A	I	I	E	I	E	E	L	F	E	F	M	E
E	T	A	X	G	N	S	A	S	S	L	I	I	A
S	E	E	Z	T	Y	R	K	I	S	S	U	D	L
S	R	E	S	T	O	H	D	W	E	I	G	H	T

Solution on Page 324

ACCESSORY
BASEBALL
BEANIE
BERET
BONNET
BOWLER
BRIM
CAPS
CLOTHING
COVERING
COWBOY HAT
CROWN
DERBY
DESIGN
FASHION
FEDORA
FELT
HARD HAT
HEAD
HELMET
HOOD
PANAMA
SHADE
SOMBRERO
STRAW HAT
STYLE
SUN
SWEATBAND
TOP HAT
TURBAN
VISOR

Hats Off

T	O	T	E	M	L	E	H	Z	W	M	O	D	N
L	P	L	Z	D	Y	G	U	U	U	E	I	C	B
O	O	E	G	N	I	R	E	V	O	C	B	R	V
G	S	F	T	A	H	Y	O	B	W	O	C	H	B
U	T	U	R	B	A	N	Y	S	W	Z	E	A	O
C	G	J	F	T	R	D	N	L	S	P	S	R	N
Z	A	Y	D	A	D	H	E	A	D	E	E	Z	S
G	U	P	E	E	H	R	P	R	B	R	C	V	T
S	X	C	S	W	A	G	Y	A	B	I	U	C	R
F	H	R	I	S	T	N	L	M	I	Y	K	W	A
T	O	O	G	E	C	L	O	T	H	I	N	G	W
E	O	W	N	L	F	S	E	I	N	A	E	B	H
R	D	N	U	Y	T	T	O	P	H	A	T	H	A
E	O	A	S	T	S	T	A	V	I	S	O	R	T
B	W	T	H	S	V	P	A	N	A	M	A	L	U
O	J	P	A	S	D	F	A	R	O	D	E	F	W

Solution on Page 324

BATHROOM
BEDROOMS
BUILDING
CABLE
CITY
COMPLEX
CONTRACT
CRAMPED
DWELLING
ELECTRIC
ELEVATOR
ENTRANCE
FLAT
FLOORS
HOME
HOUSING
KEYS
KITCHEN
LANDLORD
LAUNDRY
LEASE
LIVING
LOFT
NEIGHBOR
PARKING
PETS
RENTAL
SECURITY
SHARE
SINGLE
SMALL
SPACE
STAIRS
STORAGE
STUDIO
TENANTS
UTILITIES
WALKUP
WINDOWS

Apartment Living

J	Y	S	P	A	C	E	X	E	L	P	M	O	C
T	H	R	E	E	L	E	V	A	T	O	R	I	A
L	F	O	Q	M	E	G	A	R	O	T	S	D	B
L	H	O	U	C	O	N	T	R	A	C	T	U	L
A	L	L	L	S	Y	H	H	T	C	Y	P	T	E
M	I	F	S	E	I	T	I	L	I	T	U	S	I
S	V	D	W	Q	A	N	I	K	R	I	K	F	C
R	I	E	W	B	I	S	G	C	T	R	L	L	R
I	N	C	K	F	Y	S	E	L	C	U	A	A	A
A	G	N	I	D	L	I	U	B	E	C	W	T	M
T	N	A	T	R	A	L	B	N	L	E	E	N	P
S	I	R	C	O	U	K	I	I	E	S	F	E	E
H	K	T	H	O	N	L	A	N	D	L	O	R	D
A	R	N	E	M	D	N	E	I	G	H	B	O	R
R	A	E	N	S	R	S	T	N	A	N	E	T	K
E	P	E	T	S	Y	W	I	N	D	O	W	S	C

Solution on Page 324

AMUSEMENT
CARTOONS
COMEDY
CONTEXT
CULTURE
EMOTION
ENTERTAIN
FARCE
FUNNY
GAGS
HAPPY
HILARIOUS
HUMOR
HYPERBOLE
IMPROV
JOKES
LAUGHING
PUN
SARCASM
SATIRE
SENSE OF
SLAPSTICK
SMILE
SOCIAL
STAND UP
STORY
SURPRISE
TIMING
VERBAL
VISUAL
WIT

Humor Me

Z	S	K	C	I	T	S	P	A	L	S	N	L	O
T	U	X	S	T	O	R	Y	N	N	U	F	A	B
E	R	I	T	A	S	F	T	V	P	O	N	B	H
V	P	O	E	M	O	T	I	O	N	I	A	R	J
J	R	F	A	E	A	T	W	F	A	R	C	E	L
G	I	O	S	S	N	O	O	T	R	A	C	V	X
A	S	N	H	U	M	O	R	T	O	L	I	O	E
G	E	L	O	B	R	E	P	Y	H	I	V	R	G
S	R	U	Y	I	T	W	L	K	V	H	I	P	U
T	U	C	X	N	H	S	A	R	C	A	S	M	L
A	T	N	E	M	E	S	U	M	A	P	U	I	Z
N	L	A	I	C	O	S	G	S	Y	P	A	S	J
D	U	Y	J	U	H	O	H	E	M	Y	L	C	G
U	C	O	M	E	D	Y	I	K	C	I	P	C	F
P	N	X	T	X	E	T	N	O	C	U	L	F	Z
V	F	T	I	M	I	N	G	J	D	T	M	E	W

Solution on Page 325

ANCIENT
ANTIQUING
ARTIFACT
AUCTION
BEAUTY
BUY
CAR
CHAIR
COLLECTION
CONDITION
DEALER
DECOR
DESIRABLE
ERA
ESTATE
FURNITURE
GEORGIAN
HISTORICAL
ITEMS
LACE
MUSEUM
OBJECT
OLD
PAST
PERIOD
PORCELAIN
POTTERY
RARITY
ROADSHOW
RUGS
SALE
SHOPPING
TIME
UNIQUE
UTILITY
VALUABLE
VICTORIAN
VINTAGE
WOOD

Antiques

H	G	N	I	P	P	O	H	S	I	T	E	M	S
N	E	W	D	R	A	E	G	A	T	N	I	V	D
R	O	O	E	R	S	R	M	U	S	E	U	M	P
Y	R	O	A	O	T	U	T	I	L	I	T	Y	O
U	G	D	L	A	R	N	O	I	T	C	U	A	R
N	I	X	E	D	A	R	E	T	F	N	C	N	C
I	A	D	R	S	R	N	Y	W	O	A	O	Z	E
Q	N	V	U	H	I	S	T	O	R	I	C	A	L
U	T	A	T	O	T	R	U	I	T	I	O	T	A
E	C	L	I	W	Y	Z	A	C	Q	P	N	L	I
S	E	U	N	R	R	D	E	B	O	U	D	W	N
T	J	A	R	J	O	L	B	T	L	O	I	O	R
A	B	B	U	I	L	T	T	U	I	E	T	N	U
T	O	L	F	O	A	E	C	R	Y	C	I	C	G
E	D	E	C	O	R	H	E	I	C	A	O	C	S
S	A	L	E	Y	Z	P	C	X	V	L	N	V	Q

Solution on Page 325

ABC
BASIC
BILL
BOX
BROADCAST
CBS
CHANNELS
CHARTER
CINEMAX
COAXIAL
COMCAST
COMEDY
DIGITAL
DISCOVERY
ESPN
EXPENSIVE
FCC
FEES
FOX
HBO
LINEUP
MOVIES
MSNBC
MTV
NETWORKS
NEWS
PACKAGES
PREMIUM
PROGRAMS
PROVIDER
REMOTE
SATELLITE
SERVICE
SHOWTIME
SPORTS
STATION
TBS
TELEVISION
TNT
VERIZON

Cable Television

M	E	T	I	L	L	E	T	A	S	B	C	L	B
O	L	R	E	T	R	A	H	C	W	L	A	A	C
V	I	Y	L	L	I	B	R	T	N	T	S	M	B
I	N	F	S	A	E	D	E	P	I	I	K	U	N
E	E	E	W	I	V	V	D	G	C	M	R	I	S
S	U	E	E	X	I	Y	I	M	T	V	O	M	M
E	P	S	N	A	S	D	V	S	D	B	W	E	S
R	R	H	O	O	N	E	O	I	I	R	T	R	E
V	O	O	Z	C	E	M	R	H	S	O	E	P	T
I	G	W	I	I	P	O	P	L	C	A	N	S	O
C	R	T	R	N	X	C	E	C	O	D	O	P	M
E	A	I	E	E	E	N	F	B	V	C	I	O	E
F	M	M	V	M	N	O	W	B	E	A	T	R	R
A	S	E	G	A	K	C	A	P	R	S	A	T	F
T	B	S	H	X	O	B	H	R	Y	T	T	S	O
Z	Z	C	O	M	C	A	S	T	N	P	S	E	X

Solution on Page 325

ADMIRED
ART
ATTRACTIVE
BEAUTIFUL
BEHOLDER
CHARACTER
CHARISMA
CLASSIC
COLOR
COMPLEXION
CONCEPT
CONTEST
CULTURE
ELEGANCE
FACE
FASHION
FEATURES
GIRL
GLAMOUR
GRACE
HEALTH
HOT
IDEA
INNER
LOOKS
LOVE
MAGAZINES
MEANING
MODELS
NATURE
PERCEPTUAL
PERFECTION
PERSON
PLEASURE
PRETTY
SKIN
SPA
SYMMETRY
WOMEN
YOUTH

Beautiful

S	K	I	N	N	E	R	U	S	A	E	L	P	H
F	A	C	E	M	T	D	E	R	I	M	D	A	O
K	G	M	Y	R	E	R	U	T	L	U	C	G	T
A	O	L	A	O	U	E	Y	P	P	C	G	I	P
W	M	N	A	T	U	R	E	E	E	O	N	R	E
M	A	S	A	M	T	T	C	R	R	M	I	L	C
O	A	E	I	E	O	R	H	F	C	P	N	U	N
D	F	G	M	R	O	U	A	E	E	L	A	F	O
E	A	M	A	L	A	S	R	C	P	E	E	I	C
L	Y	E	O	Z	H	H	A	T	T	X	M	T	L
S	H	C	D	I	I	R	C	I	U	I	E	U	A
X	C	E	O	I	G	N	T	O	A	O	V	A	S
E	C	N	A	G	E	L	E	N	L	N	O	E	S
B	E	H	O	L	D	E	R	S	P	A	L	B	I
G	P	R	E	T	T	Y	T	S	E	T	N	O	C
L	O	O	K	S	K	H	P	E	R	S	O	N	Q

Solution on Page 325

ASPIRIN
BIOMEDICAL
BODY
CLINICS
DIAGNOSIS
DISEASES
DRUGS
EMERGENCY
EXAM
FEVER
FLU
GENETICS
HEALING
HEALTHCARE
HOSPITALS
ILLNESS
INJURY
INSURANCE
LAB
MEDICATION
NECESSARY
NURSES
PAIN
PATHOLOGY
PEDIATRICS
PHARMACY
PHYSICIANS
PREVENTION
RELIEF
RESEARCH
SYMPTOM
TESTS
TREATMENT

Medicine

H	C	R	A	E	S	E	R	E	L	I	E	F	B
N	N	N	O	I	T	A	C	I	D	E	M	P	A
U	Y	I	P	P	F	E	V	E	R	Y	O	R	L
R	L	D	R	A	H	N	P	A	R	R	T	E	T
S	I	F	O	I	T	Y	C	A	V	U	P	V	I
E	X	A	M	B	P	H	S	K	I	J	M	E	D
S	S	T	C	P	T	S	O	I	S	N	Y	N	I
E	Z	L	E	L	E	N	A	L	C	I	S	T	A
S	M	L	A	C	I	D	E	M	O	I	B	I	G
A	P	E	E	T	N	N	I	M	T	G	A	O	N
E	H	N	R	P	I	A	I	A	T	E	Y	N	O
S	D	R	U	G	S	P	R	C	T	A	S	B	S
I	I	L	L	N	E	S	S	U	S	R	E	T	I
D	H	E	A	L	I	N	G	O	S	S	I	R	S
O	G	E	N	E	T	I	C	S	H	N	K	C	T
A	P	H	A	R	M	A	C	Y	C	R	I	T	S

Solution on Page 326

ALIGNED
ASTRONOMY
ATMOSPHERE
BLOCK
CELESTIAL
CYCLE
DARKNESS
EARTH
ECLIPSE
EVENT
FULL MOON
HORIZON
NASA
NIGHT
OBSERVE
OMEN
ORBIT
PARTIAL
PASSES
PENUMBRAL
RARE
RAYS
REFRACTION
SCIENCE
SHADOW
SKY
SOLAR
SPACE
SUNLIGHT
TELESCOPE
TOTALITY
VIEWING
VISIBLE

Lunar Eclipse

E	L	B	I	S	I	V	P	T	N	H	Z	Z	N
C	A	V	K	R	J	F	V	D	H	W	Z	E	Y
N	A	S	A	Z	Q	Q	Q	R	S	G	M	V	Z
E	U	P	E	S	P	I	L	C	E	O	I	E	U
I	B	P	O	S	S	E	N	K	R	A	D	N	H
C	L	L	N	E	S	U	N	L	I	G	H	T	E
S	A	N	O	O	M	L	L	U	F	U	R	N	P
R	I	O	Z	C	Y	C	L	E	M	A	M	T	O
P	T	I	I	W	K	R	A	R	E	B	A	O	C
A	S	T	R	O	N	O	M	Y	R	K	R	T	S
S	E	C	O	D	N	D	E	N	G	I	L	A	E
S	L	A	H	A	B	P	A	R	T	I	A	L	L
E	E	R	E	H	P	S	O	M	T	A	I	I	E
S	C	F	A	S	V	I	E	W	I	N	G	T	T
K	L	E	V	R	E	S	B	O	R	R	A	Y	S
Y	O	R	B	I	T	E	C	A	P	S	K	N	L

Solution on Page 326

ANIMATORS
AWARDS
BUG'S LIFE
CALIFORNIA
CARS
CARTOON
CGI
CHARACTERS
COMPANY
COMPUTER
DIGITAL
DISNEY
FAMILY
FEATURE
FILMS
FUN
GRAPHICS
HOLLYWOOD
LAMP
MONSTERS
MOVIES
NEMO
RELEASE
SHORTS
STEVE JOBS
STUDIO
SUCCESS
TECHNOLOGY
TOY STORY
WALL-E

Pixar

R	M	O	V	I	E	S	C	I	H	P	A	R	G
F	D	S	S	S	E	C	C	U	S	I	E	W	S
R	I	G	C	A	R	T	O	O	N	U	F	A	M
O	N	O	L	K	Q	Z	F	R	M	K	I	L	L
I	S	T	E	V	E	J	O	B	S	P	R	L	I
D	R	S	F	F	C	F	E	R	U	T	A	E	F
U	A	R	A	N	I	M	A	T	O	R	S	N	G
T	C	E	Y	L	D	L	A	W	A	R	D	S	Y
S	R	T	A	R	N	O	S	F	V	J	I	S	E
T	E	C	H	N	O	L	O	G	Y	U	G	R	N
R	L	A	M	P	N	T	P	W	U	D	I	E	S
O	E	R	V	P	E	D	S	Z	Y	B	T	T	I
H	A	A	F	A	M	I	L	Y	F	L	A	S	D
S	S	H	T	P	O	L	Q	A	O	M	L	N	I
O	E	C	O	M	P	U	T	E	R	T	Q	O	V
Z	T	E	U	H	V	T	T	F	X	M	R	M	H

Solution on Page 326

ACES
BETTING
BLUFF
BRIDGE
CANASTA
CARDS
CASINO
CHEAT
CLUBS
CUT
DEALER
DECKS
DIAMONDS
DRAW
EUCHRE
FAMILY
GAMBLING
GIN
GO FISH
HANDS
HEARTS
JOKERS
KING
MELD
MONEY
OLD MAID
PINOCHLE
PLAYERS
PLAYING
POKER
QUEEN
RULES
RUMMY
SHUFFLE
SOLITAIRE
SPADES
SUITS
TRICK
WAGER
WINNER

Play a Card

M	Y	W	J	B	U	J	O	T	R	I	C	K	T
E	K	J	A	U	F	R	E	G	A	W	M	S	D
L	A	O	M	R	H	O	N	I	S	A	C	B	J
D	C	K	X	E	D	I	I	N	Y	M	M	U	R
E	E	E	A	L	Y	P	I	N	O	C	H	L	E
C	S	R	A	A	F	A	M	I	L	Y	T	C	L
K	T	S	L	E	T	M	G	S	D	N	A	H	F
S	I	P	D	D	O	N	G	U	M	N	T	J	F
L	U	L	G	N	I	L	B	M	A	G	G	L	U
Q	S	A	E	T	O	R	L	S	I	I	O	F	H
S	U	Y	T	W	U	M	T	W	D	B	F	R	S
W	D	E	F	L	K	A	A	F	R	U	I	E	P
K	B	R	E	R	I	A	T	I	L	O	S	K	A
A	N	S	A	N	N	T	D	B	D	D	H	O	D
T	A	E	H	C	G	G	U	C	J	Y	S	P	E
L	W	I	N	N	E	R	H	C	U	E	R	G	S

Solution on Page 326

ACCENT
ALLEGORY
ALLUSION
ANALOGY
ANECDOTE
AUTHOR
BALLAD
BOOKS
CHARACTER
CLIMAX
COMEDY
CONFLICT
DIALOGUE
DICTION
DRAMA
EPIC
ESSAY
FABLE
GENRE
GLOSSARY
HYPERBOLE
IMAGERY
IRONY
LIMERICK
LYRIC
METAPHOR
NARRATOR
NOVELLA
PLOT
POETRY
PROSE
SATIRE
SETTING
SIMILE
SONNET
STANZA
STORY
THESIS
TRAGEDY

Literary

T	O	L	P	N	K	C	I	R	E	M	I	L	E
N	Y	D	E	M	O	C	Q	U	S	K	O	O	B
E	R	I	T	A	S	I	G	N	I	T	T	E	S
C	L	I	M	A	X	O	T	C	I	R	Y	L	R
C	S	I	M	I	L	E	A	C	I	P	E	P	A
A	I	S	E	A	L	L	U	S	I	O	N	O	L
N	M	V	I	R	L	A	M	A	R	D	T	E	L
A	A	D	G	E	N	A	N	E	C	D	O	T	E
I	G	F	G	L	B	E	T	V	A	P	C	R	V
O	E	O	A	O	O	C	G	L	R	I	O	Y	O
G	R	A	S	B	A	S	L	O	L	H	D	S	N
Y	Y	U	T	R	L	A	S	F	P	E	T	O	Y
A	X	T	A	E	B	E	N	A	G	O	M	N	N
S	N	H	N	P	R	O	T	A	R	R	A	N	O
S	C	O	Z	Y	C	E	R	Y	S	Y	U	E	R
E	Y	R	A	H	M	T	S	I	S	E	H	T	I

Solution on Page 327

ATTORNEY
BAIL
BILL
BOOKS
CASE
CIVIL
CONTRACTS
COURTROOM
CRIMINAL
DECISION
DEFENDANT
ECONOMICS
EVIDENCE
FINES
GAVEL
GUILTY
JAIL
JUDGES
JUDICIARY
JUSTICE
LAWYERS
LEGAL
ORDER
PLAINTIFF
PLEA
POLITICS
PRECEDENT
PRISON
REGULATION
RIGHTS
SCHOOL
SENTENCE
SHERIFF
SOCIETY
STATUTE
SUE
TORT
WITNESS

Law

E	C	N	E	T	N	E	S	H	E	R	I	F	F
D	Y	N	V	L	E	G	A	L	U	F	M	T	R
X	E	B	I	G	D	E	C	I	S	I	O	N	G
A	N	F	D	S	T	C	A	R	T	N	O	C	S
E	R	L	E	T	N	E	D	E	C	E	R	P	C
L	O	I	N	N	J	U	D	G	E	S	T	E	H
P	T	V	C	T	D	E	L	U	I	K	R	T	O
R	T	I	E	O	L	A	S	L	V	O	U	U	O
I	A	C	G	R	F	A	N	A	I	O	O	T	L
S	S	E	N	T	I	W	N	T	C	B	C	A	A
O	O	A	J	U	D	I	C	I	A	R	Y	T	W
N	C	A	Y	E	C	O	N	O	M	I	C	S	Y
B	I	X	L	P	L	A	I	N	T	I	F	F	E
L	E	C	I	T	S	U	J	R	E	D	R	O	R
S	T	H	G	I	R	P	O	L	I	T	I	C	S
P	Y	T	L	I	U	G	A	V	E	L	I	A	B

Solution on Page 327

APPRENTICE
ARTISAN
BARBER
BLACKSMITH
BUILDER
BUSINESS
BUTCHER
CARPENTER
CHEF
COBBLER
CONTRACTOR
CRAFT
GUILD
IRONWORKER
JOURNEYMAN
KNOWLEDGE
LABORER
LOCKSMITH
MACHINIST
MANUAL
MECHANIC
PAINTER
PLUMBER
PROFESSION
ROOFER
SKILLED
STONEMASON
TOOLS
TRAINING
WATCHMAKER

Tradesman

C	L	O	C	K	S	M	I	T	H	C	H	E	F
O	H	X	A	P	P	R	E	N	T	I	C	E	C
B	T	O	O	L	S	S	E	N	I	S	U	B	A
B	B	I	E	W	A	T	C	H	M	A	K	E	R
L	S	R	E	T	N	I	A	P	S	R	A	G	P
E	T	I	R	O	N	W	O	R	K	E	R	D	E
R	O	T	C	A	R	T	N	O	C	D	T	E	N
E	N	S	I	D	K	F	A	F	A	L	I	L	T
R	F	I	N	L	D	A	M	E	L	I	S	W	E
M	M	N	A	I	V	R	Y	S	B	U	A	O	R
U	A	I	H	U	O	C	E	S	L	B	N	N	E
L	S	H	C	G	N	I	N	I	A	R	T	K	H
P	O	C	E	S	R	E	R	O	B	A	L	H	C
A	N	A	M	E	L	A	U	N	A	M	A	F	T
Y	G	M	Z	M	R	O	O	F	E	R	K	C	U
D	E	L	L	I	K	S	J	R	E	B	R	A	B

Solution on Page 327

ACTIVITY
AEROBICS
ATHLETIC
BICYCLE
BOXING
CARDIO
CIRCUIT
CYCLING
DIET
ELLIPTICAL
EQUIPMENT
FITNESS
GYM
HEALTHY
HEART RATE
HIKING
JUMP ROPE
LEG PRESS
LIFTING
MUSCLE
NUTRITION
OBESITY
PILATES
RUNNING
SPORTS
STRENGTH
STRETCHING
SWIMMING
TRAINING
TREADMILL
WALKING
WEIGHT
YOGA

Exercise

H	E	A	L	T	H	Y	D	D	W	M	S	N	I
U	A	N	W	R	U	I	I	G	U	W	S	U	S
B	P	I	L	A	T	E	S	S	I	S	E	T	C
O	S	Z	J	I	T	L	C	M	T	E	R	R	I
X	D	S	U	N	Z	L	M	R	T	E	P	I	B
I	H	T	M	I	E	I	O	A	T	Q	G	T	O
N	D	R	P	N	N	P	R	C	R	U	E	I	R
G	O	E	R	G	S	T	H	T	E	I	L	O	E
N	I	N	O	V	R	I	I	I	A	P	O	N	A
I	D	G	P	A	N	C	K	V	D	M	B	L	E
K	R	T	E	G	I	A	I	I	M	E	E	I	L
L	A	H	M	R	D	L	N	T	I	N	S	F	C
A	C	Y	C	L	I	N	G	Y	L	T	I	T	Y
W	G	U	Y	P	B	A	T	H	L	E	T	I	C
F	I	T	N	E	S	S	J	A	G	O	Y	N	I
T	H	G	I	E	W	R	U	N	N	I	N	G	B

Solution on Page 327

ACADEMIC
AUTHORITY
CAMPAIGNS
CANDIDATES
CHANGE
CITIZEN
CORPORATE
CORRUPTION
DECISIONS
DEMOCRAT
ECONOMY
ELECTIONS
EXECUTIVE
FEDERAL
GOVERNMENT
GROUP
HOUSE
LAWS
MAJORITY
MILITARY
NATIONAL
PARLIAMENT
PLATFORM
POLITICIAN
POWER
PRESIDENT
PUBLIC
REVOLUTION
STATE
TAXES
VOTING

Political

E	A	C	A	D	E	M	I	C	I	L	B	U	P
V	C	L	A	W	S	N	O	I	T	C	E	L	E
I	H	C	Y	N	C	A	M	P	A	I	G	N	S
T	A	T	M	N	O	L	A	N	O	I	T	A	N
U	N	N	P	I	O	I	D	S	E	X	A	T	L
C	G	E	P	O	L	I	T	I	C	I	A	N	A
E	E	M	M	B	D	I	T	U	V	P	S	H	R
X	P	N	E	A	U	E	T	P	L	U	C	O	E
E	R	R	T	U	I	G	C	A	U	O	T	U	D
C	E	E	A	T	A	L	T	I	R	R	V	S	E
O	S	V	T	H	V	F	R	P	S	Y	R	E	F
N	I	O	S	O	O	W	O	A	O	I	L	O	R
O	D	G	T	R	G	R	O	U	P	W	O	M	C
M	E	I	M	I	A	C	I	T	I	Z	E	N	Z
Y	N	P	R	T	A	R	C	O	M	E	D	R	S
G	T	C	E	Y	T	I	R	O	J	A	M	U	M

Solution on Page 328

AMP
ANALOG
BATTERY
BOARD
CAPACITORS
CHIP
CIRCUIT
COMPONENTS
COMPUTERS
CONDUCTOR
CONNECTION
CURRENT
DESIGN
DIAGRAM
DIGITAL
DIODES
ENGINEER
GROUND
INDUCTORS
INTEGRATED
LED
LOGIC
NEGATIVE
PARALLEL
POSITIVE
POWER
RESISTANCE
SCHEMATIC
SERIES
SIGNALS
SILICON
SUBSTRATE
TRANSISTOR
WIRES

Electronic Circuits

W	I	R	E	S	C	H	E	M	A	T	I	C	S
L	E	L	L	A	R	A	P	S	C	Y	A	I	L
A	S	N	W	W	G	X	U	O	E	P	C	G	A
T	H	R	Y	R	A	B	N	D	A	R	H	O	N
I	Y	I	O	R	S	N	N	C	O	E	I	L	G
G	D	U	E	T	E	O	I	T	D	S	P	E	I
I	N	W	R	C	C	T	C	P	R	I	C	V	S
D	O	A	T	I	O	U	T	M	A	S	I	I	P
P	T	I	L	R	D	M	D	A	O	T	R	T	O
E	O	I	S	N	P	M	P	N	B	A	C	A	S
N	S	G	O	L	A	N	A	O	I	N	U	G	I
G	E	C	U	R	R	E	N	T	N	C	I	E	T
I	D	S	G	D	E	T	A	R	G	E	T	N	I
S	O	A	D	J	R	E	E	N	I	G	N	E	V
E	I	L	R	O	T	S	I	S	N	A	R	T	E
D	D	E	L	R	C	O	M	P	U	T	E	R	S

Solution on Page 328

BACTERIA
BEHAVIOR
BIOLOGY
BREEDING
CELLS
CLONE
CODE
DISEASE
DISORDER
DNA
DOMINANT
EVOLUTION
FAMILY
GENOTYPE
HEIGHT
HEREDITY
HUMANS
INHERITED
LAB
LIFE
MEDICINE
MOLECULAR
MUTATIONS
OFFSPRING
ORGANISMS
PARENTS
RECESSIVE
RNA
SCIENTISTS
SEQUENCING
STRUCTURE
STUDY
TRAITS
VARIATION
VIRUSES

Gene Study

Y	T	I	D	E	R	E	H	E	G	B	A	L	R
G	E	V	O	L	U	T	I	O	N	K	S	N	E
E	V	I	S	S	E	C	E	R	I	O	L	V	D
N	C	R	T	T	M	O	L	E	C	U	L	A	R
O	O	U	B	N	S	B	M	Y	N	I	E	C	O
T	D	S	A	E	Y	I	U	S	E	N	C	O	S
Y	E	E	C	R	L	O	T	G	U	H	S	R	I
P	V	S	T	A	I	L	A	N	Q	E	T	G	D
F	R	A	E	P	M	O	T	I	E	R	R	A	O
N	T	O	R	N	A	G	I	R	S	I	U	N	M
I	R	N	I	I	F	Y	O	P	A	T	C	I	I
C	A	Q	A	V	A	G	N	S	E	E	T	S	N
I	I	Y	A	X	A	T	S	F	S	D	U	M	A
D	T	H	G	I	E	H	I	F	I	F	R	S	N
E	S	N	A	M	U	H	E	O	D	C	E	A	T
M	G	N	I	D	E	E	R	B	N	L	I	F	E

Solution on Page 328

ARIZONA
BEVERAGE
BLACK
BREWED
CHERRY
COLD
COOL
DRINK
FLAVORED
GLASS
GREEN
HONEY
ICE CUBES
INSTANT
LIPTON
MINT
NESTEA
PEACH
RASPBERRY
RESTAURANT
SNAPPLE
SOUTHERN
SPOON
STEEP
STIR
SUGAR
SUMMER
SUN TEA
SWEET TEA
SWEETENER
TEA BAGS
TEA LEAVES
UNSWEET
WATER

Iced Tea

H	C	S	D	E	R	O	V	A	L	F	D	P	L
O	H	B	T	K	S	E	J	K	P	E	L	M	O
N	E	E	L	N	N	U	N	S	W	E	E	T	O
E	R	V	K	O	A	I	N	E	S	T	E	A	C
Y	R	E	O	S	Q	R	R	S	T	I	R	T	I
N	Y	R	H	K	W	B	U	D	W	E	S	C	S
O	M	A	A	T	C	E	O	A	L	Q	E	C	X
O	I	G	I	S	U	A	E	L	T	C	V	W	N
P	N	E	H	N	P	O	L	T	U	S	A	Q	S
S	T	O	U	A	S	B	S	B	T	G	E	A	U
S	U	B	T	P	V	T	E	E	Z	E	L	R	B
C	S	M	E	P	P	S	A	R	W	L	A	I	W
Q	O	A	M	L	I	B	P	N	R	C	E	Z	A
O	C	L	L	E	A	L	S	N	T	Y	T	O	T
H	P	A	D	G	R	E	E	N	M	J	H	N	E
F	Z	L	S	U	N	T	E	A	S	U	G	A	R

Solution on Page 328

AIR
ANIMALS
ATMOSPHERE
COAL
COPPER
DEPLETION
EARTH
ECOLOGY
ECOSYSTEMS
ENERGY
FISH
FORESTS
FOSSIL
FUEL
GAS
GOLD
GREEN
IRON
LAKES
LAND
LIMITED
MANAGEMENT
MINERALS
MINING
NATURE
OCEANS
PETROLEUM
PROTECTION
RAIN FOREST
RENEWABLE
RIVERS
ROCKS
SILVER
SOIL
SOLAR
SUNLIGHT
WATER
WIND
WOOD

Natural Resources

D	E	T	I	M	I	L	Q	G	O	L	D	U	M
O	C	R	B	T	S	E	R	O	F	N	I	A	R
C	O	P	P	E	R	E	G	P	S	D	N	A	L
E	L	B	A	W	E	N	E	R	E	A	R	T	H
I	O	E	U	N	I	T	E	F	G	H	S	I	F
B	G	G	C	N	R	V	S	E	P	T	N	P	A
N	Y	O	I	O	I	M	M	K	S	K	A	R	Q
S	A	M	L	R	S	E	D	E	C	F	T	O	S
L	T	E	R	I	N	Y	R	I	A	O	U	T	O
A	U	H	A	T	M	O	S	P	H	E	R	E	I
M	W	E	G	X	F	C	Y	T	F	Z	E	C	L
I	A	N	O	I	T	E	L	P	E	D	G	T	S
N	T	E	W	W	L	A	K	E	S	M	A	I	O
A	E	R	O	M	I	N	E	R	A	L	S	O	L
T	R	G	O	H	S	S	U	D	N	I	W	N	A
V	G	Y	D	J	F	O	S	S	I	L	V	E	R

Solution on Page 329

ACTING
APOLLO
AWARDS
BEST ACTOR
BIG
CAST AWAY
CELEBRITY
CHARACTER
COMEDIAN
DIRECTOR
DRAGNET
FAMOUS
FATHER
FILM
FORREST
FUNNY
GREEN MILE
GUMP
HOLLYWOOD
LOVE
MEG RYAN
MOVIES
OSCARS
PRODUCER
RICH
RITA
ROLE
SEATTLE
SPLASH
STAR
TALENT
TELEVISION
TERMINAL
TOY STORY
VOICE
WOODY

Tom Hanks

A	G	Q	L	O	V	E	L	T	T	A	E	S	Y
C	T	U	T	S	R	A	C	S	O	T	H	A	A
T	W	I	M	Y	A	P	E	Z	R	E	S	G	R
I	E	B	R	P	T	R	F	S	D	R	A	W	A
N	I	L	O	G	R	I	E	U	Y	M	L	O	T
G	L	L	E	O	R	O	R	H	N	I	P	O	S
C	L	C	F	V	T	E	D	B	T	N	S	D	Y
O	H	I	A	A	I	M	E	U	E	A	Y	Y	M
M	O	A	T	S	M	S	O	N	C	L	F	D	D
E	L	O	R	N	T	O	I	V	M	E	E	I	F
D	L	O	I	A	E	A	U	O	I	I	R	C	I
I	Y	L	C	Z	C	L	W	S	N	E	L	P	L
A	W	T	H	W	P	T	A	A	C	C	S	E	M
N	O	D	R	A	G	N	E	T	Y	I	I	P	A
R	O	T	O	Y	S	T	O	R	Y	O	M	N	L
A	D	S	N	A	Y	R	G	E	M	V	N	M	L

Solution on Page 329

ANIMAL
BACON
BIG
BREEDING
DOMESTIC
FARMING
FEEDING
FERAL
FOOD
HAM
HOGS
HOUSE PET
LITTER
LIVESTOCK
MEAT
MINIATURE
PETS
PIGLETS
PORK
RUNT
SAUSAGES
SMART
SMELL
SOW
STY
SUBSPECIES
SWINE
TAIL
TRAINED
TRUFFLES
WILD BOAR

Pigs

T	B	Z	B	S	A	U	S	A	G	E	S	T	Y
T	T	N	U	R	X	J	L	Z	N	F	E	G	K
S	A	V	T	P	T	T	M	I	I	I	L	D	L
D	E	N	I	A	R	T	C	C	D	L	F	L	S
R	M	I	N	I	A	T	U	R	E	K	F	R	R
E	A	P	C	N	R	H	N	M	E	Q	U	K	O
T	H	L	I	E	O	O	S	K	R	R	R	O	H
T	X	M	P	G	P	U	F	R	B	A	T	S	M
I	A	S	D	S	L	S	G	O	H	O	F	X	G
L	C	T	M	O	T	E	B	P	O	B	E	Q	N
U	H	E	V	A	M	P	T	U	E	D	R	S	I
Z	E	P	I	S	R	E	T	S	S	L	A	D	D
Y	R	L	K	C	O	T	S	E	V	I	L	Z	E
B	V	Q	N	U	L	W	D	T	S	W	I	N	E
F	N	A	P	N	B	I	G	N	I	M	R	A	F
M	S	M	X	Y	U	B	L	B	A	C	O	N	H

Solution on Page 329

ACCESS
CARE
CLINICS
COVERAGE
DENTISTRY
DIAGNOSIS
DISEASE
DRUGS
EXAM
FAMILY
HEALTH
HMO
HOME
HOSPITALS
ILLNESS
INDUSTRY
INSURANCE
LAB
MEDICINE
NURSING
OFFICE
PATIENT
PHARMACY
PHYSICIAN
POLITICAL
PRIVATE
PROCEDURES
PROVIDER
RESEARCH
RIGHTS
SERVICES
SPENDING
THERAPY
TREATMENT
UNIVERSAL
VACCINES
WHO

Health Provider

N	S	P	R	I	V	A	T	E	C	I	F	F	O
U	C	H	Q	T	N	E	I	T	A	P	H	W	D
R	L	A	S	R	E	V	I	N	U	D	O	H	R
S	I	R	R	E	D	I	V	O	R	P	M	O	U
I	N	M	E	A	S	E	C	I	V	R	E	S	G
N	I	A	S	T	H	O	S	P	I	T	A	L	S
G	C	C	E	M	V	L	D	I	S	E	A	S	E
N	S	Y	A	E	C	N	A	R	U	S	N	I	R
I	T	M	R	N	M	B	Y	B	I	A	Z	M	U
D	H	A	C	T	Y	R	T	S	I	T	N	E	D
N	G	X	H	L	T	H	O	C	T	W	R	D	E
E	I	E	I	S	E	N	I	C	C	A	V	I	C
P	R	M	U	R	G	S	S	E	C	C	A	C	O
S	A	D	A	A	Y	S	S	E	N	L	L	I	R
F	N	P	I	H	T	L	A	E	H	M	O	N	P
I	Y	D	P	O	L	I	T	I	C	A	L	E	W

Solution on Page 329

ADAKITE
ANDESITE
APLITE
BASANITE
CHALK
COAL
DACITE
DIAMOND
DIORITE
DOLOMITE
FLINT
FOSSIL
GABBRO
GNEISS
GRANITE
IGNEOUS
JADE
LIMESTONE
MAGMA
MINERALS
MUDSTONE
OBSIDIAN
PEBBLE
PHYLLITE
QUARTZITE
RHYOLITE
SANDSTONE
SCORIA
SEDIMENT
SHALE
SILTSTONE
SLATE
TONALITE
TUFF
TURBIDITE
VOLCANIC

Rock Types

T	N	I	L	F	Q	E	T	I	N	A	R	G	J
N	Z	C	O	A	L	U	L	I	S	S	O	F	A
E	N	O	T	S	D	N	A	S	I	D	E	E	D
M	K	E	T	I	C	A	D	R	L	E	T	L	E
I	G	N	E	O	U	S	K	S	T	I	I	A	N
D	I	A	M	O	N	D	C	I	S	Z	D	H	O
E	M	U	D	S	T	O	N	E	T	P	I	S	T
S	L	A	T	E	R	A	D	V	O	E	B	T	S
R	C	P	R	I	S	N	O	O	N	P	R	T	E
G	H	H	A	A	A	B	L	L	E	E	U	O	M
A	A	Y	B	O	S	A	O	C	G	T	T	N	I
B	L	L	O	I	P	U	M	A	N	I	M	A	L
B	K	L	D	L	I	M	I	N	E	R	A	L	S
R	M	I	I	U	I	S	T	I	I	O	G	I	L
O	A	T	U	F	F	T	E	C	S	I	M	T	U
N	E	E	E	L	B	B	E	P	S	D	A	E	H

Solution on Page 330

ACRYLIC
ALPACA
ANGORA
CASHMERE
CLOTHING
COTTON
CROCHETING
DENIM
DESIGN
DYES
FABRIC
FASHION
FELT
FIBERS
FLAX
HEMP
INDUSTRY
KNITTING
LINEN
LOOM
MATERIALS
MILL
NYLON
PATTERN
POLYESTER
RAYON
SATIN
SEWING
SILK
SPANDEX
SPINNING
SYNTHETIC
TAILORING
TEXTURE
THREAD
TWILL
WEAVING
WOOL
WOVEN
YARN

Textiles

C	I	R	B	A	F	E	L	T	H	E	M	P	R
X	R	D	Y	E	S	P	I	N	N	I	N	G	J
M	A	O	A	L	P	A	C	A	N	O	N	M	S
I	N	L	C	G	N	I	R	O	L	I	A	T	G
L	G	R	F	H	L	G	T	Y	H	T	Y	E	N
L	O	X	E	Y	E	T	N	T	E	A	J	X	I
K	R	O	R	T	O	T	O	R	R	C	F	T	V
L	A	C	W	C	T	L	I	N	E	N	A	U	A
I	A	I	I	H	C	A	H	N	D	G	S	R	E
S	L	H	R	T	L	E	P	U	G	I	H	E	W
L	R	E	T	S	E	Y	L	O	P	S	I	G	M
H	A	E	C	A	S	H	M	E	R	E	O	N	I
D	L	K	B	T	Y	R	T	S	U	D	N	I	N
K	O	G	N	I	T	T	I	N	K	G	P	W	E
W	O	V	E	N	F	G	R	A	Y	O	N	E	D
C	M	J	S	X	E	D	N	A	P	S	Y	S	J

Solution on Page 330

ADDRESS
AL GORE
AOL
APPLE
ARPANET
BRIDGES
CABLE
CERN
COMPUTERS
CONNECTION
DARPA
DATA
DIGITAL
E-MAIL
GATEWAYS
GLOBAL
GOOGLE
GOPHER
HARDWARE
INTERNET
LINKS
MAINFRAME
MILITARY
MODEM
NETSCAPE
NETWORKS
ONLINE
PACKETS
PHONE
PROTOCOL
RESEARCH
ROUTER
SYSTEM
TECHNOLOGY
TELEGRAPH
URL
WEB
WWW

Internet History

Q	P	B	G	L	O	D	A	R	P	A	S	H	T
R	Y	H	L	E	N	I	L	N	O	O	F	H	E
E	L	G	O	O	G	G	H	T	N	L	S	C	N
T	W	E	B	N	R	I	P	A	E	Y	S	R	A
U	S	Y	A	W	E	T	A	G	T	R	E	A	P
O	N	G	L	W	H	A	R	D	W	A	R	E	R
R	E	O	U	W	P	L	G	C	O	T	D	S	A
U	T	L	I	I	O	G	E	E	R	I	D	E	L
H	S	O	S	T	G	O	L	R	K	L	A	R	I
E	C	N	E	W	C	R	E	N	S	I	U	M	N
M	A	H	G	S	R	E	T	U	P	M	O	C	K
O	P	C	D	M	A	I	N	F	R	A	M	E	S
D	E	E	I	N	T	E	R	N	E	T	F	L	L
E	D	T	R	L	O	C	O	T	O	R	P	P	F
M	C	A	B	L	E	S	T	E	K	C	A	P	S
U	F	L	I	A	M	E	T	S	Y	S	S	A	H

Solution on Page 330

ACID-FREE
ART
BAGS
BOOKS
CARBON
CELLULOSE
CUT
ENVELOPE
FIBER
GLOSSY
INK
JOURNAL
LETTERS
LINES
MONEY
NEWSPAPER
NOTEBOOK
PACKAGING
PAGES
PAINTING
PAPER MILL
PAPYRUS
PEN
PRINTING
PULP
REAM
RECYCLE
SANDPAPER
SHEET
STATIONERY
THIN
TISSUE
TREE
WALLPAPER
WEIGHT
WHITE
WOOD
WRAPPING
WRITING

Paper

K	J	S	R	E	A	M	E	J	D	O	O	W	J
N	O	J	T	E	N	V	E	L	O	P	E	G	T
I	A	O	P	A	P	E	R	M	I	L	L	N	B
T	M	U	B	A	T	A	F	T	Z	P	C	I	O
H	O	R	Q	E	P	I	P	I	R	R	Y	T	O
G	N	N	J	S	T	Y	O	S	B	E	C	N	K
I	E	A	G	O	R	O	R	N	W	E	E	I	S
E	Y	L	N	L	E	E	N	U	E	E	R	A	G
W	S	S	I	U	U	P	P	R	S	R	N	P	N
R	S	E	G	L	S	T	F	A	S	D	Y	N	I
I	O	G	A	L	S	D	R	E	P	R	W	O	P
T	L	A	K	E	I	K	N	A	C	L	I	B	P
I	G	P	C	C	T	I	P	U	L	P	L	R	A
N	S	G	A	B	L	E	T	T	E	R	S	A	R
G	N	E	P	P	R	I	N	T	I	N	G	C	W
N	W	H	I	T	E	E	H	S	N	I	H	T	D

Solution on Page 330

ALEJANDRO
AMERICAN
ARTIST
AWARDS
CELEBRITY
CLOTHES
CONCERT
DANCING
ECCENTRIC
FASHION
HAIR
ICON
JUST DANCE
MADONNA
MEAT DRESS
MONSTER
MTV
MUSICIAN
OUTRAGEOUS
PAPARAZZI
PERFORMING
PIANO
POKER FACE
POP SINGER
POPULAR
ROCK MUSIC
ROMANCE
SONGWRITER
STAR
STYLE
TELEPHONE
THE FAME
VIDEOS
WOMAN
YOUNG

Lady Gaga

Z	T	S	I	T	R	A	L	U	P	O	P	R	T
N	A	I	C	I	S	U	M	T	V	J	Y	O	E
A	O	U	T	R	A	G	E	O	U	S	O	M	M
M	V	I	D	E	O	S	A	S	A	E	U	A	A
O	P	R	H	A	I	R	T	T	M	H	N	N	F
W	S	E	E	S	A	D	D	Y	E	T	G	C	E
Y	C	O	G	G	A	L	R	L	R	O	N	E	H
T	T	E	N	N	N	F	E	E	I	L	I	C	T
A	R	I	C	G	I	I	S	J	C	C	C	C	E
M	N	E	R	A	W	M	S	T	A	R	N	E	L
O	A	N	C	B	F	R	R	P	N	N	A	N	E
N	W	A	O	N	E	R	I	O	O	O	D	T	P
S	A	P	N	D	O	L	E	T	F	P	C	R	H
T	R	Y	A	N	A	C	E	K	E	R	Q	I	O
E	D	C	I	S	U	M	K	C	O	R	E	C	N
R	S	U	P	I	Z	Z	A	R	A	P	A	P	E

Solution on Page 331

ALGAE
BIOLOGY
BOTANIST
BRANCH
CELLS
CLASS
DISEASES
ECOLOGY
EVOLUTION
FLOWERS
FODDER
FUNGI
GARDENS
GENETICS
GRASS
GROWTH
HERBS
LATIN
LEAVES
MEDICINE
NATURE
NUTRITION
PLANT LIFE
POLLEN
RESEARCH
SCIENCE
SEEDS
SOIL
SPECIES
STEMS
STRUCTURE
STUDY
TAXONOMY
TISSUE
VEGETABLES
VEGETATION
WATER

Studying Plants

E	N	I	C	I	D	E	M	S	F	U	N	G	I
S	T	U	D	Y	B	I	O	L	O	G	Y	E	O
H	T	W	O	R	G	P	S	L	A	T	I	N	E
Q	J	P	P	B	O	P	V	E	W	A	T	E	R
J	T	M	A	L	G	A	E	C	A	N	F	T	U
S	S	A	L	C	A	N	G	A	O	S	S	I	T
D	I	E	U	E	C	N	E	I	C	S	E	C	A
E	N	O	I	T	I	R	T	U	N	A	L	S	N
E	A	H	F	L	H	U	A	L	U	R	B	R	T
S	T	C	Z	C	L	S	T	D	I	G	A	E	I
H	O	R	N	O	M	L	I	O	S	F	T	W	S
E	B	A	V	E	Y	G	O	L	O	C	E	O	S
R	R	E	T	A	X	O	N	O	M	Y	G	L	U
B	G	S	S	T	R	U	C	T	U	R	E	F	E
S	R	E	D	D	O	F	Z	L	E	A	V	E	S
G	A	R	D	E	N	S	E	I	C	E	P	S	I

Solution on Page 331

BAKERY
BAKING
BAKLAVA
BREAD
BUTTER
CAKES
CHEF
CHOCOLATE
COOKING
CREAM PUFF
CROISSANT
CRUST
CUSTARD
DANISH
DESSERT
DISH
DOUGHNUT
EGGS
FILLING
FLAKY
FLOUR
FOOD
FRENCH
ITALIAN
MILK
NAPOLEON
OVEN
PETIT FOUR
PIES
RESTAURANT
SCONE
SHORTENING
STRUDEL
SWEET
TARTS
TORTE

Pastry

P	I	E	S	W	C	O	V	E	N	F	T	H	L
H	T	U	N	H	G	U	O	D	L	D	O	O	F
Y	Y	N	A	P	O	L	E	O	N	C	R	Y	B
B	I	C	A	V	X	C	U	R	O	H	T	B	A
U	A	A	H	S	A	R	A	O	H	S	E	R	K
T	S	K	F	E	S	L	K	T	D	I	T	E	E
T	F	E	I	F	F	I	K	N	T	N	A	A	R
E	F	S	L	N	N	N	O	A	R	A	L	D	Y
R	U	W	L	G	G	W	L	R	B	D	O	R	S
S	P	E	I	H	S	I	D	U	C	I	C	A	G
T	M	E	N	V	A	Y	K	A	L	F	O	T	G
R	A	T	G	N	I	N	E	T	R	O	H	S	E
A	E	F	Z	T	R	E	S	S	E	D	C	U	N
T	R	U	O	F	T	I	T	E	P	G	E	C	O
C	C	O	K	L	E	D	U	R	T	S	U	R	C
H	M	I	L	K	H	C	N	E	R	F	M	S	S

Solution on Page 331

ALBACORE
BIGEYE
BIOLOGY
BLUEFIN
BOATS
CANNED
CASSEROLE
CATCH
DIET
DOLPHINS
EAT
FILLET
FISHERIES
FISHING
FRESH
HELPER
IN OIL
IN WATER
LARGE
LOW FAT
MARINE
MELT
MERCURY
NETS
OCEAN
PINK
PROTEIN
RAW
RESTAURANT
SALMON
SALT WATER
SANDWICHES
SEAFOOD
STARKIST
SUSHI
SWIM
TIN
TUNA STEAK
YELLOWFIN

Tuna

C	A	N	N	E	D	M	W	J	K	N	I	P	K
E	N	L	H	C	T	A	C	Y	F	H	H	H	J
E	I	M	B	A	I	F	A	I	S	B	E	U	B
G	E	I	F	A	R	H	S	U	L	L	N	I	T
R	T	W	I	E	C	H	S	U	P	A	G	I	S
A	O	S	S	N	E	O	E	E	E	E	N	A	S
L	R	H	H	R	O	F	R	C	Y	W	N	T	T
Y	P	E	I	T	I	I	O	E	A	D	N	Y	A
E	R	E	N	N	S	A	L	T	W	A	T	E	R
N	S	U	G	W	S	M	E	I	R	E	L	L	K
I	E	A	C	A	T	R	C	U	I	B	E	L	I
R	A	W	L	R	A	H	A	D	O	K	M	O	S
A	F	M	K	A	E	T	S	A	N	U	T	W	T
M	O	H	J	S	S	M	T	E	L	L	I	F	H
N	O	V	N	E	T	S	Y	G	O	L	O	I	B
I	D	M	R	H	I	D	O	L	P	H	I	N	S

Solution on Page 331

ADVENTURE
AFRICA
ANIMATION
BROADWAY
CARTOON
CHILDREN
CLASSIC
CUB
DISNEY
FAMILY
FATHER
FILM
HAMLET
HYENAS
JUNGLE
KINGDOM
LIONS
LOVE
MEERKAT
MOVIE
MUFASA
MUSICAL
NALA
OUTLANDS
PLAY
PRINCE
PUMBAA
RAFIKI
SARABI
SCAR
SHENZI
SHOW
SIMBA
SONGS
STAMPEDE
STORY
THEATER
TIMON
WARTHOG
ZAZU

The Lion King

E	Z	F	R	H	Y	E	N	A	S	P	B	U	C
X	D	M	B	E	C	L	E	C	N	I	R	P	I
T	E	L	M	A	H	C	I	T	B	L	O	H	K
T	G	I	N	O	I	T	A	M	I	N	A	P	I
A	I	F	B	S	L	Z	A	O	A	D	D	E	F
M	L	M	S	A	D	K	N	F	V	F	W	L	A
S	L	A	O	F	R	S	I	E	X	O	A	G	R
A	L	Y	N	N	E	A	N	N	H	L	Y	N	C
C	A	J	G	X	N	T	S	S	G	S	E	U	C
I	C	G	S	O	U	T	L	A	N	D	S	J	Y
R	I	W	A	R	T	H	O	G	E	V	O	L	R
F	S	Y	E	N	S	I	D	P	L	Y	O	M	O
A	U	I	E	I	V	O	M	E	E	R	K	A	T
Z	M	X	M	S	C	A	R	T	O	O	N	I	S
Z	A	Z	U	B	T	H	E	A	T	E	R	U	T
M	U	F	A	S	A	A	B	M	U	P	L	A	Y

Solution on Page 332

AUCTION
BIDDING
BRIDGE
CALL
CARD GAME
CHANCE
CLOCKWISE
CLUBS
COMPASS
CONTRACT
DEALING
DECLARER
DIAMONDS
DOUBLE
DUMMY
DUPLICATE
EAST
FOUR
HANDS
HEARTS
LEVEL
NORTH
PARTNERS
PLAYERS
RUBBER
SCORING
SKILL
SOUTH
SPADES
STRATEGY
SUITS
TABLE
TOURNAMENT
TRICKS
TRUMP SUIT
WEST

Contract Bridge

K	E	L	B	U	O	D	U	M	M	Y	C	V	F
H	T	R	O	N	S	O	U	T	H	A	N	D	S
F	A	T	R	I	C	K	S	C	O	R	I	N	G
L	C	L	O	C	K	W	I	S	E	A	A	U	K
L	I	Y	S	T	I	U	S	P	M	U	R	T	S
A	L	G	G	U	K	R	X	O	A	C	Z	N	B
C	P	I	L	E	E	U	N	H	G	T	P	E	U
N	U	M	K	N	T	D	R	E	D	I	D	M	L
C	D	S	T	S	S	A	E	A	R	O	E	A	C
O	Q	R	A	E	E	W	R	R	A	N	A	N	H
M	A	E	B	G	D	E	A	T	C	T	L	R	A
P	W	Y	L	D	A	S	L	S	S	E	I	U	N
A	N	A	E	I	P	T	C	A	R	T	N	O	C
S	K	L	W	R	S	L	E	V	E	L	G	T	E
S	E	P	K	B	I	D	D	I	N	G	J	M	K
I	Y	M	I	R	E	B	B	U	R	U	O	F	D

Solution on Page 332

APARTMENTS
BOARD
BUILDING
BYLAWS
CITY
COMMUNITY
COMPLEX
CONDO
DWELLING
ELEVATOR
FACILITIES
FEES
FLAT
FLORIDA
HALLWAYS
HOMEOWNERS
HOUSING
LANDLORD
LEASE
LEGAL
LOFT
MORTGAGE
NEIGHBOR
OWNERSHIP
POOL
PROPERTY
RENTAL
RESIDENT
SELL
STRUCTURE
TENANT
TIME SHARE
TOWNHOUSE
UNITS
VIEW

Condominium

J	L	E	G	A	L	X	E	L	P	M	O	C	H
U	N	I	T	S	A	T	N	A	N	E	T	W	S
B	T	A	R	O	T	A	V	E	L	E	N	E	E
E	U	A	P	F	N	R	B	G	S	C	E	I	L
G	Y	I	L	A	E	L	U	E	O	O	D	V	L
A	N	T	L	F	R	E	I	C	P	M	I	Z	O
G	H	I	I	D	Q	T	S	S	T	M	S	W	O
T	A	I	L	C	I	S	M	R	O	U	E	S	P
R	L	D	B	L	O	N	O	E	W	N	R	N	R
O	L	I	I	O	E	N	G	N	N	I	A	E	O
M	W	C	S	R	A	W	D	W	H	T	H	I	P
L	A	N	D	L	O	R	D	O	O	Y	S	G	E
F	Y	E	S	A	E	L	D	E	U	L	E	H	R
M	S	W	A	L	Y	B	F	M	S	O	M	B	T
P	I	H	S	R	E	N	W	O	E	F	I	O	Y
O	V	G	N	I	S	U	O	H	B	T	T	R	S

Solution on Page 332

ACTION
ATOMS
BODIES
CALCULUS
DIRECTION
DYNAMICS
ENERGY
EQUATIONS
FORCES
GALAXIES
GALILEO
GRAVITY
INERTIA
KEPLER
KINETIC
LAWS
LIGHT
LIQUIDS
MACHINERY
MASS
MATH
MECHANICS
MOMENTUM
NEWTONIAN
PARTICLES
PHYSICS
POSITION
PROJECTILE
RELATIVITY
SPEED
STUDY
TECHNOLOGY
THEORY
TIME
VELOCITY
WORK

Classical Mechanics

L	R	Y	P	H	Y	S	I	C	S	C	H	B	F
I	W	O	R	K	D	I	R	E	C	T	I	O	N
Q	I	S	N	O	I	T	A	U	Q	E	R	D	L
U	S	N	G	D	E	E	P	S	L	C	Z	I	A
I	E	V	A	Y	O	H	W	I	E	H	S	E	W
D	L	K	L	I	G	H	T	S	V	N	C	S	S
S	C	E	I	R	N	C	P	C	M	O	I	Y	C
H	I	P	L	Y	E	O	A	U	S	L	N	T	I
A	T	L	E	J	S	L	T	S	V	O	A	I	M
I	R	E	O	I	C	N	A	W	I	G	H	V	A
T	A	R	T	U	E	M	I	T	E	Y	C	A	N
R	P	I	L	M	M	A	C	H	I	N	E	R	Y
E	O	U	O	X	M	A	T	H	U	V	M	G	D
N	S	M	O	T	A	G	A	L	A	X	I	E	S
I	S	T	U	D	Y	V	E	L	O	C	I	T	Y
A	C	I	T	E	N	I	K	E	N	E	R	G	Y

Solution on Page 332

ACORN
ALMONDS
BARLEY
BRAZIL NUT
BREADNUT
BUCKWHEAT
CASHEW
CEREALS
CHESTNUT
CHICKPEAS
COWPEAS
FLAX
FRUITS
GRAINS
HAZELNUT
HEMP
LEGUMES
LENTILS
MACADAMIA
MAIZE
MILLET
OATS
PEANUTS
PINE NUTS
PUMPKIN
QUINOA
RYE
SEEDS
SOYBEANS
SPELT
SUNFLOWER
WALNUT
WILD RICE

Edible Seeds

T	S	P	E	L	T	N	V	T	E	L	L	I	M
I	W	D	E	T	U	N	T	S	E	H	C	A	R
T	E	I	E	A	T	U	N	L	A	W	C	F	E
E	H	B	L	E	N	T	I	L	S	A	O	R	W
S	S	J	R	D	S	U	S	E	D	C	W	U	O
N	A	B	A	A	R	Z	T	A	Z	F	P	I	L
A	C	E	C	H	Z	I	M	S	N	I	E	T	F
E	R	F	O	C	H	I	C	K	P	E	A	S	N
B	S	L	R	P	A	G	L	E	I	H	S	M	U
Y	N	A	N	N	M	P	I	N	E	N	U	T	S
O	I	X	H	A	Z	E	L	N	U	T	K	D	E
S	A	B	U	C	K	W	H	E	A	T	N	N	M
N	R	T	E	Y	E	Q	U	I	N	O	A	S	U
R	G	B	S	Y	N	I	K	P	M	U	P	D	G
J	K	B	C	E	R	E	A	L	S	Q	Q	S	E
T	F	D	K	S	N	B	A	R	L	E	Y	N	L

Solution on Page 333

ALARM
ANALOG
ASTRONOMY
ATOMIC
BATTERY
BELL
BIG BEN
CUCKOO
DAY
DECORATIVE
DIGITAL
DISPLAY
ELECTRIC
FACE
HANDS
HOURGLASS
INSTRUMENT
INVENTION
LATE
METRONOME
MILITARY
MINUTES
MONTH
NOON
PENDULUM
QUARTZ
ROUND
SECONDS
SETTING
SOLAR
SUNDIAL
TICK
TIMEPIECE
TOWER
TRAVEL
WALL
WATCHES
WIND
YEAR

Telling Time

Y	H	D	I	G	I	T	A	L	E	V	A	R	T
D	A	N	N	P	Y	A	L	P	S	I	D	A	O
N	N	U	V	B	M	D	C	L	F	U	T	L	W
I	D	O	E	I	O	G	I	K	E	O	K	A	E
W	S	R	N	G	N	O	R	C	M	B	E	R	R
A	E	T	T	B	O	L	T	I	O	M	S	M	A
L	T	I	I	E	R	A	C	T	N	U	E	S	L
L	U	M	O	N	T	N	E	L	O	L	C	E	O
R	N	E	N	S	S	A	L	G	R	U	O	H	S
A	I	P	X	L	A	T	E	Z	T	D	N	C	Z
E	M	I	L	I	T	A	R	Y	E	N	D	T	F
Y	R	E	T	T	A	B	A	U	M	E	S	A	N
C	U	C	K	O	O	D	M	C	M	P	C	W	O
U	N	E	V	I	T	A	R	O	C	E	D	H	O
L	A	I	D	N	U	S	E	T	T	I	N	G	N
M	O	N	T	H	S	Q	R	Q	U	A	R	T	Z

Solution on Page 333

BRAND
BUSINESS
CALIFORNIA
CAMERAS
CARTRIDGE
COMPETITOR
COMPUTERS
COPIER
DESKTOPS
DIGITAL
FAX
GARAGE
GLOBAL
HARDWARE
INKJET
KEYBOARD
LAPTOPS
MONITORS
NETWORKING
OFFICE
PALO ALTO
PAPER
PRINTERS
SALES
SCANNER
SERVERS
SOFTWARE
STORAGE
SUPPORT
TECHNOLOGY
TONER

Hewlett-Packard

N	X	D	E	S	K	T	O	P	S	T	M	G	T
C	O	P	I	E	R	A	W	D	R	A	H	A	R
J	M	O	N	I	T	O	R	S	E	S	H	R	O
S	J	G	N	I	K	R	O	W	T	E	N	A	P
R	I	N	K	J	E	T	T	D	U	R	W	G	P
E	E	C	P	O	L	K	I	S	P	V	B	E	U
T	P	N	A	A	L	G	T	A	M	E	U	G	S
N	E	D	O	L	I	X	E	L	O	R	S	D	T
I	R	L	R	T	I	A	P	E	C	S	I	I	O
R	A	N	A	A	N	F	M	S	I	D	N	R	R
P	W	L	Y	G	O	L	O	N	H	C	E	T	A
A	T	D	N	A	R	B	C	R	R	D	S	R	G
O	F	F	I	C	E	O	Y	I	N	E	S	A	E
S	O	N	S	C	A	N	N	E	R	I	P	C	B
M	S	A	R	E	M	A	C	D	K	S	A	A	C
S	P	O	T	P	A	L	A	B	O	L	G	X	P

Solution on Page 333

AQUIFERS
BATH
BAYS
BOATING
BOIL
BOTTLED
BRIDGES
BROOK
CLEAN
CONSERVE
CREEK
CURRENT
DAM
DRINKING
DROPS
FAUCET
FISHING
ICEBERGS
MINERAL
POND
POTABLE
PUDDLE
PURIFY
RAIN
RUNOFF
SEA
SHOWER
SKIING
SPIGOT
SPRINKLER
STAGNANT
STEAM
STREAM
TAP WATER
THIRST
TIDE
TORRENT
WATERFALL
WAVES
WELL

Here's Some Water

W	R	T	L	G	N	I	I	K	S	S	S	L	M
C	R	E	E	K	N	M	D	N	O	P	P	L	V
E	P	R	W	C	O	I	I	E	K	L	I	E	W
D	C	U	O	O	U	W	T	N	L	O	G	W	H
I	R	N	D	S	H	A	A	A	E	T	O	Y	T
T	F	O	M	D	P	S	F	V	O	R	T	R	A
W	C	F	P	W	L	R	R	B	E	B	A	O	B
T	T	F	A	S	E	E	I	G	H	S	I	L	B
G	N	T	L	T	S	F	N	N	N	E	C	T	T
B	E	L	A	N	P	I	I	I	K	A	E	N	S
R	R	W	O	A	K	U	A	H	Z	L	B	E	R
I	R	C	X	N	J	Q	R	S	T	I	E	R	I
D	O	M	I	G	D	A	M	I	X	O	R	R	H
G	T	R	N	A	E	L	C	F	F	B	G	U	T
E	D	P	O	T	A	B	L	E	R	Y	S	C	V
S	B	A	Y	S	T	R	E	A	M	A	E	T	S

Solution on Page 333

AIRTIGHT
BEANS
BOILING
CANNER
COOK
FACTORY
FISH
FOODS
FRESH
FRUITS
HOME
INDUSTRY
JARS
JELLY
LIDS
MASON JAR
MEAT
METAL
PACKAGING
PICK
PRESERVING
PRESSURE
PROCESSED
QUART
RING
SALT
SEALED
SHELF LIFE
SOUP
STORAGE
TIN
TOMATOES
TUNA
VACUUM
VEGETABLES
WATER

Canning

F	Y	C	Z	S	B	M	B	Q	B	P	U	O	S
A	O	O	N	N	H	O	M	E	T	R	A	U	Q
W	U	O	G	N	I	V	R	E	S	E	R	P	G
R	A	K	D	L	W	T	V	H	E	S	A	I	D
A	I	T	I	S	T	A	E	M	V	S	J	C	F
A	O	N	E	T	E	L	G	D	A	U	N	K	I
Q	G	Y	G	R	F	O	E	E	C	R	O	H	S
S	X	P	N	L	N	D	T	L	U	E	S	N	H
T	H	G	I	T	R	I	Λ	Λ	U	J	Λ	R	S
I	R	F	G	N	K	W	B	E	M	E	M	N	A
U	E	R	A	S	D	I	L	S	B	O	A	D	R
R	N	E	K	C	Y	U	E	K	M	E	T	A	L
F	N	S	C	D	E	S	S	E	C	O	R	P	H
H	A	H	A	G	F	A	C	T	O	R	Y	F	P
A	C	P	P	G	L	E	G	A	R	O	T	S	G
F	A	N	U	T	R	J	E	L	L	Y	L	S	U

Solution on Page 334

AUTOSAVE
BACKBOX
BANK
BONUS
BOUNCE
BUMPERS
BUTTONS
COIN
COMBO
DRAIN
FLIPPERS
FREE BALL
GAME
INLANE
JACKPOT
KICKER
LAUNCH
LIGHTS
MACHINE
MAGIC POST
MATCH
MODE
MULTIBALL
ORBIT
PLAYFIELD
PLUNGER
POINTS
POPPER
RAMPS
REPLAY
ROLLOVER
SLAM TILT
SLINGSHOT
SOUNDS
SPINNER
STOPPER
SWITCHES
TARGETS

Pinball

M	U	L	T	I	B	A	L	L	D	R	A	I	N
I	P	L	A	Y	F	I	E	L	D	M	M	T	P
L	M	A	G	I	C	P	O	S	T	P	O	A	S
I	T	B	R	E	V	O	L	L	O	R	D	R	X
G	S	E	A	U	T	O	S	A	V	E	E	G	O
H	T	E	M	B	O	P	D	M	S	P	S	E	B
T	O	R	B	A	I	L	A	T	P	P	T	T	K
S	P	F	O	N	C	T	O	I	M	G	N	S	C
E	P	R	N	K	C	H	L	L	A	I	I	N	A
H	E	E	U	H	S	F	I	T	R	N	O	P	B
C	R	K	S	G	R	E	G	N	U	L	P	O	U
T	E	C	N	G	E	G	A	M	E	A	U	P	T
I	P	I	T	O	P	K	C	A	J	N	C	P	T
W	L	K	O	B	M	O	C	Y	C	E	O	E	O
S	A	H	C	N	U	A	L	E	F	J	I	R	N
Q	Y	J	O	R	B	I	T	S	O	U	N	D	S

Solution on Page 334

ALITO
APPELLATE
APPOINTED
ARGUMENTS
BENCH
CASES
CHIEF
DECISION
DOCKET
FEDERAL
GINSBURG
GOVERNMENT
HIGH COURT
JUDGES
JUDICIARY
JURY
JUSTICES
KENNEDY
LAWYERS
LEGAL
MAJORITY
NINE
OPINION
PLAINTIFF
PRECEDENT
PRESIDENT
ROBERTS
RULINGS
SCALIA
SENATE
TENURE
THOMAS
TRIAL
WASHINGTON

The Supreme Court

S	T	L	N	S	Y	V	Y	O	T	I	L	A	K
T	N	A	O	E	R	F	D	N	B	E	N	C	H
N	E	I	I	C	U	E	E	R	U	N	E	T	W
E	D	R	S	I	J	D	N	O	I	N	I	P	O
M	E	T	I	T	I	E	N	F	E	I	H	C	L
U	C	O	C	S	T	R	E	B	O	R	G	Y	A
G	E	Y	E	U	S	A	K	Y	I	O	I	E	W
R	R	R	D	J	I	L	R	Y	V	M	N	A	Y
A	P	P	E	L	L	A	T	E	S	I	S	P	E
S	E	S	A	C	I	I	R	G	N	H	B	P	R
E	C	C	X	C	R	N	N	D	I	Y	U	O	S
G	S	N	I	O	M	I	T	N	O	V	R	I	A
D	P	D	J	E	L	E	G	A	L	C	G	N	M
U	U	A	N	U	E	T	A	N	E	S	K	T	O
J	M	T	R	U	O	C	H	G	I	H	W	E	H
P	L	A	I	N	T	I	F	F	Q	M	C	D	T

Solution on Page 334

ADVENTURE
ANCHOR
ANEMONE
ANIMATION
AQUARIUM
AUSTRALIA
BARRACUDA
CARTOON
CHILDREN
CHUM
COMEDY
CORAL
CRUSH
DARLA
DENTIST
DISNEY
DIVER
DORY
FATHER
FILM
FISH TANK
GILL
JELLYFISH
JOURNEY
LOST
MARLIN
MOVIE
OCEAN
PELICAN
PIXAR
REEF
SCHOOL
SEAGULL
SHARKS
SON
SWIMMING
SYDNEY
TURTLES
WATER
WHALE

Finding Nemo

E	S	O	N	O	O	T	R	A	C	O	R	A	L
I	S	F	E	E	R	X	Q	Y	E	N	D	Y	S
V	K	Y	E	N	R	U	O	J	R	J	S	E	N
O	R	E	H	T	A	F	E	N	O	M	E	N	A
M	A	B	A	R	R	A	C	U	D	A	R	S	C
H	H	G	I	L	L	S	C	C	I	L	U	I	I
Y	S	U	K	R	D	H	U	L	N	O	T	D	L
P	M	U	A	N	I	M	A	T	I	O	N	L	E
T	I	D	R	L	A	R	U	W	L	H	E	L	P
S	Y	X	D	C	T	T	I	K	R	C	V	U	J
I	D	R	A	S	M	U	H	C	A	S	D	G	A
T	E	T	U	R	T	L	E	S	M	F	A	A	N
N	M	A	S	S	W	I	M	M	I	N	G	E	C
E	O	G	M	O	J	E	L	L	Y	F	I	S	H
D	C	W	H	A	L	E	M	X	N	A	E	C	O
F	W	A	T	E	R	Y	R	O	D	I	V	E	R

Solution on Page 334

ARTIFACTS
BEHAVIOR
BIOLOGICAL
COUNTRIES
CULTURES
DIG
ECOLOGY
ETHNICITY
ETHNOLOGY
EVOLUTION
FAMILY
FOSSIL
GENEALOGY
GENETICS
GROUPS
HISTORY
HUMANITY
KINSHIP
LANGUAGES
LINGUISTIC
NATURE
ORIGINS
PEOPLE
PHILOSOPHY
PHYSICAL
RACE
RELIGION
RESEARCH
SCIENCE
SOCIOLOGY
STUDY
TOOLS

Anthropology

W	Y	G	O	L	O	C	E	C	N	E	I	C	S
A	G	E	N	E	T	I	C	S	P	U	O	R	G
I	R	E	L	I	G	I	O	N	T	O	O	L	S
W	S	N	N	S	E	G	A	U	G	N	A	L	A
C	E	O	P	E	T	H	N	I	C	I	T	Y	K
A	I	I	C	H	A	C	U	L	T	U	R	E	S
H	R	T	P	I	I	L	A	C	I	S	Y	H	P
U	T	U	S	E	O	L	O	F	A	M	I	L	Y
M	N	L	B	I	O	L	O	G	I	C	A	L	D
A	U	O	C	O	U	P	O	S	Y	T	H	G	U
N	O	V	Q	D	I	G	L	G	O	I	R	L	T
I	C	E	R	U	T	A	N	E	Y	P	R	A	S
T	S	N	I	G	I	R	O	I	V	A	H	E	B
Y	R	A	C	E	T	H	N	O	L	O	G	Y	P
R	E	S	E	A	R	C	H	I	S	T	O	R	Y
D	P	I	H	S	N	I	K	F	O	S	S	I	L

Solution on Page 335

ACTIVIST
ALMANAC
AMBASSADOR
AMERICAN
AUTHOR
BIFOCALS
COLONIES
DIPLOMAT
FATHER
FOUNDING
GENIUS
GOVERNMENT
INVENTIONS
JEFFERSON
KEY
KITE
LIBRARY
LIGHTNING
MONEY
NEWSPAPER
PATRIOT
POLITICS
POLYMATH
POSTMASTER
PRESIDENT
PRINTING
REVOLUTION
SATIRIST
SCIENTIST
STATESMAN
STOVE

Benjamin Franklin

F	E	V	O	T	S	C	I	E	N	T	I	S	T
O	B	P	G	N	I	T	N	I	R	P	G	U	A
U	I	R	L	M	L	S	V	S	O	A	O	I	L
N	F	E	I	J	I	I	E	P	H	T	V	N	M
D	O	S	G	A	G	R	N	O	T	R	E	E	A
I	C	I	H	I	D	I	T	S	U	I	R	G	N
N	A	D	T	D	I	T	I	T	A	O	N	A	A
G	L	E	N	U	P	A	O	M	D	T	M	J	C
P	S	N	I	Y	L	S	N	A	W	S	E	L	I
O	E	T	N	R	O	O	S	S	E	F	N	M	R
L	I	R	G	A	M	S	V	T	F	Y	T	I	E
Y	N	E	G	R	A	E	A	E	Y	E	N	O	M
M	O	H	L	B	T	T	R	R	R	K	B	C	A
A	L	T	M	I	S	S	C	I	T	I	L	O	P
T	O	A	K	L	O	A	C	T	I	V	I	S	T
H	C	F	B	N	E	W	S	P	A	P	E	R	W

Solution on Page 335

AWL
BALSA
BARK
BEAD
BENCH
BLADE
BOARD
BUILDING
BURL
CARVING
CHISEL
CROSSCUT
DADO
DOVETAIL
DRILL
FACE
FENCE
FLUTE
FRAME
GOUGE
GRAIN
GRIT
GROOVE
HAMMER
HARDWOOD
HINGE
JIGSAW
JOINT
KNOT
LUMBER
MITRE
MORTISE
PATTERN
RASP
ROUTER
SCRAPER
SOFTWOOD
SQUARE
VENEER
VISE

Woodworking

M	O	I	B	L	H	Z	V	E	N	E	E	R	D
E	T	U	L	F	P	W	T	F	D	R	A	O	B
B	R	I	A	U	E	M	A	R	F	L	T	U	X
L	R	W	D	Q	D	C	C	S	G	E	N	T	H
D	L	G	E	O	E	O	F	X	G	S	I	E	A
R	K	E	G	U	O	G	O	E	I	I	O	R	E
E	C	R	R	D	E	W	R	W	N	H	J	E	Z
B	A	T	A	G	L	R	T	I	D	C	G	M	I
M	R	I	I	B	N	N	A	F	T	R	E	M	S
U	V	M	N	D	R	I	M	U	O	O	A	A	L
L	I	A	T	E	V	O	D	O	Q	S	H	H	I
R	N	R	T	I	R	E	V	L	L	S	C	M	N
A	G	T	D	T	B	E	K	A	I	C	N	H	B
S	A	H	I	N	G	E	B	N	F	U	E	Y	N
P	E	S	I	V	Q	D	A	D	O	T	B	B	H
R	E	P	A	R	C	S	T	D	H	T	V	D	F

Solution on Page 335

AFRICA
ARABICA
AROMA
ARUSHA
BEANS
BLACK
BOURBON
BRAZIL
CAFFEINE
CAPPUCCINO
CATURRA
COLOMBIAN
DARK
DECAF
DRIP
ESPRESSO
ETHIOPIAN
FLAVOR
FRENCH
HAWAIIAN
INSTANT
JAMAICAN
JAVA
KENYA
KOPI LUWAK
LATTE
MOCHA
MUNDO NOVO
PACAMARA
PANAMA
PERU
ROASTED
ROBUSTA
SANTOS
STARBUCKS
SUMATRA
TIMOR
TYPICA
UGANDA

Coffee Varieties

T	Y	P	B	R	A	Z	I	L	B	L	A	C	K
N	D	E	C	A	F	H	W	F	R	E	N	C	H
A	B	S	O	T	N	A	S	T	L	J	A	V	A
T	A	R	O	M	A	R	R	U	T	A	C	N	R
S	K	C	U	B	R	A	T	S	R	M	V	O	S
N	N	A	I	P	O	I	H	T	E	A	M	O	V
I	R	P	W	S	C	A	F	F	E	I	N	E	R
A	O	P	W	U	O	F	A	O	T	C	A	S	O
D	E	U	F	M	L	R	C	V	A	A	I	P	A
N	R	C	T	A	O	I	I	O	Y	N	I	R	S
A	O	C	M	T	M	C	P	N	N	D	A	E	T
G	B	I	O	R	B	A	Y	O	E	R	W	S	E
U	U	N	C	A	I	P	T	D	K	I	A	S	D
R	S	O	H	X	A	M	A	N	A	P	H	O	A
E	T	T	A	L	N	B	O	U	R	B	O	N	R
P	A	C	I	B	A	R	A	M	A	C	A	P	K

Solution on Page 335

ACTION
ADVENTURE
AGENT
BOND GIRLS
BRITISH
CARS
CASINO
CHARACTER
CONNERY
DALTON
DR. NO
ENEMY
FILM
FLEMING
GADGETS
GOLDENEYE
GOLDFINGER
GUNS
HERO
MARTINI
MONEYPENNY
MOONRAKER
MOVIES
OCTOPUSSY
RUSSIA
SHAKEN
SPIES
VILLAINS
WOMEN

Bond Movies

G	I	N	I	T	R	A	M	O	V	I	E	S	C
U	I	I	D	F	L	E	M	I	N	G	I	P	N
N	E	K	A	H	S	I	T	I	R	B	O	I	S
S	C	M	L	I	F	S	V	C	A	S	J	E	N
G	C	H	T	H	T	N	E	G	A	L	I	S	L
R	O	M	O	O	N	R	A	K	E	R	R	O	G
L	C	S	N	E	M	O	W	S	K	I	A	O	M
O	E	E	Y	E	N	E	D	L	O	G	L	H	O
H	W	Q	E	R	U	T	N	E	V	D	A	F	C
C	A	R	S	F	U	G	B	O	F	N	N	O	T
Y	O	S	N	I	A	L	L	I	V	O	O	N	O
M	O	N	E	Y	P	E	N	N	Y	B	I	I	P
D	N	V	N	H	R	G	A	D	G	E	T	S	U
K	R	V	E	E	E	Y	Z	J	E	M	C	A	S
O	D	R	M	R	R	R	U	S	S	I	A	C	S
A	O	D	Y	S	S	Y	S	G	X	R	K	D	Y

Solution on Page 336

AMERICAN
APPAREL
BOOKS
BULL'S EYE
BUSINESS
CHAIN
CHEAP
CLEARANCE
CLOTHING
CREDIT
DEALS
DEPARTMENT
DISCOUNT
FOOD
FURNITURE
GOODS
GROCERY
HEALTH
HOUSEWARES
JEWELRY
LOGO
MALL
MINNESOTA
MONEY
ONLINE
PHARMACY
PRODUCTS
RETAILER
SALES
SERVICE
SHOPPING
STORES
SUCCESS
TOYS
VALUE
VARIETY

Target Corporation

W	K	Y	E	N	I	L	N	O	T	S	Y	O	T
S	S	E	C	C	U	S	H	I	Y	R	F	G	V
D	R	N	I	A	H	C	D	S	L	A	E	D	F
O	Y	S	V	I	M	E	Y	E	S	L	L	U	B
O	P	T	R	A	R	R	W	C	E	W	R	D	S
F	R	O	E	C	L	E	A	R	A	N	C	E	A
T	O	R	S	I	J	U	A	H	I	W	R	P	L
N	D	E	O	L	R	P	E	T	P	A	G	A	E
U	U	S	N	G	P	Λ	U	R	W	T	N	R	S
O	C	P	A	A	O	R	V	E	M	O	I	T	H
C	T	H	S	I	E	L	S	L	O	S	H	M	O
S	S	E	N	I	S	U	B	I	N	E	T	E	P
I	D	A	B	O	O	K	S	A	E	N	O	N	P
D	O	L	C	H	E	A	P	T	Y	N	L	T	I
R	O	T	U	L	L	A	M	E	R	I	C	A	N
M	G	H	Y	R	E	C	O	R	G	M	J	Z	G

Solution on Page 336

AIRCRAFT
ANT FARM
ASSEMBLY
BALLS
BARBIE
BLOCKS
BRATZ
DOLLS
FIGURES
FRISBEE
GAME
HOT WHEELS
HULA HOOP
JACKS
KEN
LEGO
MARBLES
NERF
POGO STICK
PUZZLE
STUFFED
TEDDY BEAR
TINKERTOY
TOY CARS
TRUCKS
WEBKINZ
WHISTLES

F	N	X	D	O	L	L	S	A	A	S	N	B	Z
R	I	Y	Z	G	D	L	N	U	I	E	Z	F	U
I	S	R	Y	D	L	W	Y	A	R	R	N	O	G
S	E	R	L	A	A	N	T	F	A	R	M	N	J
B	L	A	B	S	E	R	U	G	I	F	S	W	P
E	B	E	M	T	O	Y	C	A	R	S	T	H	V
E	R	B	E	R	N	K	K	Z	C	B	U	I	K
L	A	Y	S	H	E	C	N	X	R	L	F	S	F
Z	M	D	S	F	W	I	X	L	A	O	F	T	S
Z	D	D	A	M	K	T	F	H	F	C	E	L	K
U	K	E	N	B	J	S	O	X	T	K	D	E	C
P	S	T	E	A	B	O	M	H	D	S	V	S	U
N	S	W	C	R	P	G	F	L	H	E	W	C	R
U	P	K	A	B	Y	O	T	R	E	K	N	I	T
M	S	T	T	I	C	P	O	T	J	G	T	T	N
B	Z	N	F	E	M	A	G	B	F	X	O	N	I

Solution on Page 336

AIM
ALTITUDE
APOGEE
ASSEMBLY
BUILD
CONSTRUCT
DEPLOYMENT
EJECTION
ENGINES
ESTES
EXPLOSIVE
FINS
FIRE
FLIGHT
FLYING
FUN
GLIDE
HIGH POWER
HOBBY
IGNITION
KITS
LAUNCHER
MODEL
MOTORS
NOSE CONE
PAPER
PARACHUTE
PLASTIC
RECOVERY
ROCKETRY
SAFETY
SCALE
SHOOT
SKY
SMALL
SPACE
SPEED
STREAMER
THRUST
WOOD

Model Rocket

S	P	A	C	E	R	E	H	C	N	U	A	L	P
N	N	P	I	N	Y	J	S	E	T	S	E	M	J
F	R	O	T	K	V	E	N	S	R	O	T	O	M
L	E	G	S	R	E	C	O	V	E	R	Y	D	I
I	D	E	A	E	T	T	I	Y	M	O	T	E	A
G	U	E	L	V	C	I	T	L	A	C	E	L	Q
H	T	E	P	I	U	O	I	B	E	K	F	F	I
T	I	N	H	S	R	N	N	M	R	E	A	I	G
H	T	G	S	O	T	V	G	E	T	T	S	N	F
R	L	I	H	L	S	S	I	S	S	R	I	S	U
U	A	N	O	P	N	A	C	S	D	Y	G	T	N
S	S	E	O	X	O	S	M	A	L	L	L	I	H
T	P	S	T	E	C	W	E	F	L	I	I	K	O
D	E	P	L	O	Y	M	E	N	T	E	D	U	B
C	E	E	T	U	H	C	A	R	A	P	E	G	B
P	D	O	O	W	U	F	I	R	E	P	A	P	Y

Solution on Page 336

ACTIVITIES
ART
AUDITORIUM
BUILDING
BUSES
CAFETERIA
CHILDREN
CLASSROOMS
COLLEGE
COMPUTERS
CURRICULUM
EDUCATION
ELEMENTARY
ENGLISH
EXAM
GRADUATE
GYM
LEARNING
MATH
MIDDLE
MUSIC
PAPER
PEN
PLAYGROUND
PRESCHOOL
READING
SCIENCE
SECONDARY
STUDENTS
TEACHERS
TESTS
TEXTBOOKS
UNIVERSITY

Going to School

Y	T	E	X	T	B	O	O	K	S	G	Y	M	H
O	Y	E	L	S	T	U	D	E	N	T	S	U	S
P	T	C	O	L	L	E	G	E	M	V	C	S	I
E	I	N	O	I	T	A	C	U	D	E	O	I	L
N	S	E	H	T	A	M	L	S	S	Y	M	C	G
E	R	I	C	G	S	U	A	D	E	R	P	A	N
R	E	C	S	N	C	P	S	Y	I	A	U	F	E
D	V	S	E	I	B	L	S	R	T	D	T	E	T
L	I	G	R	N	U	A	R	A	I	N	E	T	E
I	N	R	P	R	I	Y	O	T	V	O	R	E	A
H	U	A	A	A	L	G	O	N	I	C	S	R	C
C	T	D	P	E	D	R	M	E	T	E	T	I	H
E	E	U	E	L	I	O	S	M	C	S	X	A	E
X	S	A	R	U	N	U	G	E	A	A	M	G	R
A	T	T	M	Y	G	N	E	L	D	D	I	M	S
M	S	E	S	U	B	D	R	E	A	D	I	N	G

Solution on Page 337

BARK
BASEBALL
BOARDS
BOTTLE
BULLETIN
BUOYANT
CAP
CHAMPAGNE
CORK OAK
CORKSCREW
ELASTICITY
FLOATS
FLOORING
HANDLES
INDUSTRY
MATERIAL
NATURAL
PORTUGAL
RECYCLING
SEAL
STOPPER
SUBERIN
TILES
TISSUE
TREE
WALL
WINE
WOOD

Cork

H	T	N	A	Y	O	U	B	O	A	R	D	S	R
Q	N	A	T	U	R	A	L	R	F	B	A	R	K
R	C	L	S	S	S	T	A	O	L	F	F	E	U
N	H	A	N	D	L	E	S	I	B	Z	L	P	F
O	A	E	L	O	L	A	G	U	T	R	O	P	I
F	M	S	L	L	A	W	C	D	D	D	O	O	W
K	P	K	A	O	K	R	O	C	T	N	R	T	T
V	A	B	B	E	N	O	R	X	S	E	I	S	H
E	G	U	E	U	W	A	K	L	C	L	N	U	G
U	N	L	S	S	Y	X	S	Y	A	S	G	B	V
S	E	L	A	S	T	I	C	I	T	Y	O	E	V
Q	N	E	B	I	V	L	R	S	F	T	R	R	P
U	L	T	W	T	I	E	E	E	T	N	P	I	U
M	J	I	P	N	T	E	W	L	E	Z	L	N	L
F	N	N	G	A	E	C	E	I	R	R	Z	A	R
E	S	B	M	V	C	L	L	T	T	L	T	I	R

Solution on Page 337

BOOKS
BORROW
CATALOG
CDS
CHILDREN
CLASSES
COLLECTION
COMPUTERS
DICTIONARY
DVDS
EDUCATION
FINES
FREE
GOVERNMENT
HELP
INTERNET
KNOWLEDGE
LEARNING
LENDING
LIBRARIANS
LOAN
MAGAZINES
MEDIA
MOVIES
NONFICTION
NOVELS
OVERDUE
PUBLIC
READING
REFERENCES
RESEARCH
RESOURCES
SCHOOL
TABLE
TAPES

At the Library

S	G	I	N	T	E	R	N	E	T	A	P	E	S
L	D	Y	E	L	E	A	R	N	I	N	G	X	E
S	O	V	R	E	S	R	E	T	U	P	M	O	C
R	C	A	D	A	R	M	E	D	I	A	N	K	R
E	A	H	N	O	N	F	I	C	T	I	O	N	U
A	T	S	O	R	W	O	R	R	O	B	I	O	O
D	A	F	E	O	N	F	I	N	E	S	T	W	S
I	L	V	H	E	L	P	C	T	Y	N	A	L	E
N	O	I	T	C	E	L	L	O	C	A	C	E	R
G	G	N	I	D	N	E	L	Q	Y	I	U	D	M
C	S	E	C	N	E	R	E	F	E	R	D	G	O
H	C	R	A	E	S	E	R	V	I	A	E	E	V
P	U	B	L	I	C	H	I	L	D	R	E	N	I
E	U	D	R	E	V	O	F	E	L	B	A	T	E
B	O	O	K	S	M	A	G	A	Z	I	N	E	S
N	O	V	E	L	S	E	S	S	A	L	C	D	S

Solution on Page 337

APRON
BROOM
CARPET
CHILDCARE
CHILDREN
CHORES
CLEANING
CLOTHES
COOKING
DOMESTIC
DUSTING
FOOD
FURNITURE
GROCERIES
HOMEMAKER
HOUSEHOLD
HOUSEWORK
HUSBAND
IRONING
JOB
KITCHEN
LAUNDRY
LAWN
MANAGEMENT
MEALS
NUTRITION
PURCHASING
REPAIRS
SERVICES
SWEEPING
VACUUMING
WASHING
WIFE
WOMEN

Homemaking

R	H	G	N	I	H	S	A	W	M	E	A	L	S
E	U	I	T	Y	R	D	N	U	A	L	A	W	N
P	S	B	R	X	J	K	I	T	C	H	E	N	S
A	B	K	R	O	W	E	S	U	O	H	H	O	E
I	A	T	B	O	N	W	O	M	E	N	O	R	C
R	N	G	T	S	O	I	E	P	C	U	U	P	I
S	D	R	N	Y	E	M	N	A	H	T	S	A	V
C	C	O	E	I	A	R	R	G	I	R	E	G	R
L	H	C	M	K	S	P	O	N	L	I	H	N	E
E	I	E	E	E	E	A	R	H	D	T	O	I	S
A	L	R	G	T	S	U	H	O	C	I	L	P	E
N	D	I	A	T	F	T	O	C	A	O	D	E	H
I	R	E	N	W	E	F	I	W	R	N	H	E	T
N	E	S	A	C	G	T	K	C	E	U	K	W	O
G	N	I	M	U	U	C	A	V	F	B	P	S	L
O	D	U	S	T	I	N	G	N	I	K	O	O	C

Solution on Page 337

ACTIVIST
ALBUMS
APPLE
ARTIST
BAND
BASS
BEATLES
BRITISH
CELEBRITY
COMPOSER
CONCERTS
DIVORCE
ENGLAND
FAMOUS
GRAMMY
GUITAR
HARRISON
HEY JUDE
HISTORY
KNIGHTED
LENNON
LINDA
LIVERPOOL
LONDON
MUSICIAN
PAINTER
PERFORMER
PIANO
POP
RICH
RINGO
ROCK
SOLO
STAR
SUCCESSFUL
VEGETARIAN
WINGS
YESTERDAY

Paul McCartney

L	O	N	D	O	N	D	N	A	L	G	N	E	L
G	H	G	R	A	T	I	U	G	I	R	O	C	K
E	S	C	N	S	T	R	E	C	N	O	C	R	H
Y	T	U	I	I	Y	S	C	L	D	I	Y	O	S
M	A	T	C	R	R	A	I	S	A	T	B	V	I
M	R	H	R	C	O	V	D	V	I	D	A	I	T
A	P	V	E	G	E	T	A	R	I	A	N	D	I
R	E	Y	L	R	P	S	B	L	E	T	E	A	R
G	R	R	P	O	M	E	S	D	B	T	C	E	B
S	F	O	P	K	L	E	U	F	H	U	S	A	R
E	O	T	A	E	B	J	F	G	U	O	M	E	Z
L	R	S	C	C	Y	A	I	C	P	L	T	S	Y
T	M	I	G	E	M	N	S	M	O	N	A	I	P
A	E	H	H	O	K	N	O	S	I	R	R	A	H
E	R	M	U	S	I	C	I	A	N	S	O	L	O
B	L	S	G	N	I	W	P	L	E	N	N	O	N

Solution on Page 338

ADVERTISE
BOUTIQUE
BUSINESS
BUYERS
BUYING
CHECKOUT
CLOTHING
COMMERCE
CONSUMERS
CREDIT
CUSTOMERS
DELIVERY
DEPARTMENT
DISCOUNT
DISPLAYS
GOODS
ITEMS
KIOSK
MAIL
MALL
MANAGER
MARKETING
MONEY
OUTLETS
PRICING
PRODUCTS
PROFIT
PURCHASES
SALES
SELLING
SERVICE
SHOPPING
STORES
WHOLESALER

S	E	L	L	I	N	G	N	I	P	P	O	H	S
P	R	O	F	I	T	N	U	O	C	S	I	D	T
D	U	Y	R	E	V	I	L	E	D	E	M	B	E
D	E	S	E	S	A	H	C	R	U	P	O	U	L
R	C	P	C	U	S	T	O	M	E	R	S	Y	T
S	R	M	A	K	M	O	N	E	Y	W	W	E	U
G	E	A	V	R	E	L	S	C	W	H	W	R	O
N	M	R	Q	S	T	C	U	D	O	R	P	S	P
I	M	K	V	E	I	M	M	L	Z	H	Y	B	R
Y	O	E	S	I	T	R	E	V	D	A	O	E	I
U	C	T	T	S	C	S	R	N	L	U	G	W	C
B	R	I	O	A	A	E	S	P	T	A	K	A	I
L	E	N	R	L	B	U	S	I	N	E	S	S	N
L	D	G	E	E	R	I	Q	A	S	D	O	O	G
A	I	R	S	S	D	U	M	A	I	L	I	U	L
M	T	A	C	H	E	C	K	O	U	T	K	Q	S

Solution on Page 338

BATHTUB
BRASS
COPPER
COUPLING
DRAINAGE
DRINKING
EQUIPMENT
FITTINGS
FIXTURES
FLANGES
HEATERS
KITCHEN
LEAD PIPE
LINES
METERS
PIPING
PLASTIC
PLUMBER
PUMPS
SEPTIC
SEWAGE
SHOWER
SINKS
SKILL
SYSTEMS
TOILETS
TOOLS
TRAP
TUBING
VALVES
WASTE
WATER MAIN
WRENCH

Plumbing

D	N	S	E	N	I	L	R	U	L	G	L	J	C
T	N	E	M	P	I	U	Q	E	N	L	E	F	J
U	I	V	G	Q	D	R	A	I	N	A	G	E	Q
B	A	L	C	A	X	D	P	W	R	E	N	C	H
I	M	A	O	F	P	I	R	F	S	L	O	O	T
N	R	V	U	I	P	B	K	I	T	C	H	E	N
G	E	R	P	T	R	S	U	X	N	G	G	P	F
K	T	E	L	T	Q	T	S	T	S	K	I	L	L
Z	A	B	I	I	E	E	P	U	H	C	I	S	A
I	W	M	N	N	G	L	M	R	E	T	Y	N	N
C	R	U	G	G	A	I	U	E	A	S	A	Q	G
I	O	L	Y	S	W	O	P	S	T	R	S	B	E
T	K	P	T	F	E	T	N	E	E	E	K	R	S
P	P	I	P	E	S	B	M	D	R	T	N	A	N
E	C	A	W	E	T	S	A	W	S	E	I	S	E
S	H	O	W	E	R	T	R	A	P	M	S	S	R

Solution on Page 338

AEROBICS
BARBELLS
BIKES
CARDIO
CLASSES
CYCLE
DUMBBELLS
ELLIPTICAL
EQUIPMENT
EXERCISE
FACILITY
FEES
FITNESS
GOLD'S GYM
GYMNASIUM
HEALTH
INSTRUCTOR
MACHINES
MEMBERSHIP
MUSCLE
PILATES
POOLS
SAUNA
SPORTS
STEAM
SWIMMING
TRAINERS
TRAINING
TREADMILLS
WEIGHTS
WELLNESS
WORKOUT
YMCA
YOGA

Health Club

G	N	I	N	I	A	R	T	U	O	K	R	O	W
Y	S	E	E	F	B	A	R	B	E	L	L	S	E
M	E	M	B	E	R	S	H	I	P	O	O	C	F
N	N	W	E	L	L	N	E	S	S	E	K	I	B
A	I	E	O	L	G	E	L	C	S	U	M	B	T
S	H	I	I	I	N	S	T	R	U	C	T	O	R
I	C	G	D	P	I	L	A	T	E	S	F	R	E
U	A	H	R	T	M	L	C	O	L	E	F	E	A
M	M	T	A	I	M	E	B	Q	C	S	F	A	D
M	T	S	C	C	I	B	X	L	Y	S	A	F	M
A	G	O	Y	A	W	B	S	E	C	A	C	I	I
E	P	O	O	L	S	M	N	P	R	L	I	T	L
T	N	E	M	P	I	U	Q	E	O	C	L	N	L
S	V	M	Y	G	S	D	L	O	G	R	I	E	S
A	N	U	A	S	R	E	N	I	A	R	T	S	N
D	M	H	E	A	L	T	H	A	C	M	Y	S	E

Solution on Page 338

ARTIFICIAL
BEVERAGE
BOTTLED
BUBBLES
CAFFEINE
CALORIES
CANNED
CARBONATED
COKE
CORN SYRUP
CREAM SODA
DEPOSIT
DIET
DR PEPPER
DRINK
FANTA
FIZZY
FLAVORS
FOUNTAIN
GINGER ALE
GLASS
GRAPE
ICED TEA
JUICE
LEMONADE
LITER
ORANGE
PEPSI
REFRESHING
ROOT BEER
SEVEN UP
SODA POP
SPRITE
STRAW
SUGAR
SWEET
TAB

Soft Drinks

D	H	S	U	G	A	R	E	T	I	L	S	C	V
O	R	A	N	G	E	I	C	E	D	T	E	A	P
W	P	U	R	Y	S	N	R	O	C	G	P	C	U
S	E	B	Y	T	G	P	E	X	A	P	O	T	N
R	P	O	T	E	I	D	R	R	N	K	P	I	E
O	S	T	R	R	N	F	E	I	E	I	A	S	V
V	I	T	E	E	G	V	I	N	T	T	D	O	E
A	Y	L	P	E	E	P	A	C	N	E	O	P	S
L	Z	E	P	B	R	U	D	U	I	A	S	E	E
F	Z	D	E	T	A	N	O	B	R	A	C	D	L
A	I	R	P	O	L	F	S	S	S	A	L	G	B
N	F	I	R	O	E	W	M	J	U	I	C	E	B
T	G	N	D	R	E	D	A	N	O	M	E	L	U
A	H	K	R	E	F	R	E	S	H	I	N	G	B
W	A	R	T	S	E	I	R	O	L	A	C	B	A
E	N	I	E	F	F	A	C	E	P	A	R	G	T

Solution on Page 339

AMPLIFIER
ANALOG
APPLIANCES
BIT
BOARD
CAPACITORS
CIRCUIT
COMPLEX
COMPONENTS
COMPUTERS
CONDUCTOR
CORE
DESIGN
DEVICE
DIGITAL
ELECTRONIC
ELEMENTS
ENGINEER
HARDWARE
MEMORY
MICROCHIP
MODERN
PASSIVE
POWER
PROCESSOR
RAM
RESISTOR
SILICON
SOLDER
SUBSTRATE
TECHNOLOGY
TRANSISTOR
VLSI
WIRE

Integrated Circuits

R	J	M	A	R	O	T	S	I	S	N	A	R	T
O	R	E	D	L	O	S	C	O	M	P	L	E	X
T	I	U	C	R	I	C	S	W	P	B	R	J	P
C	E	R	O	C	A	M	P	L	I	F	I	E	R
U	E	C	A	P	A	C	I	T	O	R	S	T	O
D	L	L	H	A	N	A	L	O	G	E	T	A	C
N	E	A	E	N	N	W	R	D	M	E	N	R	E
O	M	V	T	C	O	O	O	E	E	N	E	T	S
C	E	L	E	I	T	L	W	S	M	I	N	S	S
I	N	S	A	S	G	R	O	I	O	G	O	B	O
L	T	I	I	Z	A	I	O	G	R	N	P	U	R
I	S	S	B	O	A	R	D	N	Y	E	M	S	E
S	E	P	I	H	C	O	R	C	I	M	O	K	W
R	N	S	R	E	T	U	P	M	O	C	C	T	O
H	A	R	D	W	A	R	E	V	I	S	S	A	P
C	Q	E	C	I	V	E	D	N	R	E	D	O	M

Solution on Page 339

APPRENTICE
APRON
BAKE
BURN
CATERING
COOKING
CREATE
CUISINE
CULINARY
DESSERT
DINNER
DISHES
EXECUTIVE
FOOD
FRENCH
GRILL
HAT
HEAD
HOTELS
KITCHENS
KNIVES
LINE COOK
MEAT
MENU
ORDER
OVEN
PANTRY
PASTRY
PLATING
POT
PREPARE
PROFESSION
RESTAURANT
SALAD
SKILLED
SOUS
SPECIAL
TRAINING
UNIFORM

Professional Chef

S	P	E	C	I	A	L	X	H	G	S	O	U	S
Y	R	T	N	A	P	R	O	N	N	Y	F	K	G
Y	R	T	S	A	P	E	L	L	I	R	G	B	T
S	O	R	D	E	R	N	V	E	K	A	B	O	M
K	I	T	C	H	E	N	S	E	O	N	P	V	M
I	T	R	F	A	N	I	R	V	O	I	W	E	T
L	E	E	L	T	T	D	E	I	C	L	N	N	M
L	E	S	I	U	I	Y	S	T	B	U	R	N	R
E	R	S	N	N	C	S	T	U	G	C	G	P	C
D	A	E	E	I	E	E	A	C	N	R	C	L	S
I	P	D	C	F	F	V	U	E	I	E	U	A	M
S	E	L	O	O	R	I	R	X	N	A	I	T	B
H	R	R	O	R	E	N	A	E	I	T	S	I	O
E	P	D	K	M	N	K	N	K	A	E	I	N	E
S	A	L	A	D	C	A	T	E	R	I	N	G	H
S	L	E	T	O	H	M	E	A	T	H	E	A	D

Solution on Page 339

ABDOMEN
ANIMAL
ANTENNAE
BRIGHT
BUTTERFLY
CHANGE
CHRYSALIS
DAMAGE
EAT
EGGS
EYES
FUZZY
GARDEN
GREEN
HAIRY
HERBIVORE
INCHWORMS
INSECT
LARVAL
LEAVES
MONARCH
MOTHS
PESTS
PLANTS
PUPA
SEGMENTED
SILK
SLIDING
SMALL
SPECIES
SPRING
STAGE
SUMMER
TREE
TUBULAR
YELLOW

Caterpillar

W	D	E	T	N	E	M	G	E	S	L	T	K	T
O	N	E	E	R	G	F	B	R	P	A	G	L	R
L	E	A	V	E	S	R	A	O	R	R	N	I	E
L	P	T	E	Y	I	R	Y	V	I	V	I	S	E
E	F	D	C	G	L	A	M	I	N	A	D	P	K
Y	U	S	H	E	A	F	S	B	G	L	I	U	Y
Q	Z	T	A	S	S	T	R	R	O	N	L	P	P
P	Z	N	I	U	Y	N	S	E	C	O	S	A	D
E	Y	A	R	M	R	E	I	H	T	P	N	A	N
S	J	L	Y	M	H	H	W	U	E	T	M	V	E
T	E	P	W	E	C	O	B	C	E	A	U	A	G
S	Y	Q	G	R	R	U	I	N	G	R	T	B	N
H	E	G	A	M	L	E	N	E	M	O	D	B	A
T	S	N	S	A	S	A	L	L	A	M	S	S	H
O	O	H	R	N	E	D	R	A	G	W	X	H	C
M	U	O	W	N	T	B	Q	J	I	I	V	B	H

Solution on Page 339

AFRICA
ANIMAL
BANANA
BONOBO
BRAIN
CAPTIVITY
CHIMP
CIRCUS
CLIMBING
COMMUNITY
CONGO
EVOLUTION
FAMILY
FOREST
FUNNY
GOODALL
GORILLA
GREAT APE
HABITAT
HANG
LONG ARMS
MAMMAL
MONKEY
NO TAIL
OMNIVOROUS
ORANGUTAN
PET
PRIMATE
RESEARCH
SCIENCE
SOCIAL
SPACE
STRENGTH
STRONG
STUDY
TOOLS
WALK
WILD
ZOO

Chimpanzees

A	S	N	T	F	B	G	C	I	R	C	U	S	V
B	O	O	E	O	O	L	S	P	A	C	E	C	T
R	C	A	P	R	N	A	U	Z	O	O	A	I	A
A	I	F	O	E	O	M	O	P	S	P	W	E	T
I	A	R	R	S	B	I	R	R	T	M	I	N	I
N	L	I	A	T	O	N	O	I	R	I	L	C	B
S	U	C	N	C	M	A	V	M	O	H	D	E	A
T	V	A	G	S	O	I	I	A	N	C	V	L	H
U	S	G	U	R	T	M	N	T	G	O	L	A	Y
D	T	N	T	Y	E	G	M	E	L	I	N	F	E
Y	R	I	A	M	N	A	O	U	R	A	Y	A	K
N	E	B	N	A	M	O	T	O	N	W	B	M	N
N	N	M	H	M	G	I	G	A	D	I	A	I	O
U	G	I	A	N	O	G	B	J	P	A	T	L	M
F	T	L	O	N	G	A	R	M	S	E	L	Y	K
Z	H	C	R	A	E	S	E	R	T	O	O	L	S

Solution on Page 340

ALARM
ANALOG
BAND
BATTERY
BRACELET
CASIO
CHAIN
CITIZEN
CLOCK
DATE
DIAMOND
DIGITAL
ELECTRONIC
EXPENSIVE
FASHION
GOLD
HOUR HAND
JEWELS
MECHANICAL
METAL
MINUTES
NUMBERS
PLASTIC
POCKET
QUARTZ
REPAIR
SECONDS
SEIKO
SILVER
SPRING
STOPWATCH
STRAP
SWATCH
SWISS
TIMEPIECE
WATERPROOF
WRISTWATCH

Watch It

S	O	E	X	P	E	N	S	I	V	E	L	Z	D
W	K	C	F	G	O	L	A	N	A	L	M	T	Y
I	I	E	O	O	C	I	T	I	Z	E	N	R	J
S	E	I	O	I	S	A	C	P	C	C	E	A	E
S	S	P	R	I	N	G	O	H	H	T	M	U	W
W	K	E	P	L	G	C	A	A	T	R	G	Q	E
A	C	M	R	K	K	N	I	A	A	O	T	H	L
T	O	I	E	E	I	N	B	L	L	N	E	O	S
C	L	T	T	C	E	T	A	D	D	I	L	U	R
H	C	T	A	W	P	O	T	S	I	C	E	R	I
S	I	L	W	R	I	S	T	W	A	T	C	H	A
I	T	A	S	E	T	U	N	I	M	A	A	A	P
L	S	T	D	F	A	S	H	I	O	N	R	N	E
V	A	E	S	R	E	B	M	U	N	W	B	D	R
E	L	M	L	A	T	I	G	I	D	N	A	B	Q
R	P	A	R	T	S	D	N	O	C	E	S	U	B

Solution on Page 340

ASH
BAMBOO
BARK
BIRCH
BOARDS
BUILD
BURN
CARVING
CEDAR
CHERRY
CHOP
CUT
ELM
FIBROUS
FINISH
FLOORING
FOREST
FUEL
GRAIN
HARDWOOD
HICKORY
HOUSES
KNOTS
LOG
LUMBER
MAHOGANY
MAPLE
OAK
PAINT
PAPER
PINE
PLYWOOD
SAND
SAWDUST
SOFTWOOD
STAIN
TABLE
TIMBER
TREES
WALNUT

Wood

L	D	X	E	L	P	A	M	F	P	A	P	E	R
V	T	D	D	E	L	M	S	U	I	A	X	Z	Y
A	I	M	S	U	Y	R	R	E	H	C	I	E	H
M	M	H	M	O	W	A	G	L	S	T	O	N	K
M	B	B	A	F	O	R	E	S	T	U	Y	I	T
K	E	K	Y	R	O	K	C	I	H	N	O	P	E
R	R	S	C	E	D	A	R	D	A	S	F	H	R
A	T	U	N	L	A	W	T	G	L	L	A	N	Y
B	D	O	O	W	T	F	O	S	O	I	C	O	L
S	T	R	E	E	S	H	H	O	U	G	U	O	G
T	A	B	L	E	A	O	R	H	D	D	T	B	C
A	Q	I	O	M	P	I	S	A	N	D	W	M	L
I	F	F	G	G	N	I	V	R	A	C	P	A	X
N	I	A	R	G	N	K	S	D	R	A	O	B	S
N	R	U	B	I	R	C	H	Q	B	L	H	G	F
G	G	R	F	L	F	M	N	C	N	S	C	E	G

Solution on Page 340

ABALONE
ALGAE
BACTERIA
BALEEN
CAVIAR
CETACEAN
CLAMS
COPEPODS
CORAL
CRAB
DETRITUS
DIATOMS
DIVER
DOLPHIN
EEL
EGGS
HUMPBACK
KRILL
MARLIN
MOLLUSK
NARWHAL
NAUTILUS
OCTOPUS
OYSTERS
PORPOISE
SALMON
SCALLOPS
SEA LIONS
SEA OTTER
SEAWEED
SHARK
SHRIMP
SPONGES
SQUID
STARFISH
STURGEON
SUBMARINE
SWORDFISH
TUNA

Marine Wildlife

D	I	U	Q	S	F	G	C	R	A	B	S	N	E
A	D	E	E	W	A	E	S	I	O	P	R	O	P
S	E	A	O	T	T	E	R	S	H	M	A	M	K
E	E	N	I	R	A	M	B	U	S	I	I	L	R
G	G	U	L	L	A	A	A	P	I	R	V	A	A
N	G	T	I	R	C	K	B	O	F	H	A	S	H
O	S	O	L	T	E	C	A	T	D	S	C	N	S
P	N	I	E	C	T	A	L	C	R	O	L	O	M
S	N	R	O	K	A	B	O	O	O	Y	A	E	O
C	I	R	R	L	C	P	N	L	W	S	H	G	L
A	A	I	G	L	E	M	E	G	S	T	W	R	L
L	L	A	A	P	A	U	D	I	V	E	R	U	U
L	E	M	O	C	N	H	S	I	F	R	A	T	S
O	S	D	E	T	R	I	T	U	S	S	N	S	K
P	S	U	L	I	T	U	A	N	E	E	L	A	B
S	M	O	T	A	I	D	O	L	P	H	I	N	N

Solution on Page 340

AGENTS
APARTMENTS
APPRAISAL
BANK
BROKER
BUILDING
BUSINESS
BUYING
CLOSING
COMMERCIAL
COMMON LAW
CONTRACT
DUPLEX
EQUITY
FOR SALE
HOMES
HOUSING
INTEREST
INVESTMENT
LAND
LEASE
LICENSE
LISTING
LOANS
LOCATION
MARKET
MORTGAGES
OFFER
OWNERS
PRICE
PROPERTY
REALTOR
RENT
SALES
SELLING
TAXES
VALUE
VIEW
YARD

Real Estate

R	E	E	S	N	E	C	I	L	B	V	G	H	L
P	Q	E	Z	L	O	C	A	T	I	O	N	A	I
B	U	S	I	N	E	S	S	E	B	V	I	G	S
P	I	A	A	W	I	R	W	K	U	A	S	E	T
O	T	E	P	A	S	E	C	R	I	L	U	N	I
S	Y	L	R	L	E	N	O	A	L	U	O	T	N
T	T	P	O	N	X	W	M	M	D	E	H	S	G
C	P	N	P	O	A	O	M	K	I	C	N	E	N
A	T	N	E	M	T	S	E	V	N	I	Y	R	I
R	I	K	R	M	M	O	R	T	G	A	G	E	S
T	O	T	T	O	T	E	C	I	R	P	B	T	O
N	N	T	Y	C	J	R	I	D	H	E	S	N	L
O	B	E	L	S	E	L	A	S	R	O	F	I	C
C	C	A	R	A	X	E	L	P	U	D	M	F	G
G	N	I	L	L	E	S	S	N	A	O	L	E	O
D	B	R	O	K	E	R	G	N	I	Y	U	B	S

Solution on Page 341

ANIMALS
ARTIFACTS
AUTOGRAPHS
BOOKS
BOTTLES
BUTTONS
CANS
CDS
CHINA
COINS
CURRENCY
DISNEY
DOLLS
FIGURINES
FILMS
FURNITURE
GLASS
GUNS
HATS
JEWELRY
KEYS
MAGAZINES
MAPS
MODEL CARS
MUSIC
NEWSPAPERS
PLATES
POST CARDS
POTTERY
RECORDS
ROCKS
SEASHELLS
STAMPS
TEAPOTS
THIMBLES
TOYS
TRAINS
WINE

Collectibles

Q	Y	D	Y	E	S	E	N	I	R	U	G	I	F
B	R	O	U	H	A	T	S	S	K	O	O	B	J
S	E	L	T	T	O	B	C	L	A	N	I	H	C
D	T	L	E	N	S	D	R	A	C	T	S	O	P
R	T	S	A	E	H	L	W	M	F	B	N	C	A
O	O	S	P	W	P	M	I	I	I	I	O	U	O
C	P	A	O	S	A	J	N	N	L	C	T	R	E
E	L	L	T	P	R	T	E	A	M	P	T	R	M
R	A	G	S	A	G	A	R	W	S	S	U	E	A
O	T	Y	P	P	O	Y	C	A	E	T	B	N	G
C	E	T	M	E	T	J	E	L	I	L	R	C	A
K	S	O	A	R	U	C	B	N	E	N	R	Y	Z
S	N	Y	T	S	A	M	R	S	S	D	S	Y	I
N	I	S	S	N	I	U	V	F	D	I	O	L	N
U	O	E	S	H	F	M	U	S	I	C	D	M	E
G	C	X	T	O	S	E	A	S	H	E	L	L	S

Solution on Page 341

Answers

B	X	O	P	O	C	K	E	T	E	S	S	U	G
K	A	L	A	I	R	E	T	A	M	Y	T	N	N
H	R	C	E	L	B	M	I	H	T	E	I	I	I
D	T	O	K	F	A	B	R	I	C	T	T	B	N
A	R	O	W	S	V	R	A	H	T	P	C	B	I
E	Y	E	L	E	T	O	N	A	A	H	H	O	L
R	J	S	T	C	L	I	B	T	E	G	E	B	G
H	M	R	R	L	Q	D	T	M	L	A	S	P	N
T	A	O	A	U	A	E	E	C	O	T	T	L	I
D	C	S	E	R	R	R	P	E	H	H	A	E	W
E	H	S	N	N	I	Y	A	R	N	E	C	A	E
S	I	I	P	A	T	C	H	W	O	R	K	T	S
I	N	C	I	H	C	G	N	I	T	L	I	U	Q
G	E	S	N	S	E	A	M	S	T	R	E	S	S
N	R	O	L	I	A	T	C	Q	U	U	I	U	U
C	Q	L	G	N	I	D	N	I	B	B	C	M	A

Sewing Circle

T	J	Z	E	Q	Y	B	Q	E	U	L	A	V	Y
N	P	T	M	T	S	T	L	S	A	D	S	S	Z
E	Y	R	U	S	A	E	R	T	L	M	U	B	S
D	M	E	N	U	B	D	E	E	I	A	R	E	L
I	O	L	I	C	R	M	I	N	B	O	R	Y	I
S	N	H	M	O	A	H	T	M	N	I	N	A	A
E	E	F	U	I	S	H	N	Z	E	L	L	U	T
R	Y	U	L	N	S	F	E	S	B	L	O	Z	A
P	Q	Y	A	A	G	M	C	A	O	A	C	Q	E
J	P	R	H	G	T	R	E	N	D	M	N	R	H
A	R	O	R	E	A	I	N	M	I	S	I	K	W
R	O	T	C	E	L	L	O	C	O	Z	L	V	G
X	F	S	Y	V	P	Y	C	N	E	R	R	U	C
D	I	I	J	A	S	P	E	N	D	J	I	F	I
C	L	H	R	S	X	R	O	U	N	D	P	A	H
Q	E	G	N	A	H	C	F	C	S	T	E	E	L

Penny

P	P	K	W	Y	V	U	E	U	V	F	H	X	R
W	O	P	M	X	O	I	F	D	D	O	O	F	E
H	W	M	I	L	K	I	N	G	E	C	C	O	D
O	D	H	E	A	L	T	H	Y	H	G	Q	C	D
L	E	I	G	N	I	T	S	E	V	R	A	H	U
E	R	U	N	A	M	A	E	R	C	E	C	I	C
F	A	R	M	E	R	S	C	Y	E	H	W	P	H
G	N	I	S	S	E	C	O	R	P	G	R	A	S
C	L	V	F	R	T	X	A	T	C	O	W	S	W
A	S	A	A	E	T	M	L	S	D	H	A	T	B
T	T	A	M	F	U	N	A	U	E	R	U	U	A
T	A	N	V	I	B	M	C	D	G	I	C	R	R
L	O	F	C	E	N	T	T	N	N	K	N	E	N
E	G	L	W	H	S	A	O	I	E	L	S	B	L
F	A	C	T	O	R	Y	S	T	R	U	G	O	Y
C	U	R	D	S	L	D	E	M	M	I	K	S	E

Dairy

K	D	R	F	O	I	L	E	I	K	O	O	R	S
C	S	C	O	N	D	I	T	I	O	N	R	C	G
A	T	A	O	T	E	L	E	V	I	S	I	O	N
P	R	T	T	R	C	S	P	P	O	T	L	R	I
Y	O	H	B	A	S	E	L	L	S	F	L	A	X
E	P	L	A	D	P	D	L	I	K	D	A	C	O
K	S	E	L	I	I	R	T	L	O	G	B	I	B
C	C	T	L	N	C	A	M	Y	O	U	E	N	L
O	A	E	E	G	T	O	U	B	B	C	S	G	A
H	R	L	D	S	U	B	B	B	C	A	A	W	S
P	C	B	A	R	R	R	L	O	I	R	B	R	R
E	I	A	Z	E	E	E	A	H	M	T	M	A	E
R	T	U	R	E	G	P	E	D	O	O	I	P	Y
S	Y	L	B	U	E	A	P	L	C	O	N	P	A
O	G	A	M	E	S	P	M	U	F	N	T	E	L
N	Y	V	R	A	R	E	N	I	T	S	I	R	P

Trading Cards

S	N	I	A	G	K	Q	Z	L	S	D	N	O	B
S	E	I	C	P	Q	C	A	P	I	T	A	L	S
G	D	L	G	E	U	P	O	V	P	I	T	F	I
N	A	O	L	R	I	R	I	T	L	F	T	U	L
I	T	S	W	C	A	D	C	A	S	O	I	T	V
V	Z	S	N	E	E	M	I	H	B	R	S	U	E
A	D	I	Y	N	P	C	O	U	A	P	O	R	R
S	R	L	D	T	N	E	S	N	F	S	P	E	E
P	E	S	O	A	I	I	N	T	E	R	E	S	T
E	B	C	N	G	N	D	I	S	I	Y	D	K	U
U	L	I	U	E	R	N	O	S	I	M	Z	N	R
L	F	A	S	R	C	W	K	M	A	O	E	A	N
A	U	S	N	O	I	T	P	O	M	N	N	B	S
V	N	S	M	D	Y	T	R	E	P	O	R	P	W
F	D	E	D	A	R	T	Y	P	Q	C	C	H	B
Z	S	T	T	J	K	M	A	R	K	E	T	G	S

Financial Investment

I	M	R	T	R	A	N	S	M	I	T	A	L	K
S	R	U	A	S	T	A	T	I	O	N	S	Q	P
H	E	F	S	I	M	U	L	C	A	S	T	N	Q
O	N	S	R	I	N	T	E	R	N	E	T	S	B
R	E	I	L	E	C	A	E	O	T	D	N	A	B
T	T	G	R	A	Q	V	S	P	E	P	A	T	C
W	S	N	R	U	I	U	H	H	N	U	U	E	N
A	I	A	V	E	I	D	E	O	N	R	D	L	E
V	L	L	C	R	F	P	I	N	A	C	I	L	T
E	O	E	I	D	E	T	J	E	C	Q	E	I	W
S	R	S	E	V	A	W	R	I	A	Y	N	T	O
R	O	U	E	L	N	O	I	T	P	E	C	E	R
Q	A	N	U	Z	V	V	R	T	O	W	E	R	K
A	P	D	A	M	F	E	L	B	A	C	C	F	S
R	O	Y	I	I	C	H	A	N	N	E	L	I	C
M	A	R	G	O	R	P	U	B	L	I	C	Z	L

Radio Broadcasting

D	B	W	V	D	M	Y	C	U	N	H	D	H	C
R	S	U	V	I	K	S	Y	Y	R	E	D	D	R
M	S	O	D	N	O	O	D	L	E	I	M	M	L
S	A	D	U	D	V	P	R	O	D	U	C	T	S
H	J	H	I	P	M	E	A	L	S	X	R	E	D
N	C	U	K	K	L	E	G	H	D	W	E	N	H
E	M	A	T	L	A	S	R	E	K	C	A	R	C
H	N	L	S	T	D	O	S	F	T	R	M	V	O
C	E	E	E	S	O	N	O	U	B	A	C	N	O
T	K	A	J	M	E	X	H	T	O	R	B	J	K
I	C	F	L	D	P	R	L	L	A	B	E	L	S
K	I	O	N	T	D	O	O	G	M	M	M	X	E
K	H	O	M	E	H	J	P	L	K	C	O	T	S
T	C	D	Y	R	V	Y	T	A	E	D	E	T	I
D	S	N	A	C	U	C	V	A	R	I	E	T	Y
I	G	W	V	X	Z	J	W	H	I	T	E	N	Y

Campbell's Soup

C	B	I	O	L	O	G	Y	D	U	T	S	A	B
I	M	U	S	E	U	M	S	L	A	M	I	N	A
O	N	O	I	S	O	R	E	S	E	A	R	C	H
Z	J	F	L	T	G	P	E	N	S	D	R	I	B
O	U	U	A	Q	L	H	A	P	H	N	W	E	S
E	R	N	B	R	T	M	N	T	T	O	S	N	S
L	A	G	S	R	U	A	S	O	N	I	D	T	L
A	S	I	A	H	G	I	T	O	E	T	L	G	I
P	S	E	N	N	T	R	I	C	M	U	S	E	S
C	I	E	I	N	I	T	O	E	I	L	K	O	S
A	C	T	E	A	C	S	F	A	R	O	C	L	O
N	A	I	S	N	Y	I	M	N	E	V	O	O	F
D	C	S	I	S	L	Y	Y	S	P	E	R	G	I
S	I	T	T	Y	M	O	N	O	X	A	T	Y	S
C	X	E	D	I	S	C	O	V	E	R	Y	T	H
E	M	E	S	O	Z	O	I	C	S	E	N	O	B

Paleontology

B	T	N	W	Y	F	O	M	F	L	A	T	E	M
E	E	A	S	D	R	A	O	B	P	U	C	G	O
N	N	M	Q	A	W	O	O	D	E	N	D	T	O
C	I	O	B	H	T	O	R	S	A	R	A	P	R
H	B	T	U	S	K	A	G	Z	A	E	L	E	D
E	A	T	T	C	O	S	N	W	S	A	K	T	E
S	C	O	A	B	R	E	I	E	S	C	R	S	B
H	O	S	D	E	D	N	V	T	I	S	E	E	O
L	E	A	W	E	G	O	I	W	B	E	N	H	R
F	E	A	R	B	L	C	L	Z	E	L	I	C	D
H	R	C	O	F	F	E	E	T	A	B	L	E	R
D	N	A	T	S	T	H	G	I	N	A	C	P	A
T	R	O	P	N	E	V	A	D	B	T	E	O	W
D	R	E	S	S	E	R	S	K	A	D	R	H	W
A	F	O	S	E	A	T	I	N	G	N	J	E	N
C	O	U	C	H	D	R	A	O	B	E	D	I	S

Furniture Types

C	A	R	P	E	N	T	E	R	S	U	N	C	G
F	R	A	M	E	P	S	P	R	G	S	G	N	E
S	C	W	M	S	R	K	K	E	N	E	I	E	R
R	H	O	V	C	O	Y	C	E	I	D	S	M	E
E	I	O	N	I	P	S	I	N	D	A	E	A	G
K	T	D	A	T	E	C	R	I	L	R	D	T	A
R	E	T	N	S	R	R	B	G	I	T	J	E	N
O	C	N	O	I	T	A	D	N	U	O	F	R	A
W	T	E	I	G	Y	P	C	E	B	C	E	I	M
H	C	M	T	O	T	E	L	T	R	Z	R	A	S
O	E	P	U	L	E	R	D	A	O	I	E	L	Y
U	J	I	C	B	F	N	N	D	N	R	C	S	A
S	O	U	E	K	A	E	L	S	L	N	T	T	L
E	R	Q	X	L	S	L	E	E	T	S	I	O	E
S	P	E	E	R	U	T	C	U	R	T	S	N	D
W	Z	L	A	B	O	R	E	R	S	I	T	E	G

Construction

W	D	G	U	B	R	T	H	F	Z	X	N	Q	E
D	E	Z	O	L	Y	H	E	T	P	E	Z	G	Y
H	T	M	C	O	N	T	E	N	T	X	A	A	V
S	E	M	A	G	G	M	N	W	R	P	B	U	I
M	S	O	C	I	A	L	O	I	E	E	L	Y	S
U	S	K	N	I	L	R	E	M	A	R	T	R	I
R	E	K	S	M	K	D	O	C	U	M	E	N	T
O	G	N	S	G	S	H	S	P	L	T	O	F	I
F	A	C	E	B	O	O	K	S	U	I	U	D	O
H	M	K	N	I	L	R	E	P	Y	H	C	N	Q
C	I	R	I	U	D	G	M	D	S	K	L	K	D
R	D	E	S	A	A	O	H	S	I	I	W	E	P
A	K	V	U	P	C	A	O	W	N	V	S	W	S
E	F	R	B	R	O	W	S	E	R	I	W	I	G
S	S	E	R	D	D	A	T	N	G	W	T	G	Y
J	W	S	S	P	L	A	I	N	T	E	X	T	E

On the Web

Y	M	J	G	N	I	S	A	H	C	R	U	P	G
P	L	Z	R	P	A	C	K	A	G	I	N	G	X
Z	B	P	S	H	O	P	P	I	N	G	T	P	G
T	U	J	P	G	N	I	Y	U	B	D	Q	A	O
S	S	Y	K	U	T	U	N	N	Z	D	Q	U	O
G	I	T	W	A	S	T	E	D	E	M	A	N	D
H	N	E	L	D	N	E	P	S	U	T	A	T	S
R	E	I	S	E	R	V	I	C	E	S	Y	U	E
E	S	C	T	L	J	R	L	C	I	M	T	P	L
T	S	O	S	E	E	A	T	O	O	Z	P	R	L
A	J	S	X	C	K	M	O	N	E	Y	R	O	Y
I	S	T	H	G	I	R	O	S	A	W	O	D	R
L	T	Z	W	V	T	C	A	U	N	W	F	U	M
P	E	O	P	L	E	V	A	M	E	R	I	C	A
H	T	L	A	E	W	C	R	E	D	I	T	T	L
C	O	S	T	R	A	D	E	R	O	T	S	S	L

Consumerism

E	S	R	E	V	I	N	U	C	L	E	A	R	W
M	U	D	C	X	T	H	E	O	R	Y	M	D	R
A	L	I	G	H	T	Y	T	I	C	O	L	E	V
S	U	X	P	A	R	T	I	C	L	E	S	E	S
S	C	I	E	N	T	I	S	T	U	D	Y	P	K
N	L	P	Y	T	I	V	A	R	G	A	S	S	R
O	A	H	G	S	C	I	N	A	H	C	E	M	A
T	C	E	M	A	T	T	E	R	U	T	A	N	U
W	I	N	H	C	R	A	E	S	E	R	K	S	Q
E	S	O	Y	G	O	L	O	N	H	C	E	T	U
N	Y	M	S	I	T	E	N	G	A	M	I	P	A
E	H	E	X	P	E	R	I	M	E	N	T	E	N
R	P	N	I	E	T	S	N	I	E	S	R	C	T
G	L	A	W	S	E	L	E	C	T	R	O	N	U
Y	N	O	I	T	O	M	U	T	N	E	M	O	M
S	M	O	T	A	F	O	R	M	U	L	A	C	E

Physics Class

S	D	A	O	L	A	C	I	N	A	H	C	E	M
S	K	C	O	L	C	S	T	O	V	E	N	S	G
G	N	I	N	A	E	L	C	I	H	D	Y	Y	N
N	N	E	H	C	T	I	K	T	R	L	G	R	I
I	R	E	X	I	M	U	M	A	J	O	R	E	K
H	F	X	R	R	R	S	N	M	L	H	U	T	O
S	R	B	E	T	E	G	Z	O	L	E	E	A	O
A	E	M	T	C	E	H	N	T	A	S	C	E	C
W	E	I	S	E	A	H	S	U	M	U	I	H	I
R	Z	C	A	L	C	M	S	A	S	O	V	D	T
E	E	R	O	E	J	K	C	E	W	H	R	N	S
P	R	O	T	C	A	P	M	O	C	H	E	O	E
A	N	W	B	L	E	N	D	E	R	I	S	R	M
I	S	A	R	E	M	A	C	F	P	D	V	I	O
R	Q	V	T	E	L	E	P	H	O	N	E	E	D
X	S	E	N	I	H	C	A	M	R	E	Y	R	D

Home Appliance

C	Y	D	N	A	H	I	N	T	E	R	I	O	R
A	X	P	O	P	R	O	J	E	C	T	S	O	E
R	N	L	I	O	A	S	G	N	I	X	I	F	P
P	E	U	D	P	W	I	B	R	A	R	U	O	A
E	I	M	L	A	E	L	N	O	E	I	Z	O	I
N	G	B	O	E	L	S	I	T	J	M	L	C	R
T	H	I	H	D	L	L	X	C	I	D	O	S	S
R	B	N	E	R	E	E	T	A	E	N	D	H	B
Y	O	G	S	Y	Z	L	C	R	S	N	G	O	U
R	R	R	U	W	P	H	I	T	A	K	S	R	I
E	U	O	O	A	E	Z	R	N	R	D	A	E	L
M	S	O	H	L	L	U	A	O	G	I	E	E	D
M	E	L	P	L	C	V	W	C	G	F	C	S	L
A	F	F	A	T	E	C	I	V	R	E	S	A	W
H	U	C	F	H	B	L	U	B	T	H	G	I	L
L	L	I	R	D	E	L	L	I	K	S	O	T	W

Handyman

A	N	P	A	R	Y	S	U	O	L	A	E	J	I
E	T	I	N	M	U	Z	C	L	O	S	E	K	Q
R	M	O	F	R	J	G	P	I	H	S	N	I	K
A	Z	O	L	Q	C	R	E	H	T	O	M	H	E
H	V	U	H	F	R	I	E	N	D	E	G	K	R
S	N	I	W	T	P	J	V	O	X	I	N	R	T
T	I	X	Y	G	O	L	O	M	Y	T	E	E	O
N	S	G	I	A	B	H	L	F	S	L	R	H	G
E	U	N	M	I	D	D	L	E	A	L	D	T	E
R	G	I	R	L	X	A	G	T	B	S	L	A	T
A	E	T	I	F	H	N	I	Y	O	I	I	F	H
P	H	H	J	K	U	V	J	L	N	S	H	S	E
N	C	G	T	O	E	L	D	I	D	T	C	A	R
O	U	I	Y	O	U	E	L	M	P	E	T	S	A
N	E	F	A	U	R	I	V	A	L	R	Y	D	H
U	F	P	T	G	A	B	K	F	O	S	T	E	R

Siblings

W	I	M	O	R	T	A	R	O	L	O	C	A	Y
K	R	O	O	F	S	E	G	F	L	A	T	W	H
U	L	K	O	S	S	R	E	W	O	H	S	E	A
Q	O	D	Q	U	A	R	R	Y	W	A	T	E	R
K	G	R	E	N	G	I	S	E	D	A	T	F	D
J	I	U	I	C	D	G	C	S	L	I	C	G	M
B	A	T	H	R	O	O	M	S	H	H	E	L	Q
S	E	N	C	P	F	R	O	W	A	N	R	A	P
Q	C	T	I	H	L	P	A	W	O	W	A	Z	S
U	G	T	R	A	E	A	A	T	N	E	M	E	C
A	M	E	T	A	L	N	S	T	I	L	I	D	R
R	G	N	I	L	I	E	C	T	T	V	C	J	X
E	L	B	R	A	M	J	C	F	I	E	E	F	Z
J	U	L	F	I	T	U	O	R	G	C	R	O	T
W	A	L	L	S	C	F	L	O	O	R	I	N	G
Y	N	F	G	S	L	J	C	N	F	P	B	Y	S

Tiles

A	T	H	L	E	T	I	C	U	R	L	I	N	G
S	C	O	R	E	Q	S	O	F	T	B	A	L	L
R	A	M	A	T	E	U	R	U	N	N	I	N	G
E	Z	Y	N	O	I	T	I	R	T	U	N	O	G
Y	B	G	U	R	B	N	G	P	E	M	A	G	N
A	L	N	Y	T	R	O	P	S	M	A	E	T	I
L	T	I	T	M	L	I	Y	L	P	E	G	L	L
P	E	N	E	F	N	T	L	L	O	T	N	H	W
H	K	I	N	E	I	A	M	A	L	H	I	T	O
Y	C	A	N	V	B	E	S	B	I	I	M	Y	B
S	I	R	I	E	D	R	X	T	T	C	M	R	O
I	R	T	S	I	R	C	V	E	I	S	I	E	X
C	C	A	C	U	V	E	X	K	C	C	W	H	I
A	B	I	L	A	C	R	O	S	S	E	S	C	N
L	N	E	F	O	O	T	B	A	L	L	L	R	G
E	S	N	S	C	I	T	A	B	O	R	E	A	T

Sporting Chance

L	K	C	I	T	S	N	O	N	Q	R	Z	S	A
A	A	F	E	N	O	C	I	L	I	S	S	L	Q
T	P	D	P	I	E	P	A	N	C	A	U	I	C
E	P	C	L	X	R	O	K	H	U	M	X	S	I
M	C	A	K	E	P	A	N	C	I	Q	S	N	M
J	V	S	E	R	A	W	E	N	O	T	S	E	A
Z	N	S	Q	Y	X	P	U	A	O	T	Q	T	R
Y	A	E	C	P	A	M	E	P	S	E	S	U	E
H	P	R	V	N	Z	K	B	F	S	F	E	B	C
T	G	O	S	O	O	I	U	A	A	L	L	B	O
T	N	L	K	R	H	T	N	O	L	O	D	O	P
W	I	E	I	I	R	C	D	L	G	N	D	W	P
K	Y	F	L	T	F	H	T	O	B	W	I	L	E
A	R	R	L	S	M	E	P	U	O	M	R	S	R
T	F	K	E	A	F	N	A	K	D	F	G	D	T
P	P	S	T	C	K	G	N	I	T	S	A	O	R

Cookware

S	E	G	A	E	N	I	L	D	O	O	L	B	P
U	U	T	P	K	S	O	F	T	W	A	R	E	R
P	A	S	T	N	O	I	T	A	C	O	L	T	E
D	D	N	N	R	O	B	E	I	M	B	F	Y	L
H	C	R	A	E	S	E	R	E	A	R	A	R	A
B	Y	T	E	I	C	O	S	N	R	O	M	D	T
A	S	N	O	I	T	I	D	A	R	T	I	L	I
P	Y	R	T	S	E	C	N	A	I	H	L	A	V
T	R	S	I	S	Y	L	A	N	A	E	I	R	E
I	A	H	F	J	P	E	D	I	G	R	E	E	S
S	R	N	C	H	I	L	D	R	E	N	S	H	T
M	B	S	G	N	I	L	B	I	S	E	M	A	N
N	I	S	U	O	C	P	S	U	R	N	A	M	E
E	L	P	O	E	P	P	S	D	R	O	C	E	R
K	X	R	E	H	T	A	F	B	I	R	T	H	A
M	O	T	H	E	R	K	I	N	S	H	I	P	P

Family Tree

T	A	L	E	N	T	E	D	S	I	N	G	E	R
D	B	S	M	S	O	N	G	W	R	I	T	E	R
C	R	T	N	O	S	N	B	Y	M	M	A	R	G
T	O	A	C	N	V	E	T	H	E	V	I	E	W
D	S	K	W	A	F	I	L	M	L	S	S	L	B
P	N	I	I	A	R	D	E	V	I	U	L	L	G
D	U	I	V	B	Y	E	U	S	O	C	A	V	H
D	N	D	E	I	T	M	T	W	N	C	N	K	O
R	I	L	N	Y	T	O	M	S	K	E	F	E	S
A	E	A	M	A	V	C	N	E	I	S	E	R	T
C	M	W	I	W	T	W	A	Y	N	S	M	T	V
S	O	A	P	D	I	S	H	G	G	F	A	R	O
O	T	R	N	A	N	I	U	G	A	U	L	A	I
G	H	D	N	O	I	S	I	V	E	L	E	T	C
S	E	S	J	R	E	C	U	D	O	R	P	S	E
O	R	I	Q	B	S	A	C	T	R	E	S	S	N

Whoopi Goldberg

F	R	A	L	A	T	E	M	E	S	A	B	G	S
R	E	T	R	A	U	Q	D	E	S	I	G	N	C
E	V	N	O	I	T	I	D	N	O	C	O	U	L
V	C	O	P	P	E	R	A	R	O	I	R	E	Y
L	A	I	R	E	T	S	U	L	L	R	K	E	E
I	M	L	E	M	F	E	L	L	E	C	E	L	N
S	E	L	T	I	A	E	A	N	I	U	S	G	O
D	O	U	A	N	C	D	C	N	G	L	R	A	M
B	J	B	D	T	E	Y	E	O	P	A	E	E	O
R	R	N	I	M	V	M	L	M	D	T	V	R	T
A	S	O	I	T	A	D	Y	I	E	E	B	R	T
S	N	D	N	S	L	C	N	A	T	D	O	O	O
S	E	I	N	Z	U	G	A	I	P	N	A	R	Z
A	K	I	T	R	E	V	A	R	G	N	E	R	B
Y	O	W	Z	A	L	L	O	Y	A	X	K	C	T
C	T	S	H	E	P	R	O	O	F	T	W	W	I

Numismatics

P	S	O	U	R	C	E	D	I	T	I	N	G	Z
R	T	R	E	N	D	S	A	S	R	I	D	N	C
E	V	E	N	T	S	I	I	A	N	A	W	I	L
S	N	D	L	C	E	L	D	T	E	N	D	T	B
S	C	I	H	E	A	C	E	L	E	F	K	I	L
M	T	O	Z	N	V	R	M	W	C	A	Q	R	O
V	O	O	R	A	V	I	S	P	I	C	H	W	G
L	G	U	R	I	G	P	S	R	N	T	A	D	E
B	O	N	E	Y	A	A	A	I	F	S	U	U	X
J	S	W	I	P	P	R	M	N	O	I	D	E	I
Q	E	Z	E	T	A	O	T	T	R	N	I	D	M
H	U	R	M	W	R	B	C	I	M	M	E	I	T
T	S	A	C	D	A	O	R	B	C	U	N	T	G
U	S	N	O	I	N	I	P	O	N	L	C	O	R
R	I	O	O	N	L	I	N	E	H	O	E	R	Y
T	W	H	M	R	E	S	E	A	R	C	H	S	V

Journalism

C	E	L	L	U	L	A	R	D	A	R	W	I	N
A	N	D	A	H	G	N	I	E	T	O	R	P	A
Z	I	S	Z	B	N	O	I	T	C	N	U	F	M
S	C	E	Y	G	O	L	O	I	S	Y	H	P	U
P	I	U	T	I	I	R	E	S	E	A	R	C	H
E	D	S	I	E	T	B	A	N	I	M	A	L	S
C	E	S	D	E	U	A	N	T	L	I	F	E	A
I	M	I	E	R	L	C	A	S	O	C	L	C	O
E	O	T	R	U	O	T	T	U	H	R	P	N	R
S	D	A	E	T	V	E	O	E	Y	O	Y	E	G
Y	G	X	H	C	E	R	M	L	G	S	D	I	A
N	N	O	T	U	U	I	Y	C	O	C	U	C	N
A	I	N	W	R	S	A	L	U	L	O	T	S	I
T	K	O	O	T	N	A	N	N	O	P	S	M	S
O	G	M	R	S	S	E	L	U	C	E	L	O	M
B	F	Y	G	S	K	G	E	N	E	T	I	C	S

Biology

P	A	S	T	S	R	U	A	S	O	N	I	D	N
A	N	E	H	A	B	I	T	A	T	E	E	O	A
M	O	C	S	D	E	A	T	H	R	R	E	D	M
B	I	O	L	O	G	Y	R	A	E	A	S	O	U
P	T	L	E	N	M	E	R	G	I	C	A	U	H
L	U	O	V	R	A	I	N	F	O	R	E	S	T
A	L	G	R	T	R	A	E	P	P	A	S	I	D
N	O	Y	E	Y	D	U	T	S	O	L	I	M	H
T	V	N	S	N	N	U	G	R	L	S	D	S	U
S	E	G	E	N	E	P	O	O	L	L	C	I	N
D	S	U	R	V	I	V	E	T	U	I	H	N	T
L	X	S	P	E	C	I	E	S	T	S	A	A	I
V	H	I	S	T	O	R	Y	E	I	S	N	G	N
H	T	O	M	M	A	M	N	C	O	O	G	R	G
S	C	I	E	N	C	E	V	N	N	F	E	O	Y
K	D	E	N	O	G	S	L	A	M	I	N	A	B

Extinction

R	M	S	A	V	I	N	G	P	V	S	N	I	B
E	R	E	M	U	S	N	O	C	A	N	S	O	G
U	C	D	T	S	E	L	I	T	X	E	T	N	N
S	C	O	S	A	L	V	A	G	E	T	I	E	Y
E	O	N	L	U	L	P	S	I	L	T	E	G	V
R	M	Y	T	L	L	S	H	E	R	R	R	N	X
L	P	I	G	A	E	S	S	O	G	E	S	I	A
A	O	R	N	O	A	C	S	S	N	N	T	G	L
N	S	E	E	R	L	E	T	E	F	I	E	A	U
D	T	S	T	T	G	O	W	I	M	A	E	K	M
F	H	O	A	A	N	S	C	R	O	T	L	C	I
I	T	U	B	L	P	E	E	E	N	N	C	A	N
L	R	R	X	A	G	D	C	T	E	O	Y	P	U
L	A	C	P	Q	U	Z	U	T	Y	C	C	I	M
G	E	E	S	C	I	T	S	A	L	P	E	R	T
R	R	S	E	C	A	R	D	B	O	A	R	D	S

Recyclable

G	Y	N	O	C	I	J	P	G	U	I	T	A	R
S	M	M	Y	R	T	N	U	O	C	R	I	L	C
Y	R	E	C	O	R	D	S	M	P	N	D	B	O
M	A	M	B	A	C	T	O	R	P	U	O	U	N
M	P	P	L	A	S	V	E	G	A	S	L	M	C
A	E	H	U	H	I	P	S	G	A	T	U	A	E
R	R	I	E	E	K	C	O	R	R	C	S	I	R
G	F	S	S	I	B	I	R	A	T	O	O	N	T
O	O	I	U	P	R	I	S	C	I	L	L	A	H
S	R	D	E	O	A	A	K	E	S	O	E	I	E
P	M	E	D	H	M	W	M	L	T	N	P	C	K
E	E	B	E	N	K	A	W	A	D	E	U	I	I
L	R	U	O	T	U	H	F	N	S	L	T	S	N
M	L	R	S	G	N	O	S	D	N	I	T	U	G
S	I	N	G	E	R	E	H	T	A	E	L	M	B
E	E	S	S	E	N	N	E	T	D	A	N	C	E

Elvis

A	Y	D	S	M	X	Z	W	R	O	D	E	O	G
E	N	A	M	K	X	H	O	Y	E	K	C	O	J
E	G	E	G	R	I	D	I	N	G	I	A	G	R
B	R	H	R	N	W	E	S	T	E	R	N	K	R
R	F	A	N	A	B	A	G	E	L	X	T	S	T
I	I	Y	M	G	O	M	A	N	D	R	E	O	F
D	L	B	P	N	L	A	S	I	I	E	R	O	N
L	L	T	E	O	T	T	T	U	N	T	A	K	Y
E	Y	I	D	L	I	E	A	Q	G	L	S	P	N
N	J	Q	I	R	N	U	L	E	N	A	A	O	O
G	U	H	R	U	G	R	L	A	I	H	D	L	P
L	M	U	T	F	Y	J	I	X	K	H	D	L	K
I	P	P	S	L	C	B	O	O	C	O	L	A	C
S	I	N	O	O	A	E	N	W	U	O	E	G	A
H	N	H	A	R	N	E	S	S	B	F	L	J	T
G	G	T	A	E	C	A	R	J	G	A	I	T	Y

Speaking of Horses

X	W	G	M	S	T	O	R	A	G	E	L	O	P
S	P	A	C	E	S	R	F	A	N	X	L	L	N
E	P	A	I	N	T	B	R	N	I	V	A	O	Y
D	R	A	Y	K	C	A	B	G	T	S	M	C	S
I	E	E	L	Q	G	R	L	N	T	N	S	K	L
S	T	R	W	E	G	N	U	I	O	M	S	E	L
T	L	U	O	O	E	N	C	N	P	H	E	D	A
U	E	T	R	M	M	T	I	E	O	O	I	K	W
O	H	C	K	J	R	N	S	D	U	B	L	H	T
Y	S	U	S	E	A	E	W	R	L	B	P	U	O
M	K	R	H	S	F	M	O	A	V	I	P	K	O
T	O	T	O	U	Y	P	O	G	L	E	U	I	L
E	O	S	P	O	I	I	D	K	C	S	S	B	S
G	H	C	E	H	D	U	E	V	I	N	Y	L	P
L	J	P	E	P	H	Q	N	F	O	O	R	T	E
B	B	I	K	E	S	E	V	L	E	H	S	L	M

Shed

S	T	L	U	S	E	R	E	S	E	A	R	C	H
E	V	I	T	C	E	J	B	O	P	T	U	H	T
G	N	I	N	O	S	A	E	R	H	A	S	E	I
D	P	R	O	C	E	D	U	R	E	D	C	M	N
E	M	P	I	R	I	C	A	L	N	N	I	I	Q
L	O	R	T	N	O	C	R	S	O	M	E	S	U
W	S	E	E	X	P	E	R	I	M	E	N	T	I
O	E	D	J	R	T	Q	S	S	E	A	T	R	R
N	U	I	L	E	L	U	L	E	N	S	I	Y	Y
K	Q	C	S	A	L	E	A	H	A	U	S	G	E
D	I	T	B	C	O	S	N	T	L	R	T	O	V
O	N	I	N	T	G	T	A	O	E	A	S	L	R
H	H	O	W	I	I	I	L	P	D	B	T	O	E
T	C	N	P	O	C	O	Y	Y	O	L	E	I	S
E	E	B	S	N	X	N	Z	H	M	E	P	B	B
M	T	H	E	O	R	I	E	S	J	F	S	Y	O

The Scientific Method

C	G	N	I	M	M	I	W	S	A	L	O	N	H
O	G	N	P	T	A	H	T	B	O	O	T	H	S
P	O	V	I	T	A	M	I	N	D	T	C	U	T
P	H	K	K	H	E	A	L	T	H	L	E	V	B
E	S	H	N	O	T	O	Y	G	S	E	T	R	I
R	K	R	E	T	M	A	I	T	S	S	O	A	K
T	T	O	E	G	K	L	B	T	U	N	R	Y	I
O	R	L	R	B	N	A	O	N	Z	A	P	S	N
N	E	O	C	U	G	B	G	E	U	R	E	B	I
E	M	C	S	I	O	L	R	X	Q	S	R	B	P
L	M	U	N	E	A	R	I	P	A	L	E	K	W
K	U	G	U	S	R	A	N	O	I	T	O	L	P
N	S	I	S	P	F	J	S	S	Y	C	K	L	K
I	N	E	N	R	U	B	N	U	S	B	W	R	F
R	S	S	E	L	K	C	E	R	F	Q	A	U	P
W	L	G	N	I	X	A	L	E	R	D	R	B	S

Get Some Sun

R	H	G	U	O	D	N	U	O	R	L	F	E	Y
U	E	K	E	G	I	R	L	S	C	O	U	T	Q
O	K	C	H	I	P	S	C	H	E	F	H	S	X
L	C	W	I	C	H	O	C	O	L	A	T	E	L
F	R	U	T	P	E	E	P	R	J	E	I	I	Z
Q	B	U	T	T	E	R	B	T	Y	G	U	N	N
S	W	E	E	T	E	O	R	B	N	G	C	W	X
O	P	M	X	S	E	E	V	R	H	S	S	O	U
F	O	F	S	A	S	R	J	E	T	P	I	R	S
R	R	E	T	S	N	O	M	A	N	I	B	B	U
C	D	A	E	R	S	A	F	D	R	C	A	S	G
A	L	D	E	T	I	T	F	O	S	E	K	N	A
F	K	M	L	C	R	M	I	N	I	S	I	A	R
Q	T	G	I	N	G	E	R	U	T	J	N	C	H
V	A	N	I	L	L	A	A	U	R	L	G	K	O
B	G	T	H	H	K	L	N	T	C	F	B	X	A

Cookies

O	T	L	N	G	I	S	E	D	O	C	T	T	C
B	Y	P	R	E	E	N	I	G	N	E	F	S	N
J	P	A	V	E	I	N	F	C	C	O	B	O	L
E	E	S	U	H	P	O	O	H	S	A	H	F	Y
C	H	C	C	U	R	M	N	O	S	T	C	T	H
T	T	A	T	T	M	O	R	M	Y	A	O	W	C
P	M	L	R	A	L	C	H	P	I	D	M	A	I
I	L	A	N	O	I	T	C	N	U	F	P	R	S
R	N	D	G	M	I	G	U	B	E	D	U	E	A
C	S	Y	P	R	O	G	R	A	M	S	T	T	B
S	A	N	O	I	S	S	E	R	P	X	E	U	R
A	Q	G	B	C	O	M	P	I	L	E	R	C	U
V	L	L	S	E	M	A	N	T	I	C	S	E	B
A	S	Y	M	B	O	L	S	E	N	I	L	X	Y
J	X	A	T	N	Y	S	C	I	E	N	C	E	I
L	O	G	I	C	W	D	N	U	M	B	E	R	G

Programming Languages

O	G	L	Y	P	A	R	E	H	T	E	I	D	R
R	Y	C	A	H	E	R	B	A	L	I	S	M	O
D	G	G	H	U	T	N	E	M	T	A	E	R	T
S	R	N	O	I	T	A	T	I	D	E	M	G	C
S	E	I	A	L	N	I	P	K	K	Y	H	N	O
E	N	T	R	G	O	E	R	O	N	I	T	I	D
N	E	S	E	N	E	B	S	I	E	E	A	L	F
L	C	A	M	T	W	V	R	E	P	M	P	A	K
L	I	F	E	S	T	Y	L	E	T	S	O	E	R
E	T	A	D	U	S	T	A	I	H	S	R	H	O
W	S	D	I	S	E	A	S	E	E	R	U	C	W
A	I	N	E	O	S	T	E	O	P	A	T	H	Y
T	L	I	S	A	D	E	V	R	U	Y	A	R	D
E	O	M	S	U	P	P	L	E	M	E	N	T	O
R	H	Y	P	N	O	S	I	S	Y	O	G	A	B
V	M	A	S	S	A	G	E	P	L	A	N	T	S

Alternative Medicine

M	A	W	N	J	N	L	R	J	B	Q	Q	G	P
U	K	S	H	R	B	O	T	T	L	E	E	W	Z
E	D	H	P	I	V	H	B	T	D	E	X	I	M
F	O	O	R	P	S	P	I	R	I	T	S	S	U
P	V	P	Z	E	A	K	I	Y	U	J	C	W	R
H	U	S	E	A	E	N	E	F	D	O	I	Z	G
H	C	V	H	T	K	B	H	Y	T	N	B	L	Y
T	B	A	T	I	H	Y	R	C	E	J	A	R	P
U	J	B	N	L	O	A	H	A	S	S	R	R	U
O	Y	G	I	G	O	L	N	K	S	E	L	O	B
M	V	I	S	T	O	H	S	O	H	M	E	U	O
R	L	N	B	P	E	C	O	S	L	B	Y	Q	O
E	N	G	A	P	M	A	H	C	A	H	Q	I	Z
V	R	R	O	T	E	Q	U	I	L	A	D	L	E
Q	T	R	O	P	A	O	R	E	G	A	L	U	A
Y	T	Y	D	B	D	J	X	A	M	J	Q	D	Z

Intoxicating

Y	D	U	T	S	W	E	A	T	H	E	R	O	C
T	H	N	A	T	U	R	E	C	O	L	O	G	Y
E	N	E	R	G	Y	X	Y	G	O	L	O	E	G
T	E	N	A	L	P	L	A	T	E	S	J	F	O
A	G	E	O	S	P	H	E	R	E	S	O	I	L
M	E	S	E	K	A	U	Q	H	T	R	A	E	O
I	O	C	H	R	O	N	O	L	O	G	Y	N	I
L	G	I	N	Y	E	R	E	H	P	S	O	I	B
C	R	S	T	E	D	H	E	F	I	L	M	A	A
I	A	Y	S	A	I	R	P	L	A	V	A	T	N
N	P	H	U	C	H	C	O	S	T	Q	G	N	I
O	H	P	R	O	C	K	S	L	O	N	M	U	M
T	Y	O	C	E	A	N	S	O	O	M	A	O	A
C	H	E	M	I	S	T	R	Y	E	G	T	M	L
E	Y	G	O	L	O	I	C	A	L	G	Y	A	S
T	Q	B	B	V	O	L	C	A	N	O	E	S	G

Earth Science

F	E	E	S	R	E	L	L	E	T	H	E	H	D
M	O	R	T	G	A	G	E	H	R	C	Y	S	R
N	Z	G	N	I	K	C	E	H	C	N	C	W	A
A	Y	T	U	W	L	A	I	C	N	A	N	I	F
T	M	L	O	I	A	I	N	T	E	R	E	S	T
I	O	U	C	L	W	R	C	L	O	B	R	E	N
O	N	A	C	I	A	C	D	A	S	O	R	C	E
N	O	V	A	N	R	U	E	R	S	Y	U	U	M
A	C	S	E	E	D	S	G	C	E	H	C	R	Y
L	E	N	D	S	H	T	T	N	N	V	K	I	A
A	E	I	E	L	T	O	O	I	I	A	O	T	P
T	T	O	B	L	I	M	F	K	S	D	L	Y	L
I	A	C	T	I	W	E	E	U	U	O	N	A	U
P	R	O	B	B	E	R	Y	N	B	I	P	E	B
A	A	B	O	N	D	S	C	A	T	M	S	E	L
C	H	A	N	G	E	R	E	G	A	N	A	M	D

Bank Terms

T	G	E	N	I	U	S	T	E	N	A	L	P	T
M	A	T	H	S	R	A	T	S	I	S	K	Y	R
U	G	G	E	O	C	E	N	T	R	I	C	L	O
L	H	M	C	X	P	J	M	W	H	P	C	Z	R
U	N	B	Y	H	P	O	S	O	L	I	H	P	B
D	I	S	C	O	V	E	R	Y	O	Z	U	Y	I
N	G	E	O	M	E	T	R	Y	Q	N	R	M	T
E	K	I	N	E	M	A	T	I	C	S	C	O	E
P	S	S	C	I	S	Y	H	P	M	Y	H	N	L
C	E	N	O	I	T	U	L	O	V	E	R	O	E
I	I	E	M	H	I	S	T	O	R	Y	N	R	S
T	R	A	P	S	C	I	E	N	T	I	S	T	C
E	O	R	A	F	S	U	N	S	P	O	T	S	O
R	E	T	S	N	A	I	L	A	T	I	K	A	P
E	H	H	S	C	O	E	L	I	L	A	G	R	E
H	T	B	J	U	P	I	T	E	R	O	M	A	N

Galileo Galilei

F	R	E	N	C	H	V	A	T	I	C	A	N	Z
S	X	L	K	Q	E	R	U	T	L	U	C	E	N
C	V	O	C	A	B	U	L	A	R	Y	H	K	E
B	H	E	M	I	M	U	S	I	C	G	H	O	T
T	I	U	R	U	F	S	X	Y	I	R	I	P	T
E	E	B	R	U	I	I	J	P	N	E	S	S	I
C	R	B	L	C	T	T	T	P	F	L	T	C	R
N	I	E	A	E	H	A	A	N	L	C	O	H	W
A	R	L	F	H	N	G	R	L	E	G	R	O	L
M	I	A	O	S	P	I	T	E	C	I	I	O	E
O	R	N	M	H	P	L	C	N	T	D	C	L	G
R	O	G	M	M	T	A	A	I	E	I	A	S	A
V	O	U	M	E	A	A	N	M	D	I	L	E	L
I	T	A	L	Y	C	R	C	I	R	E	C	D	D
Y	S	G	R	E	E	K	G	Y	S	O	M	N	O
S	M	E	D	I	E	V	A	L	E	H	F	F	A

Latin

E	E	L	T	T	O	B	X	Y	L	A	T	I	A
S	Y	D	N	U	G	R	U	B	R	G	V	P	M
O	R	V	A	R	I	E	T	A	L	E	I	W	O
N	R	S	M	B	J	A	V	S	F	D	N	H	R
Y	E	P	E	A	J	T	L	R	E	R	T	I	A
V	H	A	R	V	K	H	U	C	E	Y	A	T	W
W	S	R	L	A	I	I	A	E	O	S	G	E	H
E	R	K	O	Y	T	N	N	L	B	H	E	T	C
R	A	L	T	S	T	G	E	O	P	A	O	R	N
C	L	I	G	I	A	R	U	Y	I	J	T	L	E
S	L	N	N	P	R	Q	P	R	A	A	W	C	R
K	E	G	M	A	U	O	G	Y	S	R	N	T	F
R	C	A	B	E	R	N	E	T	E	A	D	E	J
O	H	O	T	T	A	X	I	G	R	A	P	E	S
C	D	G	H	S	I	N	I	F	W	C	R	W	V
Y	I	E	L	D	G	L	A	S	S	C	A	S	K

Speaking of Wine

Domesticated Animals

W	D	M	T	L	C	K	V	Q	I	D	F	B	Z
Y	X	C	A	U	G	O	O	S	E	C	M	L	P
J	J	N	H	S	I	F	D	L	O	G	T	S	O
I	G	X	D	T	A	F	Q	C	A	D	B	T	Q
G	C	E	E	O	N	F	K	H	A	F	U	A	H
U	L	A	E	D	N	A	I	A	S	N	F	C	Q
I	Z	C	B	S	T	K	H	N	Y	X	A	U	K
N	K	A	Y	I	E	S	E	P	C	M	F	R	B
E	B	P	E	D	G	K	S	Y	E	H	N	F	Y
A	T	L	N	Y	C	R	Y	L	S	L	O	E	E
P	L	A	O	I	R	E	E	D	N	I	E	R	K
I	J	S	H	T	U	A	S	T	A	O	G	R	R
G	W	C	O	I	I	M	B	U	S	D	I	E	U
I	Z	R	R	S	W	A	N	B	O	M	P	T	T
G	E	T	S	T	B	L	O	V	I	M	A	T	O
S	H	E	E	P	E	L	E	P	E	T	X	H	N

Emotional

C	R	G	B	A	H	A	T	R	E	D	F	S	S
A	W	E	L	T	I	X	Q	R	O	T	O	W	X
B	T	P	L	E	F	W	I	D	E	R	O	B	L
H	S	I	D	I	E	S	B	Y	R	U	R	U	J
G	U	T	E	A	E	E	V	O	L	S	S	O	S
G	L	Y	V	D	L	F	W	J	Y	T	U	S	H
F	Z	D	P	U	I	G	Y	H	J	W	O	S	A
N	M	I	A	T	N	E	T	N	O	C	V	E	M
O	E	S	N	V	G	A	E	X	N	F	R	N	E
I	T	G	I	P	P	R	I	A	P	S	E	D	G
T	H	U	C	M	P	F	X	R	E	G	N	A	A
A	G	S	E	E	I	J	N	Y	E	G	X	S	R
L	I	T	K	Y	H	T	A	P	M	Y	S	Y	H
E	R	U	S	A	E	L	P	R	I	D	E	V	F
J	F	E	I	R	G	V	L	O	N	G	I	N	G
P	A	C	Z	E	S	T	R	U	H	O	P	E	H

String Instruments

A	H	K	R	S	A	R	U	B	M	A	T	J	L
N	N	P	E	A	N	I	L	O	D	N	A	M	Q
M	H	R	E	H	T	I	Z	E	E	R	R	V	G
Z	R	C	S	S	O	I	K	M	N	U	U	G	G
S	A	E	I	M	F	C	U	A	W	B	D	B	V
Q	T	L	M	R	U	R	T	G	C	N	N	V	D
A	I	L	C	I	T	S	U	O	C	A	A	N	C
W	S	O	F	S	C	C	I	N	B	T	P	G	N
J	V	E	N	H	U	L	E	C	Q	A	T	I	J
S	P	I	O	K	B	D	U	L	A	P	S	U	D
Y	L	R	O	N	A	I	P	D	E	L	K	S	C
A	D	T	A	L	R	V	E	B	Y	U	T	E	N
I	O	S	J	H	I	W	A	R	L	C	F	T	K
V	V	R	O	R	O	N	E	E	M	K	E	U	G
R	E	B	A	B	J	Z	L	R	Z	E	B	L	Q
Y	S	N	G	O	I	E	E	L	D	D	I	F	I

Entertainment

H	O	B	B	I	E	S	Y	A	L	P	B	X	Y
R	E	L	A	X	M	O	N	O	P	O	L	Y	T
V	A	P	E	O	P	L	E	O	W	R	S	H	R
Y	I	M	U	S	I	C	A	L	O	E	U	Y	E
S	D	D	Z	P	Y	T	I	V	I	T	C	A	C
C	E	E	E	B	P	N	Q	L	D	H	R	G	N
I	M	L	M	O	G	E	S	H	I	G	I	A	O
M	S	E	A	O	R	M	T	A	V	U	C	M	C
O	I	I	G	K	C	E	U	S	E	A	L	B	I
C	N	S	D	S	R	S	A	N	R	L	O	L	N
S	G	U	R	T	H	U	F	D	S	F	W	I	E
P	E	R	A	R	O	M	U	H	I	U	N	N	M
O	R	E	C	R	E	A	T	I	O	N	S	G	A
R	H	E	N	J	O	Y	M	E	N	T	G	B	Q
T	D	A	N	C	E	I	V	O	M	L	I	F	M
S	T	O	R	Y	A	R	E	P	O	I	D	A	R

G	H	H	T	R	I	B	C	H	A	N	G	E	S
E	L	N	B	P	R	E	S	C	H	O	O	L	T
N	E	R	D	L	I	H	C	P	N	I	E	E	U
E	A	O	L	A	T	A	T	H	U	T	V	M	D
T	R	B	A	Y	P	V	N	Y	R	I	N	O	Y
I	N	W	T	I	S	I	A	S	T	R	I	T	T
C	I	E	N	N	Y	O	F	I	U	T	A	I	R
S	N	N	E	G	C	R	N	C	R	U	R	O	E
P	G	S	M	J	H	G	I	A	E	N	B	N	B
A	N	K	D	O	O	H	D	L	I	H	C	A	U
R	I	I	Y	C	L	M	S	I	T	U	A	L	P
E	H	L	B	N	O	I	T	A	C	U	D	E	S
N	C	L	A	N	G	U	A	G	E	V	O	L	K
T	A	S	B	C	Y	M	O	N	O	T	U	A	D
S	E	I	R	O	E	H	T	O	D	D	L	E	R
N	T	E	E	T	H	I	N	G	R	O	W	T	H

Child Development

E	H	C	N	U	L	N	O	I	T	R	O	P	X
T	C	U	A	S	T	A	R	C	H	C	D	V	H
B	S	I	K	P	C	L	C	A	R	R	O	T	S
R	N	S	R	O	P	O	T	A	T	O	E	S	E
E	E	I	R	R	L	E	B	D	I	N	N	E	R
A	E	N	V	E	G	E	T	A	B	L	E	S	V
D	R	E	S	S	I	N	G	I	W	Y	E	M	I
S	G	L	T	T	S	C	D	O	Z	G	E	O	N
L	A	E	M	A	O	C	B	O	A	E	B	O	G
W	S	U	E	U	L	L	O	B	O	S	R	R	N
S	N	P	R	R	L	P	B	U	A	F	O	H	I
O	A	S	P	A	R	A	G	U	S	L	C	S	F
U	E	T	M	N	C	S	C	N	L	C	C	U	F
P	B	S	S	T	R	E	S	S	E	D	O	M	U
S	D	A	L	A	S	Q	U	A	S	H	L	U	T
O	O	S	I	S	P	I	H	C	F	R	I	E	S

Side Dish

A	R	S	K	E	C	I	R	P	M	U	X	F	R
P	I	C	T	U	R	E	A	S	E	P	I	I	C
O	D	R	O	L	L	C	P	S	T	E	E	H	S
S	T	E	M	Y	K	E	O	N	E	R	B	X	T
T	E	A	L	A	L	P	S	G	R	F	G	U	I
M	L	S	G	I	I	O	T	I	J	O	N	S	C
A	K	E	C	I	V	L	C	S	V	R	I	P	K
R	O	K	X	C	Q	E	A	E	G	A	L	S	C
K	O	E	Y	C	A	V	R	D	U	T	I	M	C
O	B	T	V	S	E	N	D	Y	F	E	A	A	Q
T	S	O	C	I	M	E	S	O	Z	D	M	L	J
A	D	D	R	E	S	S	R	E	T	T	E	L	P
H	D	K	N	Y	L	E	T	A	L	I	H	P	I
R	T	T	B	G	V	L	H	O	B	B	Y	F	Q
M	P	A	P	E	R	D	O	D	X	N	L	V	C
U	T	Y	R	T	N	U	O	C	A	I	V	Y	A

Stamp It

S	M	H	M	J	W	I	R	E	L	E	S	S	Z
C	P	O	C	K	A	E	R	B	L	I	A	J	T
R	R	P	B	U	I	N	T	E	R	N	E	T	E
E	E	Y	A	I	O	S	C	P	O	T	P	A	L
E	T	A	S	Y	L	T	Y	R	E	T	T	A	B
N	U	L	I	G	R	E	I	E	O	I	D	U	A
O	P	P	N	O	A	V	P	T	C	M	S	P	T
E	M	S	N	L	L	E	O	M	L	I	V	A	R
D	O	I	O	O	U	J	D	W	N	U	V	T	O
I	C	D	V	N	P	O	B	E	I	S	M	E	P
V	I	M	A	H	O	B	S	B	R	K	D	G	D
I	S	O	T	C	P	S	C	Z	A	O	E	D	G
F	U	V	I	E	R	A	W	T	F	O	S	A	A
I	M	I	O	T	M	E	D	I	A	B	I	G	M
W	A	E	N	O	H	P	I	C	S	E	G	O	E
B	M	S	O	T	O	H	P	I	T	U	N	E	S

iPad

T	O	X	I	C	F	L	O	A	T	I	N	G	T
G	A	D	U	M	B	R	E	L	L	A	M	S	F
O	B	L	O	O	M	S	I	N	A	G	R	O	O
D	E	R	F	O	P	G	N	I	M	M	I	W	S
S	A	I	R	E	F	S	F	N	A	T	U	R	E
W	C	G	E	L	A	T	I	N	O	U	S	C	I
A	H	D	S	M	U	I	R	A	U	Q	A	U	L
R	P	E	H	C	R	N	S	O	R	A	O	B	L
M	A	A	W	L	E	G	T	Z	A	N	Z	O	E
S	I	D	A	E	L	I	A	O	G	I	O	Z	J
G	N	L	T	A	I	N	I	H	E	M	S	O	N
O	F	Y	E	R	A	G	D	P	N	A	U	A	O
C	U	R	R	E	N	T	S	Y	I	L	D	H	S
E	L	U	F	R	O	L	O	C	V	A	E	S	I
A	O	Z	O	R	U	A	T	S	A	F	M	I	O
N	X	S	E	L	C	A	T	N	E	T	S	F	P

Jellyfish

I	P	U	T	O	O	L	S	Y	S	T	E	M	E
N	F	R	E	E	W	A	R	E	M	L	I	S	C
S	S	C	O	M	P	U	T	E	R	D	E	W	I
T	J	E	C	C	W	P	M	A	D	M	I	T	F
A	F	B	C	O	E	O	V	L	A	N	U	U	F
L	I	O	R	A	R	D	E	G	D	S	N	E	O
L	R	D	S	Y	F	W	U	O	E	C	D	R	T
W	M	A	S	O	A	R	W	R	T	D	A	A	J
V	W	P	S	R	R	S	E	I	E	I	O	W	A
D	A	R	E	D	O	C	O	T	N	S	L	E	V
R	R	O	N	G	A	N	I	H	N	K	N	R	A
I	E	G	I	P	P	C	A	M	G	I	W	A	P
V	J	R	S	M	P	O	H	S	O	T	O	H	P
E	G	A	U	G	N	A	L	A	T	A	D	S	L
R	D	M	B	H	A	R	D	W	A	R	E	M	E
S	U	S	Y	N	T	A	X	U	N	I	L	Q	L

Computer Software

Y	T	G	E	H	W	J	S	B	X	P	Z	M	G
T	U	N	I	O	A	T	M	E	A	L	F	D	I
I	X	A	K	G	S	O	I	R	E	E	H	C	E
U	C	R	U	N	C	H	Y	K	I	X	E	F	M
R	W	B	L	Y	P	C	N	X	E	C	I	G	C
F	I	B	E	R	O	N	E	H	X	L	R	R	S
V	D	N	S	Q	X	H	C	I	T	U	I	E	L
N	O	I	U	M	C	E	R	U	S	S	I	S	A
H	K	L	G	T	C	T	N	E	P	T	P	P	T
I	A	S	A	I	S	Y	L	I	A	E	U	O	O
E	S	E	R	O	E	B	X	E	C	R	M	P	T
O	H	U	P	N	B	K	H	I	V	S	K	N	I
W	I	M	O	E	J	W	A	L	O	N	A	R	G
Q	M	H	P	K	E	L	L	O	G	G	S	O	P
Z	E	X	S	E	K	A	L	F	N	R	O	C	X
P	N	B	C	G	U	K	W	R	Q	U	P	S	I

Breakfast Cereals

C	S	R	Y	T	N	A	R	R	A	W	S	B	E
S	E	E	N	I	L	N	O	P	S	A	T	L	V
O	N	M	T	S	Q	R	P	R	L	O	E	U	I
F	O	U	A	A	E	L	E	E	H	C	C	E	S
T	H	S	B	O	I	M	S	T	T	D	H	C	N
W	P	N	P	A	O	C	A	R	A	Z	N	C	E
A	L	O	N	T	Z	A	O	G	J	I	O	A	P
R	L	C	S	S	E	N	I	S	U	B	L	M	X
E	E	U	E	C	I	V	R	E	S	S	O	E	E
S	C	Y	E	C	S	T	E	G	D	A	G	R	R
F	X	D	A	U	Q	S	K	E	E	G	Y	A	O
Y	Y	E	L	L	O	W	T	A	G	T	V	S	E
S	R	E	T	U	P	M	O	C	I	S	U	M	R
E	I	V	O	M	E	D	I	A	S	T	O	R	E
F	I	N	O	I	S	I	V	E	L	E	T	S	T
S	H	O	P	P	I	N	G	D	R	Y	E	R	S

Best Buy

Y	H	L	Y	S	G	Z	B	T	H	B	F	K	Y
U	G	O	L	V	R	A	G	R	O	W	L	E	O
P	W	R	M	A	S	E	R	I	U	Y	O	B	N
H	E	I	A	E	B	S	W	D	S	S	W	E	T
H	D	S	B	S	T	T	E	O	E	F	E	R	F
K	P	A	T	C	S	H	O	E	M	N	R	M	E
Y	L	Q	E	I	V	E	R	O	D	N	S	U	R
L	A	S	Q	N	C	T	S	D	F	S	W	D	T
I	N	R	S	P	R	I	N	K	L	E	R	A	I
I	T	S	D	O	L	C	D	W	O	R	S	C	L
G	I	R	R	I	G	A	T	E	G	V	K	U	I
G	N	I	R	E	T	A	W	I	M	I	R	T	Z
R	G	I	R	H	L	A	N	D	S	C	A	P	E
E	G	A	W	S	H	R	U	B	S	E	P	D	R
E	C	L	I	O	S	I	N	N	E	T	G	Q	L
N	C	S	U	M	M	E	R	W	E	E	D	K	A

Lawns

E	C	U	A	S	W	D	H	J	P	S	Y	A	S
R	I	H	O	N	I	O	N	S	O	H	T	S	P
G	R	E	E	N	S	O	N	U	T	S	N	G	E
V	A	T	G	E	K	F	B	L	A	O	P	C	P
I	D	A	G	H	S	A	A	P	T	T	U	A	P
N	I	L	S	S	G	E	C	U	O	C	P	S	E
E	S	P	R	I	H	S	O	J	U	P	E	E	R
G	H	T	A	D	Z	R	N	M	E	L	D	O	S
A	E	I	S	E	C	C	B	T	B	R	L	T	N
R	C	U	E	D	H	E	I	A	E	I	O	A	C
O	U	R	A	I	R	Z	T	S	V	R	I	M	O
M	T	F	C	S	E	E	S	E	R	L	W	O	B
A	T	K	R	R	G	I	S	A	A	N	U	T	B
I	E	Y	M	E	N	K	C	T	O	S	S	E	D
N	L	K	V	G	S	P	I	N	A	C	H	A	M
E	U	R	A	N	C	H	M	E	A	T	U	N	C

Toss a Salad

N	G	I	S	E	D	N	U	O	R	T	U	U	Y
T	P	T	E	K	C	O	P	E	I	G	G	A	P
O	N	R	I	S	I	R	S	H	N	G	G	L	Z
Y	H	I	S	L	M	E	T	A	G	A	A	L	X
S	A	D	P	P	R	A	L	L	E	Y	E	E	X
E	Q	S	E	C	H	I	L	D	R	E	N	X	E
M	P	E	E	N	L	E	W	L	T	G	S	H	W
A	I	I	K	Y	O	A	R	S	N	Q	T	E	I
G	Q	S	I	Z	E	S	Y	I	R	O	O	K	C
L	N	T	P	T	J	S	T	E	C	T	N	A	S
A	I	I	H	E	R	C	T	A	R	A	E	T	G
S	W	U	L	O	E	O	F	A	L	L	L	E	H
S	M	Q	L	L	O	K	D	R	C	G	S	G	S
B	A	O	L	H	O	E	R	R	E	O	I	R	F
M	C	O	S	V	K	R	I	O	L	L	L	A	B
Q	C	R	F	L	I	C	K	J	F	O	X	T	U

Marbles

I	N	T	E	R	A	C	T	M	S	O	N	G	S
G	C	H	I	L	D	H	O	O	D	F	T	G	Y
N	H	N	O	M	E	O	G	N	I	T	I	R	W
I	S	O	A	U	R	M	S	L	L	I	K	S	A
G	K	I	W	S	T	N	E	D	U	T	S	J	C
N	C	T	S	I	U	L	A	N	G	U	A	G	E
I	O	A	A	C	T	I	V	I	T	I	E	S	N
S	L	C	V	O	C	A	B	U	L	A	R	Y	T
C	B	U	Y	O	U	N	G	O	G	M	R	K	E
H	A	D	D	I	T	I	O	N	P	J	A	Y	R
I	Q	E	N	I	L	H	I	K	I	D	S	T	S
L	L	A	P	I	C	N	I	R	P	W	A	N	H
D	Y	A	Z	S	R	E	B	M	U	N	A	E	P
R	A	T	E	A	C	H	E	R	S	T	O	R	Y
E	L	R	E	A	D	I	N	G	F	U	N	A	D
N	P	L	A	I	C	O	S	K	O	O	B	P	F

Kindergarten

S	M	C	H	I	N	E	S	E	N	A	P	A	J
E	Y	G	M	T	R	E	E	S	U	E	O	H	M
L	R	G	N	I	N	U	R	P	R	B	Z	J	K
Y	O	U	A	I	D	L	O	E	S	G	J	U	G
T	T	B	T	B	J	W	N	E	E	R	G	N	N
S	S	A	U	A	O	N	A	E	R	A	C	I	I
C	I	R	R	P	I	N	E	R	Y	F	C	P	T
I	H	K	E	A	C	N	D	P	F	T	M	E	N
S	T	S	L	S	R	C	I	T	S	I	T	R	A
L	W	L	N	A	Z	T	G	M	R	N	N	A	L
E	O	O	S	M	R	O	F	O	K	G	T	G	P
A	R	O	O	U	T	D	O	O	R	Z	E	E	O
V	G	T	I	R	Y	D	G	A	R	D	E	N	T
E	S	N	L	A	N	G	N	I	M	M	I	R	T
S	H	A	P	I	N	G	N	I	R	I	W	M	E
W	A	T	E	R	H	O	B	B	Y	J	Z	M	D

Bonsai

T	R	A	M	K	E	R	U	T	I	N	R	U	F
N	T	J	C	O	R	E	L	I	A	T	E	R	R
B	O	S	H	O	P	P	I	N	G	S	D	R	O
G	Y	S	I	B	S	G	T	I	D	E	R	C	E
O	S	E	C	H	R	N	S	F	P	H	O	T	B
L	E	N	A	S	E	I	E	A	E	O	L	O	U
A	C	I	G	I	W	H	R	P	C	U	I	W	C
T	N	S	O	W	O	T	O	A	I	S	A	E	K
A	A	U	T	O	M	O	T	I	V	E	M	R	B
C	I	B	L	E	N	L	S	N	R	W	A	A	E
H	L	D	N	F	W	C	U	T	E	A	L	W	D
A	P	T	R	I	A	P	E	R	S	R	L	D	D
I	P	S	E	I	L	P	P	U	S	E	S	R	I
N	A	S	O	H	C	R	A	F	T	S	M	A	N
J	E	W	E	L	R	Y	S	A	L	E	S	H	G
S	L	O	O	T	E	R	O	M	N	E	K	D	N

Sears

S	B	S	L	Y	G	O	L	O	N	H	C	E	T
A	U	E	A	U	M	P	R	O	B	L	E	M	S
F	I	G	I	S	L	A	I	R	E	T	A	M	W
E	L	D	R	N	S	T	B	O	J	N	Q	A	O
T	D	I	T	A	A	H	C	R	A	E	S	E	R
Y	I	R	S	L	C	O	L	L	E	G	E	R	K
T	N	B	U	P	P	H	Y	S	I	C	S	O	T
I	G	G	D	S	Y	S	T	E	M	S	T	S	K
S	E	S	N	O	I	T	C	U	D	O	R	P	N
R	N	O	I	S	S	E	F	O	R	P	U	A	O
E	U	F	O	L	A	C	I	M	E	H	C	C	W
V	I	T	C	O	N	S	T	R	U	C	T	E	L
I	T	W	C	I	N	O	I	T	A	C	U	D	E
N	Y	A	A	C	O	M	P	U	T	E	R	S	D
U	T	R	C	L	A	C	I	N	H	C	E	T	G
I	T	E	M	E	C	H	A	N	I	C	S	O	E

Engineering

C	P	C	D	F	S	E	I	C	E	P	S	Y	N
O	J	Y	E	N	M	G	C	I	T	A	U	Q	A
R	B	D	E	R	E	G	N	A	D	N	E	C	T
L	I	L	L	E	L	E	E	I	P	N	O	M	U
H	O	O	T	S	T	I	R	C	M	A	A	T	R
N	H	O	R	I	R	T	A	G	P	M	R	L	E
P	A	Z	U	O	U	E	H	T	T	M	I	A	X
P	F	V	T	T	T	E	P	U	R	G	D	W	C
Q	E	M	A	R	X	R	E	P	T	I	L	E	S
J	W	T	E	O	O	D	L	E	I	H	S	L	N
L	S	A	S	T	B	A	H	E	N	L	L	T	A
R	O	C	T	H	G	F	N	C	G	E	F	R	P
G	U	C	R	E	C	I	L	I	H	G	C	W	P
W	P	H	E	A	R	A	B	S	M	W	S	K	I
F	U	K	E	A	W	T	E	R	R	A	P	I	N
E	T	P	M	S	N	L	C	B	W	O	L	S	G

Turtle Life

T	A	L	F	G	D	T	B	A	L	W	O	O	D
I	T	F	O	Y	E	N	M	I	H	C	G	B	E
L	L	A	I	R	E	T	A	M	O	N	W	U	K
E	A	V	E	S	G	R	O	V	I	O	M	I	A
S	H	V	Y	N	A	S	E	H	G	A	B	L	E
W	P	S	C	T	N	R	C	W	J	J	E	D	P
A	S	H	N	O	I	T	A	L	U	S	N	I	I
R	A	I	W	N	A	L	N	L	P	Q	L	N	T
T	O	N	G	H	R	J	I	A	O	J	L	G	C
S	C	G	T	L	D	W	L	B	I	S	N	C	H
L	R	L	P	T	E	L	E	C	A	L	P	E	R
A	L	E	O	A	O	P	R	Z	L	R	S	E	E
T	A	S	T	C	E	T	O	R	P	T	U	P	P
E	T	H	R	T	G	N	I	L	L	E	W	D	A
U	E	A	H	O	U	S	E	E	S	S	H	S	I
R	M	Q	S	V	C	G	F	R	O	O	F	E	R

Roofs

B	O	A	R	D	G	A	M	E	R	P	N	T	O
C	A	P	T	U	R	E	E	I	W	I	N	A	O
F	B	L	N	E	T	A	M	K	C	E	H	C	A
P	A	W	N	S	E	V	O	M	C	C	E	T	J
X	S	S	P	O	H	S	I	B	A	E	T	I	D
A	C	M	A	S	T	E	R	S	S	S	A	C	E
T	E	T	I	H	W	C	K	S	T	S	M	S	R
T	K	V	G	K	R	O	F	K	L	E	E	H	E
A	I	I	V	U	O	M	R	O	I	R	L	H	K
C	N	C	H	A	M	P	I	O	N	A	A	K	C
K	G	B	H	N	J	U	P	R	G	U	T	G	E
Z	S	S	L	Q	E	T	E	O	J	Q	S	A	H
N	S	T	R	A	T	E	G	Y	N	S	R	M	C
R	U	L	E	S	C	R	U	H	N	E	E	B	L
U	R	Z	L	L	I	K	S	Q	F	U	N	I	U
T	U	S	C	U	G	N	I	K	N	I	H	T	B

The Game of Kings

E	C	N	O	C	S	H	A	D	O	W	L	L	S
W	R	S	F	C	A	N	D	L	E	S	Z	A	B
O	E	U	P	L	V	I	E	W	P	L	G	R	L
L	T	H	T	M	O	R	O	O	D	N	I	U	U
G	A	Z	C	X	A	O	T	D	I	M	N	T	B
L	N	T	L	T	I	L	D	R	E	B	O	A	J
P	I	E	H	A	I	F	I	L	A	M	E	N	T
O	M	G	G	G	I	W	E	E	I	D	N	N	H
K	U	A	H	A	I	C	S	G	T	G	T	R	A
C	L	T	L	T	T	R	I	Y	H	D	H	E	L
A	L	N	D	R	B	S	B	F	G	Y	G	T	O
R	I	E	I	O	O	U	C	E	I	L	I	N	G
T	C	C	N	K	O	O	L	C	L	T	N	A	E
K	A	C	R	U	D	R	L	B	Y	U	R	L	N
L	R	A	L	O	S	E	E	F	A	T	T	A	W
U	D	R	E	C	E	S	S	E	D	W	O	H	S

Lighting

B	H	I	H	L	H	C	G	X	M	S	L	Y	G
W	A	V	Y	S	U	U	N	L	Z	O	E	C	R
I	P	L	A	C	S	H	A	V	I	N	G	T	O
G	G	W	D	K	E	R	A	T	I	N	F	H	W
S	V	K	Z	X	D	E	O	C	N	O	T	G	T
G	S	Z	C	A	N	B	U	S	S	W	N	I	H
N	H	J	E	A	O	R	G	N	S	I	O	A	V
O	O	H	L	D	L	A	U	E	T	I	I	R	P
L	R	I	Y	Y	B	B	H	T	L	R	C	T	B
C	T	E	T	A	N	S	U	T	C	O	O	S	D
F	H	S	S	I	A	C	E	U	G	A	M	T	D
Q	T	L	I	L	D	X	T	Q	R	A	B	E	B
E	G	O	E	M	T	N	E	N	A	M	R	E	P
X	N	Y	O	U	R	Y	O	D	Y	E	K	I	Y
P	E	I	R	R	S	E	L	C	I	L	L	O	F
D	L	E	F	L	B	U	D	M	A	C	T	Q	U

Hair

N	E	L	S	O	R	B	O	I	R	A	M	J	A
W	T	E	K	K	E	N	G	X	I	Q	G	P	Z
H	N	A	M	C	A	P	U	A	M	B	U	S	H
L	U	E	N	O	Z	E	L	T	T	A	B	S	D
R	H	T	E	T	R	I	S	Y	C	F	D	R	I
E	K	A	S	O	I	J	L	Z	Y	I	I	A	X
D	C	L	I	I	R	X	A	A	O	P	P	W	L
N	U	I	M	I	A	R	T	R	D	I	P	R	I
E	D	E	P	I	T	N	E	C	N	G	W	A	D
F	J	N	S	N	A	T	M	B	A	A	R	T	M
E	P	S	O	M	S	P	A	L	M	U	E	S	E
D	O	C	N	A	P	L	A	Y	M	N	D	U	V
Q	N	N	S	Y	L	X	W	M	O	T	A	O	D
R	G	U	D	G	I	D	B	Y	C	L	C	J	K
A	C	S	G	A	F	R	O	G	G	E	R	I	Q
T	R	O	N	A	M	T	A	B	C	T	A	M	G

Classic Arcade Games

S	R	E	L	L	I	H	I	M	S	E	L	F	C
T	S	E	I	L	L	I	H	I	C	K	O	R	Y
S	H	L	Y	T	I	R	A	L	I	H	J	D	P
S	I	B	S	U	A	T	S	E	H	G	I	H	S
E	P	A	Y	T	T	S	O	M	D	N	I	H	T
L	S	R	A	G	H	I	L	L	T	O	P	S	X
E	T	I	W	S	G	N	I	S	S	I	H	E	H
V	E	H	H	H	I	P	B	O	N	E	S	N	I
I	R	F	G	Q	H	I	C	C	U	P	S	I	T
H	S	T	I	H	I	T	H	E	R	T	O	L	C
I	Y	O	H	L	G	N	I	T	L	I	H	P	H
D	E	H	I	G	H	N	E	S	S	O	F	I	I
I	K	S	K	K	R	G	N	I	T	N	I	H	N
N	C	P	I	E	O	H	I	R	E	L	I	N	G
G	I	I	N	F	A	S	C	H	I	R	I	N	G
S	H	H	G	E	D	I	S	L	L	I	H	N	V

Starts with HI

Y	N	R	S	C	I	T	A	B	O	R	C	A	G
P	N	X	S	G	H	R	A	S	E	V	I	N	K
R	P	C	E	H	U	A	B	W	S	K	I	L	L
L	E	F	H	O	O	C	I	Q	X	W	M	L	M
P	I	M	C	P	G	W	I	N	O	N	P	A	Z
H	Y	O	R	C	M	N	X	R	S	I	X	V	D
V	A	O	O	O	A	J	H	I	C	A	G	I	S
B	P	P	T	A	F	T	F	V	Z	U	W	T	T
R	U	I	P	J	C	R	C	I	I	D	S	S	C
I	O	O	Q	L	U	R	E	H	R	I	A	E	E
N	G	K	O	S	E	G	D	P	I	E	F	F	J
G	X	W	L	T	M	S	G	A	B	N	A	E	B
S	N	L	S	R	S	B	U	L	C	C	G	U	O
X	A	E	H	O	B	B	Y	X	E	E	R	P	Q
B	J	I	T	P	M	H	T	Y	H	R	R	T	D
H	A	N	D	S	V	T	R	I	C	K	S	A	T

Juggling

H	R	E	E	S	O	R	P	O	E	T	S	N	E
S	E	N	I	L	I	M	E	R	I	C	K	U	P
P	T	O	S	E	C	N	A	M	O	R	W	W	I
W	E	T	C	O	B	A	L	L	A	D	R	R	C
F	M	E	I	F	D	E	L	I	M	I	S	I	S
S	E	S	R	E	V	E	E	R	F	S	B	T	T
P	A	E	Y	U	C	E	S	S	T	M	E	I	O
R	S	S	L	T	T	G	T	H	A	C	A	N	R
W	S	K	I	I	E	A	G	I	S	L	U	G	Y
R	O	O	M	K	N	U	R	O	F	A	T	N	L
H	N	O	T	Z	O	G	N	E	E	S	I	I	D
Y	A	B	A	H	U	N	S	V	T	S	F	M	R
T	N	S	T	K	E	A	O	V	J	I	U	Y	A
H	C	X	I	T	E	L	P	U	O	C	L	H	M
M	E	A	N	I	N	G	N	I	D	A	E	R	A
T	H	S	D	R	O	W	H	I	T	M	A	N	E

Poetic

S	Y	T	G	L	I	M	A	R	T	S	A	P	O
K	O	S	H	E	R	K	S	N	U	M	B	E	R
C	O	O	K	I	E	S	P	O	G	C	K	N	D
Q	U	F	R	N	B	Y	I	S	D	O	W	I	E
F	P	T	O	D	I	C	D	A	H	F	L	W	R
T	I	U	Y	K	I	R	E	N	A	F	S	O	J
D	C	N	W	L	E	R	D	D	M	E	N	E	B
H	K	A	E	T	B	N	S	W	V	E	W	R	P
G	L	D	N	F	C	T	Z	I	K	I	A	V	O
R	E	U	X	A	O	K	L	C	S	E	E	T	H
O	O	N	V	R	L	O	I	H	T	G	S	N	S
C	U	I	E	I	D	H	D	E	A	L	A	N	H
E	A	Z	M	D	C	S	E	S	E	E	H	C	C
R	Y	E	K	R	U	T	U	G	E	R	M	A	N
Y	B	B	U	G	T	A	A	W	F	U	K	E	U
I	M	A	L	A	S	B	K	C	B	E	H	M	L

Delicatessen

Y	N	O	S	F	T	E	N	R	E	T	N	I	R
Q	S	F	I	L	T	E	R	X	L	E	N	S	O
W	S	A	M	A	R	D	P	A	F	O	C	U	S
C	C	W	E	S	M	O	O	Z	W	E	I	V	N
R	A	W	M	H	S	W	C	A	P	T	U	R	E
W	N	J	O	U	I	N	G	C	C	T	F	P	S
P	N	H	R	C	K	L	R	S	C	A	N	O	N
G	I	E	Y	O	B	O	O	L	Y	M	P	U	S
W	N	C	D	M	P	A	P	E	R	T	U	R	E
I	G	A	T	P	P	D	E	X	G	E	S	G	E
T	K	A	I	U	P	P	R	I	N	T	I	N	G
H	C	N	R	T	R	W	A	P	I	E	Z	I	A
G	G	E	D	E	U	E	H	A	T	L	I	G	R
I	W	R	P	R	M	H	S	G	I	E	N	A	O
L	A	N	D	S	C	A	P	E	D	D	G	M	T
C	U	P	L	O	A	D	C	M	E	I	Y	I	S

Digital Photography

X	T	O	S	H	I	B	A	K	S	I	D	J	M
C	Z	E	G	A	R	O	T	S	E	E	Q	H	L
O	X	H	C	T	A	R	C	S	E	S	M	C	I
M	I	G	P	H	I	L	I	P	S	R	U	T	F
P	L	H	S	O	N	Y	S	R	U	Z	S	A	V
A	F	T	A	M	R	O	F	E	C	K	I	W	P
C	T	P	R	E	S	A	L	C	C	I	C	C	S
T	E	L	E	V	I	S	I	O	N	S	R	A	D
K	N	A	L	B	S	L	M	R	G	E	C	S	B
M	U	A	C	N	D	P	Y	D	Y	Y	I	E	M
E	V	E	C	R	U	L	L	A	C	I	T	P	O
D	I	G	I	T	A	L	L	B	R	A	S	N	V
I	D	V	E	T	I	P	W	L	O	U	A	R	I
U	E	R	N	O	D	O	Y	E	U	D	L	U	E
M	O	E	Z	V	H	S	N	F	N	I	P	B	S
S	R	N	D	S	P	A	T	A	D	O	Z	O	D

DVD

T	N	A	I	D	N	I	H	U	S	K	N	C	T
R	T	S	L	H	C	R	A	T	S	T	I	R	G
A	L	A	E	M	N	R	O	C	X	A	D	O	Z
D	I	V	S	E	S	N	U	C	L	F	K	P	E
E	O	E	S	K	D	L	A	L	P	E	F	M	V
B	N	G	A	S	T	S	I	Z	R	O	L	A	Y
I	R	E	T	I	C	T	E	N	T	F	P	Y	E
O	O	T	V	A	R	I	E	T	I	E	S	A	L
F	C	A	P	O	R	L	T	E	H	A	C	N	L
U	T	B	T	C	S	F	L	E	G	A	R	S	O
E	E	L	S	I	C	D	Y	L	N	Z	N	G	W
L	E	E	E	X	S	N	D	T	I	E	A	O	J
P	W	R	A	E	I	U	S	N	M	M	G	C	L
A	S	T	S	M	A	O	H	A	R	V	E	S	T
T	A	K	O	O	C	R	L	L	A	E	R	E	C
S	F	H	N	V	R	G	S	P	F	O	O	D	N

Maize

L	G	B	C	O	N	T	A	C	T	E	K	I	L
L	C	L	Y	K	S	T	S	E	R	E	T	N	I
A	H	O	A	D	V	E	R	T	I	S	E	I	N
W	A	G	M	R	E	T	U	P	M	O	C	E	K
R	T	D	P	M	J	G	N	I	R	A	H	S	E
M	E	Y	I	W	E	B	S	I	T	E	N	O	D
Y	R	T	C	O	N	N	E	C	T	I	O	N	I
S	E	I	T	I	V	I	T	C	A	N	L	E	N
P	T	N	U	I	H	I	A	S	D	T	O	T	P
A	S	U	R	E	W	N	M	T	A	E	G	W	R
C	D	M	E	N	O	T	S	N	T	R	Y	O	I
E	N	M	S	I	B	E	S	E	I	A	L	R	V
P	E	O	P	L	E	R	A	V	N	C	I	K	A
Q	I	C	K	N	B	N	L	E	G	T	A	I	C
C	R	K	O	O	B	E	C	A	F	D	M	N	Y
Y	F	M	R	O	F	T	A	L	P	J	E	G	K

Social Networks

T	H	T	L	A	E	H	R	M	Y	A	C	E	D
S	U	R	G	E	R	Y	O	U	T	L	Y	D	I
I	S	L	S	O	M	G	O	G	R	P	A	I	N
T	N	S	T	N	O	I	T	N	E	V	E	R	P
N	W	C	P	D	P	E	C	I	A	S	H	O	O
E	O	A	L	I	A	N	A	S	T	E	C	U	O
D	R	V	A	S	T	I	N	S	M	R	A	L	I
C	C	I	Q	E	I	S	A	O	E	U	H	F	W
N	H	T	U	A	E	T	L	L	N	T	T	D	C
O	A	I	E	S	N	S	I	F	T	N	O	R	L
I	I	E	Z	E	T	Z	J	V	J	E	O	I	E
T	R	S	I	S	O	N	G	A	I	D	T	L	A
A	R	A	E	F	I	L	L	I	N	G	S	L	N
D	F	E	X	T	R	A	C	T	I	O	N	S	I
E	N	I	C	I	D	E	M	O	L	A	R	I	N
S	E	G	D	I	R	B	R	U	S	H	I	N	G

Dentistry

L	E	E	T	S	Y	V	E	M	A	S	T	E	R
Q	N	C	C	P	A	D	L	O	C	K	C	I	F
D	T	M	A	G	N	E	T	I	C	E	E	R	I
O	R	R	E	D	N	I	L	Y	C	Y	T	E	D
O	Y	C	L	H	T	I	M	S	K	C	O	L	K
R	C	G	K	C	O	L	N	I	P	A	R	B	E
L	A	C	I	N	A	H	C	E	M	R	P	M	Y
O	V	G	U	D	Y	N	R	U	T	D	D	U	C
C	I	N	O	R	T	C	E	L	E	S	R	T	O
K	R	I	T	O	I	T	L	O	B	D	A	E	D
S	P	K	E	W	R	N	C	U	P	E	U	F	E
A	V	C	R	S	U	E	Y	X	G	E	G	K	S
F	A	I	C	S	C	V	C	B	R	G	N	Y	O
E	U	P	E	A	E	E	I	M	E	T	A	L	L
T	L	M	S	P	S	R	B	A	R	L	U	G	C
Y	T	H	I	E	F	P	E	D	E	V	I	C	E

Lock Up

P	E	O	P	L	E	L	A	N	O	I	T	A	N
B	R	S	T	G	O	L	D	R	O	C	E	R	A
O	U	N	C	N	O	I	T	U	L	O	V	E	R
O	T	O	T	I	E	V	E	N	T	S	J	L	R
K	L	S	N	N	T	M	U	E	S	U	M	I	A
S	U	S	E	R	A	I	N	Y	P	O	H	G	T
G	C	E	I	A	W	G	L	R	D	Q	I	I	I
N	I	L	C	E	D	M	E	O	E	U	S	O	V
I	V	N	N	L	P	H	Y	S	P	V	T	N	E
K	I	N	A	C	I	R	E	M	A	P	O	S	W
C	L	A	S	S	A	S	M	Y	S	E	R	G	E
I	W	R	T	T	C	O	U	N	T	R	I	E	S
N	A	O	I	H	D	T	I	M	E	I	A	R	T
W	R	L	O	E	G	D	E	L	W	O	N	K	E
Y	I	O	R	J	G	W	O	R	L	D	S	R	R
M	L	N	X	S	T	O	R	I	E	S	A	G	N

History

I	C	O	N	I	C	C	U	P	P	A	C	A	V
Z	I	S	L	L	I	P	L	A	N	T	L	O	J
Z	T	R	E	T	T	I	B	E	N	E	R	G	Y
U	E	E	T	E	S	S	E	N	T	R	E	L	A
B	R	T	N	S	N	O	I	T	C	I	D	D	A
K	U	T	A	P	D	F	D	Q	L	M	B	R	S
W	I	I	L	R	E	T	E	A	A	O	U	I	L
U	D	J	U	E	T	D	B	J	W	L	L	N	E
H	E	G	M	S	A	R	E	C	A	E	L	K	E
E	C	A	I	S	L	I	A	H	R	C	E	S	P
A	A	W	T	O	O	N	N	E	D	U	A	V	L
D	F	A	S	P	C	K	S	M	H	L	V	F	A
A	L	K	A	L	O	I	D	I	T	E	E	R	T
C	R	E	P	Y	H	P	G	C	I	H	S	U	T
H	C	O	C	A	C	O	L	A	W	Q	G	I	E
E	E	F	F	O	C	K	O	L	A	N	U	T	P

Caffeine

L	A	V	E	I	D	E	M	N	R	E	D	O	M
I	N	C	E	N	A	E	P	O	R	U	E	A	E
L	O	U	X	T	R	A	D	I	T	I	O	N	M
L	I	L	P	H	I	L	O	S	O	P	H	Y	S
A	T	T	R	E	Z	A	I	I	Y	A	Y	F	I
C	A	U	E	M	O	L	I	V	C	S	T	E	L
I	C	R	S	R	A	P	K	E	A	T	I	B	A
S	U	E	S	T	A	I	L	L	R	C	L	A	B
S	D	S	I	X	K	T	N	E	C	A	A	S	O
A	E	P	O	W	E	R	U	T	O	F	U	E	L
L	A	S	N	A	M	O	R	R	M	I	Q	B	G
C	Y	G	O	L	O	N	H	C	E	T	E	A	R
I	H	O	L	L	Y	W	O	O	D	R	Q	L	E
S	C	B	C	H	R	I	S	T	I	A	N	L	E
U	H	E	R	I	T	A	G	E	F	I	L	N	K
M	L	C	Q	L	L	A	B	T	O	O	F	N	S

Western Culture

X	J	N	O	N	F	L	Y	I	N	G	B	O	F
T	S	R	E	L	L	E	P	O	R	P	K	D	E
G	E	Y	E	N	E	N	A	L	P	R	I	A	L
Q	L	V	O	T	G	T	E	K	C	O	R	I	E
B	W	I	I	T	P	I	R	O	T	O	M	R	C
A	P	I	D	S	C	O	N	S	T	R	U	C	T
L	A	I	N	E	N	T	C	E	R	M	Y	R	R
S	S	A	L	G	R	E	B	I	F	O	B	A	I
A	S	A	V	O	S	N	P	T	L	D	B	F	C
W	E	I	L	O	T	E	E	X	I	E	O	T	A
O	M	I	N	I	A	T	U	R	E	L	H	V	T
O	B	U	I	L	D	I	N	G	D	S	T	E	J
D	L	I	A	T	O	F	U	S	E	L	A	G	E
Z	Y	R	A	T	I	L	I	M	T	N	I	A	P
S	C	A	L	E	M	A	O	F	L	I	G	H	T
K	I	T	S	T	R	A	P	L	A	S	T	I	C

Model Aircraft

D	I	U	E	V	E	I	S	E	V	I	N	K	K
D	R	E	D	E	E	T	M	N	X	N	F	V	O
O	O	A	S	O	R	E	D	N	A	L	O	C	O
O	N	T	W	A	A	A	R	A	T	R	O	M	B
F	O	I	I	E	W	Q	W	E	V	O	T	S	K
P	R	N	B	A	R	E	W	E	K	S	P	E	O
Y	E	G	S	S	E	R	P	I	K	A	T	C	O
R	T	H	B	P	V	G	N	I	N	A	E	L	C
E	A	B	O	W	L	G	I	S	L	R	B	E	S
L	R	F	R	Y	I	N	G	P	A	N	C	A	K
T	G	H	T	U	S	K	G	W	H	O	T	V	R
U	A	L	U	T	A	P	S	S	P	C	P	E	O
C	K	T	O	O	L	S	U	P	J	V	D	R	F
F	L	A	T	W	A	R	E	R	E	L	E	E	P
R	M	W	C	L	B	R	S	P	O	O	N	S	N
A	S	F	G	M	B	U	T	H	U	K	M	X	U

Kitchen Utensils

```
E M S C O I L E D D R T P L
T A P F R E E N A D W H A O
R C O R B O U N C I N G D O
A R R A C O G H S Y T I S H
P O T M B E I T T A U L O C
E B S E R G N I L L A F M S
Z A R O H H C T E R T S E Y
E T U N O I T A E R C E R R
S S C I T S A N M Y G V S U
I Y I S A F E T Y N E T A J
C A A T U M B L I N G T U N
R L A S P R I N G S H M L I
E P G R A V I T Y L P A T E
X C I R B A F O E I N T I C
E S U C R I C T N D N U O R
L E E T S X E G N I V I D Q
```

Trampolines

```
G N I K O M S N I A R B Y X
P P U Q I L L N E S S O Y N
H L A T N E M U E S S D H O
Y C A M R A H P C I E Y E I
S H I E C I N I L C N M A T
I I F T A C T I V I T Y L A
C L O N G E V I T Y I B T C
A D W Y N I L B O E F R H I
L R A E N F E Y S N E M Y D
E E G G L N O I T A C U D E
S N N A E L C O T S P A S M
T W E F R R N M D T E A R R
R A I I E I E E L F E F M E
E T A X G N S A S S L I I A
S E E Z T Y R K I S S U D L
S R E S T O H D W E I G H T
```

Health

```
T O T E M L E H Z W M O D N
L P L Z D Y G U U U E I C B
O O E G N I R E V O C B R V
G S F T A H Y O B W O C H B
U T U R B A N Y S W Z E A O
C G J F T R D N L S P S R N
Z A Y D A D H E A D E E Z S
G U P E E H R P R B R C V T
S X C S W A G Y A B I U C R
F H R I S T N L M I Y K W A
T O O G E C L O T H I N G W
E O W N L F S E I N A E B H
R D N U Y T T O P H A T H A
E O A S T S T A V I S O R T
B W T H S V P A N A M A L U
O J P A S D F A R O D E F W
```

Hats Off

```
J Y S P A C E X E L P M O C
T H R E E L E V A T O R I A
L F O Q M E G A R O T S D B
L H O U C O N T R A C T U L
A L L L S Y H H T C Y P T E
M I F S E I T I L I T U S I
S V D W Q A N I K R I K F C
R I E W B I S G C T R L L R
I N C K E Y S E L C U A A A
A G N I D L I U B E C W T M
T N A T R A L B N L E E N P
S I R C O U K I I E S F E E
H K T H O N L A N D L O R D
A R N E M D N E I G H B O R
R A E N S R S T N A N E T K
E P E T S Y W I N D O W S C
```

Apartment Living

Z	S	K	C	I	T	S	P	A	L	S	N	L	O
T	U	X	S	T	O	R	Y	N	N	U	F	A	B
E	R	I	T	A	S	F	T	V	P	O	N	B	H
V	P	O	E	M	O	T	I	O	N	I	A	R	J
J	R	F	A	E	A	T	W	F	A	R	C	E	L
G	I	O	S	S	N	O	O	T	R	A	C	V	X
A	S	N	H	U	M	O	R	T	O	L	I	O	E
G	E	L	O	B	R	E	P	Y	H	I	V	R	G
S	R	U	Y	I	T	W	L	K	V	H	I	P	U
T	U	C	X	N	H	S	A	R	C	A	S	M	L
A	T	N	E	M	E	S	U	M	A	P	U	I	Z
N	L	A	I	C	O	S	G	S	Y	P	A	S	J
D	U	Y	J	U	H	O	H	E	M	Y	L	C	G
U	C	O	M	E	D	Y	I	K	C	I	P	C	F
P	N	X	T	X	E	T	N	O	C	U	L	F	Z
V	F	T	I	M	I	N	G	J	D	T	M	E	W

Humor Me

H	G	N	I	P	P	O	H	S	I	T	E	M	S
N	E	W	D	R	A	E	G	A	T	N	I	V	D
R	O	O	E	R	S	R	M	U	S	E	U	M	P
Y	R	O	A	O	T	U	T	I	L	I	T	Y	O
U	G	D	L	A	R	N	O	I	T	C	U	A	R
N	I	X	E	D	A	R	E	T	F	N	C	N	C
I	A	D	R	S	R	N	Y	W	O	A	O	Z	E
Q	N	V	U	H	I	S	T	O	R	I	C	A	L
U	T	A	T	O	T	R	U	I	T	I	O	T	A
E	C	L	I	W	Y	Z	A	C	Q	P	N	L	I
S	E	U	N	R	R	D	E	B	O	U	D	W	N
T	J	A	R	J	O	L	B	T	L	O	I	O	R
A	B	B	U	I	L	T	T	U	I	E	T	N	U
T	O	L	F	O	A	E	C	R	Y	C	I	C	G
E	D	E	C	O	R	H	E	I	C	A	O	C	S
S	A	L	E	Y	Z	P	C	X	V	L	N	V	Q

Antiques

M	E	T	I	L	L	E	T	A	S	B	C	L	B
O	L	R	E	T	R	A	H	C	W	L	A	A	C
V	I	Y	L	L	I	B	R	T	N	T	S	M	B
I	N	F	S	A	E	D	E	P	I	I	K	U	N
E	E	E	W	I	V	V	D	G	C	M	R	I	S
S	U	E	E	X	I	Y	I	M	T	V	O	M	M
E	P	S	N	A	S	D	V	S	D	B	W	E	S
R	R	H	O	O	N	E	O	I	I	R	T	R	E
V	O	O	Z	C	E	M	R	H	S	O	E	P	T
I	G	W	I	I	P	O	P	L	C	A	N	S	O
C	R	T	R	N	X	C	E	C	O	D	O	P	M
E	A	I	E	E	E	N	F	B	V	C	I	O	E
F	M	M	V	M	N	O	W	B	E	A	T	R	R
A	S	E	G	A	K	C	A	P	R	S	A	T	F
T	B	S	H	X	O	B	H	R	Y	T	T	S	O
Z	Z	C	O	M	C	A	S	T	N	P	S	E	X

Cable Television

S	K	I	N	N	E	R	U	S	A	E	L	P	H
F	A	C	E	M	T	D	E	R	I	M	D	A	O
K	G	M	Y	R	E	R	U	T	L	U	C	G	T
A	O	L	A	O	U	E	Y	P	P	C	G	I	P
W	M	N	A	T	U	R	E	E	E	O	N	R	E
M	A	S	A	M	T	T	C	R	R	M	I	L	C
O	A	E	I	E	O	R	H	F	C	P	N	U	N
D	F	G	M	R	O	U	A	E	E	L	A	F	O
E	A	M	A	L	A	S	R	C	P	E	E	I	C
L	Y	E	O	Z	H	H	A	T	T	X	M	T	L
S	H	C	D	I	I	R	C	I	U	I	E	U	A
X	C	E	O	I	G	N	T	O	A	O	V	A	S
E	C	N	A	G	E	L	E	N	L	N	O	E	S
B	E	H	O	L	D	E	R	S	P	A	L	B	I
G	P	R	E	T	T	Y	T	S	E	T	N	O	C
L	O	O	K	S	K	H	P	E	R	S	O	N	Q

Beautiful

H	C	R	A	E	S	E	R	E	L	I	E	F	B
N	N	N	O	I	T	A	C	I	D	E	M	P	A
U	Y	I	P	P	F	E	V	E	R	Y	O	R	L
R	L	D	R	A	H	N	P	A	R	R	T	E	T
S	I	F	O	I	T	Y	C	A	V	U	P	V	I
E	X	A	M	B	P	H	S	K	I	J	M	E	D
S	S	T	C	P	T	S	O	I	S	N	Y	N	I
E	Z	L	E	L	E	N	A	L	C	I	S	T	A
S	M	L	A	C	I	D	E	M	O	I	B	I	G
A	P	E	E	T	N	N	I	M	T	G	A	O	N
E	H	N	R	P	I	A	I	A	T	E	Y	N	O
S	D	R	U	G	S	P	R	C	T	A	S	B	S
I	I	L	L	N	E	S	S	U	S	R	E	T	I
D	H	E	A	L	I	N	G	O	S	S	I	R	S
O	G	E	N	E	T	I	C	S	H	N	K	C	T
A	P	H	A	R	M	A	C	Y	C	R	I	T	S

Medicine

E	L	B	I	S	I	V	P	T	N	H	Z	Z	N
C	A	V	K	R	J	F	V	D	H	W	Z	E	Y
N	A	S	A	Z	Q	Q	Q	R	S	G	M	V	Z
E	U	P	E	S	P	I	L	C	E	O	I	E	U
I	B	P	O	S	S	E	N	K	R	A	D	N	H
C	L	L	N	E	S	U	N	L	I	G	H	T	E
S	A	N	O	O	M	L	L	U	F	U	R	N	P
R	I	O	Z	C	Y	C	L	E	M	A	M	T	O
P	T	I	I	W	K	R	A	R	E	B	A	O	C
A	S	T	R	O	N	O	M	Y	R	K	R	T	S
S	E	C	O	D	N	D	E	N	G	I	L	A	E
S	L	A	H	A	B	P	A	R	T	I	A	L	L
E	E	R	E	H	P	S	O	M	T	A	I	I	E
S	C	F	A	S	V	I	E	W	I	N	G	T	T
K	L	E	V	R	E	S	B	O	R	R	A	Y	S
Y	O	R	B	I	T	E	C	A	P	S	K	N	L

Lunar Eclipse

R	M	O	V	I	E	S	C	I	H	P	A	R	G
F	D	S	S	S	E	C	C	U	S	I	E	W	S
R	I	G	C	A	R	T	O	O	N	U	F	A	M
O	N	O	L	K	Q	Z	F	R	M	K	I	L	L
I	S	T	E	V	E	J	O	B	S	P	R	L	I
D	R	S	F	F	C	F	E	R	U	T	A	E	F
U	A	R	A	N	I	M	A	T	O	R	S	N	G
T	C	E	Y	L	D	L	A	W	A	R	D	S	Y
S	R	T	A	R	N	O	S	F	V	J	I	S	E
T	E	C	H	N	O	L	O	G	Y	U	G	R	N
R	L	A	M	P	N	T	P	W	U	D	I	E	S
O	E	R	V	P	E	D	S	Z	Y	B	T	T	I
H	A	A	F	A	M	I	L	Y	F	L	A	S	D
S	S	H	T	P	O	L	Q	A	O	M	L	N	I
O	E	C	O	M	P	U	T	E	R	T	Q	O	V
Z	T	E	U	H	V	T	T	F	X	M	R	M	H

Pixar

M	Y	W	J	B	U	J	O	T	R	I	C	K	T
E	K	J	A	U	F	R	E	G	A	W	M	S	D
L	A	O	M	R	H	O	N	I	S	A	C	B	J
D	C	K	X	E	D	I	I	N	Y	M	M	U	R
E	E	E	A	L	Y	P	I	N	O	C	H	L	E
C	S	R	A	A	F	A	M	I	L	Y	T	C	L
K	T	S	L	E	T	M	G	S	D	N	A	H	F
S	I	P	D	D	O	N	G	U	M	N	T	J	F
L	U	L	G	N	I	L	B	M	A	G	G	L	U
Q	S	A	E	T	O	R	L	S	I	I	O	F	H
S	U	Y	T	W	U	M	T	W	D	B	F	R	S
W	D	E	F	L	K	A	A	F	R	U	I	E	P
K	B	R	E	R	I	A	T	I	L	O	S	K	A
A	N	S	A	N	N	T	D	B	D	D	H	O	D
T	A	E	H	C	G	G	U	C	J	Y	S	P	E
L	W	I	N	N	E	R	H	C	U	E	R	G	S

Play a Card

T	O	L	P	N	K	C	I	R	E	M	I	L	E
N	Y	D	E	M	O	C	Q	U	S	K	O	O	B
E	R	I	T	A	S	I	G	N	I	T	T	E	S
C	L	I	M	A	X	O	T	C	I	R	Y	L	R
C	S	I	M	I	L	E	A	C	I	P	E	P	A
A	I	S	E	A	L	L	U	S	I	O	N	O	L
N	M	V	I	R	L	A	M	A	R	D	T	E	L
A	A	D	G	E	N	A	N	E	C	D	O	T	E
L	G	F	G	L	B	E	T	V	A	P	C	R	V
O	E	O	A	O	O	C	G	L	R	I	O	Y	O
G	R	A	S	B	A	S	L	O	L	H	D	S	N
Y	Y	U	T	R	L	A	S	F	P	E	T	O	Y
A	X	T	A	E	B	E	N	A	G	O	M	N	N
S	N	H	N	P	R	O	T	A	R	R	A	N	O
S	C	O	Z	Y	C	E	R	Y	S	Y	U	E	R
E	Y	R	A	H	M	T	S	I	S	E	H	T	I

Literary

E	C	N	E	T	N	E	S	H	E	R	I	F	F
D	Y	N	V	L	E	G	A	L	U	F	M	T	R
X	E	B	I	G	D	E	C	I	S	I	O	N	G
A	N	F	D	S	T	C	A	R	T	N	O	C	S
E	R	L	E	T	N	E	D	E	C	E	R	P	C
L	O	I	N	N	J	U	D	G	E	S	T	E	H
P	T	V	C	T	D	E	L	U	I	K	R	T	O
R	T	I	E	O	L	A	S	L	V	O	U	U	O
I	A	C	G	R	F	A	N	A	I	O	O	T	L
S	S	E	N	T	I	W	N	T	C	B	C	A	A
O	O	A	J	U	D	I	C	I	A	R	Y	T	W
N	C	A	Y	E	C	O	N	O	M	I	C	S	Y
B	I	X	L	P	L	A	I	N	T	I	F	F	E
L	E	C	I	T	S	U	J	R	E	D	R	O	R
S	T	H	G	I	R	P	O	L	I	T	I	C	S
P	Y	T	L	I	U	G	A	V	E	L	I	A	B

Law

C	L	O	C	K	S	M	I	T	H	C	H	E	F
O	H	X	A	P	P	R	E	N	T	I	C	E	C
B	T	O	O	L	S	S	E	N	I	S	U	B	A
B	B	I	E	W	A	T	C	H	M	A	K	E	R
L	S	R	E	T	N	I	A	P	S	R	A	G	P
E	T	I	R	O	N	W	O	R	K	E	R	D	E
R	O	T	C	A	R	T	N	O	C	D	T	E	N
E	N	S	I	D	K	F	A	F	A	L	I	L	T
B	E	I	N	L	D	A	M	E	L	I	S	W	E
M	M	N	A	I	V	R	Y	S	B	U	A	O	R
U	A	I	H	U	O	C	E	S	L	B	N	N	E
L	S	H	C	G	N	I	N	I	A	R	T	K	H
P	O	C	E	S	R	E	R	O	B	A	L	H	C
A	N	A	M	E	L	A	U	N	A	M	A	F	T
Y	G	M	Z	M	R	O	O	F	E	R	K	C	U
D	E	L	L	I	K	S	J	R	E	B	R	A	B

Tradesman

H	E	A	L	T	H	Y	D	D	W	M	S	N	I
U	A	N	W	R	U	I	I	G	U	W	S	U	S
B	P	I	L	A	T	E	S	S	I	S	E	T	C
O	S	Z	J	I	T	L	C	M	T	E	R	R	I
X	D	S	U	N	Z	L	M	R	T	E	P	I	B
I	H	T	M	I	E	I	O	A	T	Q	G	T	O
N	D	R	P	N	N	P	R	C	R	U	E	I	R
G	O	E	R	G	S	T	H	T	E	I	L	O	E
N	I	N	O	V	R	I	I	I	A	P	O	N	A
I	D	G	P	A	N	C	K	V	D	M	B	L	E
K	R	T	E	G	I	A	I	I	M	E	E	I	L
L	A	H	M	R	D	L	N	T	I	N	S	F	C
A	C	Y	C	L	I	N	G	Y	L	T	I	T	Y
W	G	U	Y	P	B	A	T	H	L	E	T	I	C
F	I	T	N	E	S	S	J	A	G	O	Y	N	I
T	H	G	I	E	W	R	U	N	N	I	N	G	B

Exercise

E A C A D E M I C I L B U P
V C L A W S N O I T C E L E
I H C Y N C A M P A I G N S
T A T M N O L A N O I T A N
U N N P I O I D S E X A T L
C G E P O L I T I C I A N A
E E M M B D I T U V P S H R
X P N E A U E T P L U C O E
E R R T U I G C A U O T U D
C E E A T A L T I R R V S E
O S V T H V F R P S Y R E F
N I O S O O W O A O I L O R
O D G T R G R O U P W O M C
M E I M I A C I T I Z E N Z
Y N P R T A R C O M E D R S
G T C E Y T I R O J A M U M

Political

W I R E S C H E M A T I C S
L E L L A R A P S C Y A I L
A S N W W G X U O E P C G A
T H R Y R A B N D A R H O N
I Y I O R S N N C O E I L G
G D U E T E O I T D S P E I
I N W R C C T C P R I C V S
D O A T I O U T M A S I I P
P T I L R D M D A O T R T O
E O I S N P M P N B A C A S
N S G O L A N A O I N U G I
G E C U R R E N T N C I E T
I D S G D E T A R G E T N I
S O A D J R E E N I G N E V
E I L R O T S I S N A R T E
D D E L R C O M P U T E R S

Electronic Circuits

Y T I D E R E H E G B A L R
G E V O L U T I O N K S N E
E V I S S E C E R I O L V D
N C R T T M O L E C U L A R
O O U B N S B M Y N I E C O
T D S A E Y I U S E N C O S
Y E E C R L O T G U H S R I
P V S T A I L A N Q E T G D
E R A E P M O T I E R R A O
N T O R N A G I R S I U N M
I R N I I F Y O P A T C I I
C A Q A V A G N S E E T S N
I I Y A X A T S F S D U M A
D T H G I E H I F I F R S N
E S N A M U H E O D C E A T
M G N I D E E R B N L I F E

Gene Study

H C S D E R O V A L F D P L
O H B T K S E J K P E L M O
N E E L N N U N S W E E T O
E R V K O A I N E S T E A C
Y R E O S Q R R S T I R T I
N Y R H K W B U D W E S C S
O M A A T C E O A L Q E C X
O I G I S U A E L T C V W N
P N E H N P O L T U S A Q S
S T O U A S B S B T G E A U
S U B T P V T E E Z E L R B
C S M E P P S A R W L A I W
Q O A M L I B P N R C E Z A
O C L L E A L S N T Y T O T
H P A D G R E E N M J H N E
F Z L S U N T E A S U G A R

Iced Tea

D	E	T	I	M	I	L	Q	G	O	L	D	U	M
O	C	R	B	T	S	E	R	O	F	N	I	A	R
C	O	P	P	E	R	E	G	P	S	D	N	A	L
E	L	B	A	W	E	N	E	R	E	A	R	T	H
I	O	E	U	N	I	T	E	F	G	H	S	I	F
B	G	G	C	N	R	V	S	E	P	T	N	P	A
N	Y	O	I	O	I	M	M	K	S	K	A	R	Q
S	A	M	L	R	S	E	D	E	C	F	T	O	S
L	T	E	R	I	N	Y	R	I	A	O	U	T	O
A	U	H	A	T	M	O	S	P	H	E	R	E	I
M	W	E	G	X	F	C	Y	T	F	Z	E	C	L
I	A	N	O	I	T	E	L	P	E	D	G	T	S
N	T	E	W	W	L	A	K	E	S	M	A	I	O
A	E	R	O	M	I	N	E	R	A	L	S	O	L
T	R	G	O	H	S	S	U	D	N	I	W	N	A
V	G	Y	D	J	F	O	S	S	I	L	V	E	R

Natural Resources

A	G	Q	L	O	V	E	L	T	T	A	E	S	Y
C	T	U	T	S	R	A	C	S	O	T	H	A	A
T	W	I	M	Y	A	P	E	Z	R	E	S	G	R
I	E	B	R	P	T	R	F	S	D	R	A	W	A
N	I	L	O	G	R	I	E	U	Y	M	L	O	T
G	L	L	E	O	R	O	R	H	N	I	P	O	S
C	L	C	F	V	T	E	D	B	T	N	S	D	Y
O	H	I	A	A	I	M	E	U	E	A	Y	Y	M
M	O	A	T	S	M	S	O	N	C	L	F	D	D
E	L	O	R	N	T	O	I	V	M	E	E	I	F
D	L	O	I	A	E	A	U	O	I	I	R	C	I
I	Y	L	C	Z	C	L	W	S	N	E	L	P	L
A	W	T	H	W	P	T	A	A	C	C	S	E	M
N	O	D	R	A	G	N	E	T	Y	I	I	P	A
R	O	T	O	Y	S	T	O	R	Y	O	M	N	L
A	D	S	N	A	Y	R	G	E	M	V	N	M	L

Tom Hanks

T	B	Z	B	S	A	U	S	A	G	E	S	T	Y
T	T	N	U	R	X	J	L	Z	N	F	E	G	K
S	A	V	T	P	T	T	M	I	I	I	L	D	L
D	E	N	I	A	R	T	C	C	D	L	F	L	S
R	M	I	N	I	A	T	U	R	E	K	F	R	R
E	A	P	C	N	R	H	N	M	E	Q	U	K	O
T	H	L	I	E	O	O	S	K	R	R	R	O	H
T	X	M	P	G	P	U	F	R	B	A	T	S	M
I	A	S	D	S	L	S	G	O	H	O	F	X	G
L	C	T	M	O	T	E	B	P	O	B	E	Q	N
U	H	E	V	A	M	P	T	U	E	D	R	S	I
Z	E	P	I	S	R	E	T	S	S	L	A	D	D
Y	R	L	K	C	O	T	S	E	V	I	L	Z	E
B	V	Q	N	U	L	W	D	T	S	W	I	N	E
F	N	A	P	N	B	I	G	N	I	M	R	A	F
M	S	M	X	Y	U	B	L	B	A	C	O	N	H

Pigs

N	S	P	R	I	V	A	T	E	C	I	F	F	O
U	C	H	Q	T	N	E	I	T	A	P	H	W	D
R	L	A	S	R	E	V	I	N	U	D	O	H	R
S	I	R	R	E	D	I	V	O	R	P	M	O	U
I	N	M	E	A	S	E	C	I	V	R	E	S	G
N	I	A	S	T	H	O	S	P	I	T	A	L	S
G	C	C	E	M	V	L	D	I	S	E	A	S	E
N	S	Y	A	E	C	N	A	R	U	S	N	I	R
I	T	M	R	N	M	B	Y	B	I	A	Z	M	U
D	H	A	C	T	Y	R	T	S	I	T	N	E	D
N	G	X	H	L	T	H	O	C	T	W	R	D	E
E	I	E	I	S	E	N	I	C	C	A	V	I	C
P	R	M	U	R	G	S	S	E	C	C	A	C	O
S	A	D	A	A	Y	S	S	E	N	L	L	I	R
F	N	P	I	H	T	L	A	E	H	M	O	N	P
I	Y	D	P	O	L	I	T	I	C	A	L	E	W

Health Provider

T	N	I	L	F	Q	E	T	I	N	A	R	G	J
N	Z	C	O	A	L	U	L	I	S	S	O	F	A
E	N	O	T	S	D	N	A	S	I	D	E	E	D
M	K	E	T	I	C	A	D	R	L	E	T	L	E
I	G	N	E	O	U	S	K	S	T	I	I	A	N
D	I	A	M	O	N	D	C	I	S	Z	D	H	O
E	M	U	D	S	T	O	N	E	T	P	I	S	T
S	L	A	T	E	R	A	D	V	O	E	B	T	S
R	C	P	R	I	S	N	O	O	N	P	R	T	E
G	H	H	A	A	A	B	L	L	E	E	U	O	M
A	A	Y	B	O	S	A	O	C	G	T	T	N	I
B	L	L	O	I	P	U	M	A	N	I	M	A	L
B	K	L	D	L	I	M	I	N	E	R	A	L	S
R	M	I	I	U	I	S	T	I	I	O	G	I	L
O	A	T	U	F	F	T	E	C	S	I	M	T	U
N	E	E	E	L	B	B	E	P	S	D	A	E	H

Rock Types

C	I	R	B	A	F	E	L	T	H	E	M	P	R
X	R	D	Y	E	S	P	I	N	N	I	N	G	J
M	A	O	A	L	P	A	C	A	N	O	N	M	S
I	N	L	C	G	N	I	R	O	L	I	A	T	G
L	G	R	F	H	L	G	T	Y	H	T	Y	E	N
L	O	X	E	Y	E	T	N	T	E	A	J	X	I
K	R	O	R	T	O	T	O	R	R	C	F	T	V
L	A	C	W	C	T	L	I	N	E	N	A	U	A
I	A	I	I	H	C	A	H	N	D	G	S	R	E
S	L	H	R	T	L	E	P	U	G	I	H	E	W
L	R	E	T	S	E	Y	L	O	P	S	I	G	M
H	A	E	C	A	S	H	M	E	R	E	O	N	I
D	L	K	B	T	Y	R	T	S	U	D	N	I	N
K	O	G	N	I	T	T	I	N	K	G	P	W	E
W	O	V	E	N	F	G	R	A	Y	O	N	E	D
C	M	J	S	X	E	D	N	A	P	S	Y	S	J

Textiles

Q	P	B	G	L	O	D	A	R	P	A	S	H	T
R	Y	H	L	E	N	I	L	N	O	O	F	H	E
E	L	G	O	O	G	G	H	T	N	L	S	C	N
T	W	E	B	N	R	I	P	A	E	Y	S	R	A
U	S	Y	A	W	E	T	A	G	T	R	E	A	P
O	N	G	L	W	H	A	R	D	W	A	R	E	R
R	E	O	U	W	P	L	G	C	O	T	D	S	A
U	T	L	I	I	O	G	E	E	R	I	D	E	L
H	S	O	S	T	G	O	L	R	K	L	A	R	I
E	C	N	E	W	C	R	E	N	S	I	U	M	N
M	A	H	G	S	R	E	T	U	P	M	O	C	K
O	P	C	D	M	A	I	N	F	R	A	M	E	S
D	E	E	I	N	T	E	R	N	E	T	F	L	L
E	D	T	R	L	O	C	O	T	O	R	P	P	F
M	C	A	B	L	E	S	T	E	K	C	A	P	S
U	F	L	I	A	M	E	T	S	Y	S	S	A	H

Internet History

K	J	S	R	E	A	M	E	J	D	O	O	W	J
N	O	J	T	E	N	V	E	L	O	P	E	G	T
I	A	O	P	A	P	E	R	M	I	L	L	N	B
T	M	U	B	A	T	A	F	T	Z	P	C	I	O
H	O	R	Q	E	P	I	P	I	R	R	Y	T	O
G	N	N	J	S	T	Y	O	S	B	E	C	N	K
I	E	A	G	O	R	O	R	N	W	E	E	I	S
E	Y	L	N	L	E	E	N	U	E	E	R	A	G
W	S	S	I	U	U	P	P	R	S	R	N	P	N
R	S	E	G	L	S	T	F	A	S	D	Y	N	I
I	O	G	A	L	S	D	R	E	P	R	W	O	P
T	L	A	K	E	I	K	N	A	C	L	I	B	P
I	G	P	C	C	T	I	P	U	L	P	L	R	A
N	S	G	A	B	L	E	T	T	E	R	S	A	R
G	N	E	P	P	R	I	N	T	I	N	G	C	W
N	W	H	I	T	E	E	H	S	N	I	H	T	D

Paper

Z	T	S	I	T	R	A	L	U	P	O	P	R	T
N	A	I	C	I	S	U	M	T	V	J	Y	O	E
A	O	U	T	R	A	G	E	O	U	S	O	M	M
M	V	I	D	E	O	S	A	S	A	E	U	A	A
O	P	R	H	A	I	R	T	T	M	H	N	N	F
W	S	E	E	S	A	D	D	Y	E	T	G	C	E
Y	C	O	G	G	A	L	R	L	R	O	N	E	H
T	T	E	N	N	N	F	E	E	I	L	I	C	T
A	R	I	C	G	I	I	S	J	C	C	C	C	E
M	N	E	R	A	W	M	S	T	A	R	N	E	L
O	A	N	C	B	F	R	R	P	N	N	A	N	E
N	W	A	O	N	E	R	I	O	O	O	D	T	P
S	A	P	N	D	O	L	E	T	F	P	C	R	H
T	R	Y	A	N	A	C	E	K	E	R	Q	I	O
E	D	C	I	S	U	M	K	C	O	R	E	C	N
R	S	U	P	I	Z	Z	A	R	A	P	A	P	E

Lady Gaga

E	N	I	C	I	D	E	M	S	F	U	N	G	I
S	T	U	D	Y	B	I	O	L	O	G	Y	E	O
H	T	W	O	R	G	P	S	L	A	T	I	N	E
Q	J	P	P	B	O	P	V	E	W	A	T	E	R
J	T	M	A	L	G	A	E	C	A	N	F	T	U
S	S	A	L	C	A	N	G	A	O	S	S	I	T
D	I	E	U	E	C	N	E	I	C	S	E	C	A
E	N	O	I	T	I	R	T	U	N	A	L	S	N
E	A	H	F	L	H	U	A	L	U	R	B	R	T
S	T	C	Z	C	L	S	T	D	I	G	A	E	I
H	O	R	N	O	M	L	I	O	S	F	T	W	S
E	B	A	V	E	Y	G	O	L	O	C	E	O	S
R	R	E	T	A	X	O	N	O	M	Y	G	L	U
B	G	S	S	T	R	U	C	T	U	R	E	F	E
S	R	E	D	D	O	F	Z	L	E	A	V	E	S
G	A	R	D	E	N	S	E	I	C	E	P	S	I

Studying Plants

P	I	E	S	W	C	O	V	E	N	F	T	H	L
H	T	U	N	H	G	U	O	D	L	D	O	O	F
Y	Y	N	A	P	O	L	E	O	N	C	R	Y	B
B	I	C	A	V	X	C	U	R	O	H	T	B	A
U	A	A	H	S	A	R	A	O	H	S	E	R	K
T	S	K	F	E	S	L	K	T	D	I	T	E	E
T	F	E	I	F	F	I	K	N	T	N	A	A	R
E	F	S	L	N	N	N	O	A	R	A	L	D	Y
R	U	W	L	G	G	W	L	R	B	D	O	R	S
S	P	E	I	H	S	I	D	U	C	I	C	A	G
T	M	E	N	V	A	Y	K	A	L	F	O	T	G
R	A	T	G	N	I	N	E	T	R	O	H	S	E
A	E	F	Z	T	R	E	S	S	E	D	C	U	N
T	R	U	O	F	T	I	T	E	P	G	E	C	O
C	C	O	K	L	E	D	U	R	T	S	U	R	C
H	M	I	L	K	H	C	N	E	R	F	M	S	S

Pastry

C	A	N	N	E	D	M	W	J	K	N	I	P	K
E	N	L	H	C	T	A	C	Y	F	H	H	H	J
E	I	M	B	A	I	F	A	I	S	B	E	U	B
G	E	I	F	A	R	H	S	U	L	L	N	I	T
R	T	W	I	E	C	H	S	U	P	A	G	I	S
A	O	S	S	N	E	O	E	E	E	E	N	A	S
L	R	H	H	R	O	F	R	C	Y	W	N	T	T
Y	P	E	I	T	I	I	O	E	A	D	N	Y	A
E	R	E	N	N	S	A	L	T	W	A	T	E	R
N	S	U	G	W	S	M	E	I	R	E	L	L	K
I	E	A	C	A	T	R	C	U	I	B	E	L	I
R	A	W	L	R	A	H	A	D	O	K	M	O	S
A	F	M	K	A	E	T	S	A	N	U	T	W	T
M	O	H	J	S	S	M	T	E	L	L	I	F	H
N	O	V	N	E	T	S	Y	G	O	L	O	I	B
I	D	M	R	H	I	D	O	L	P	H	I	N	S

Tuna

E	Z	F	R	H	Y	E	N	A	S	P	B	U	C
X	D	M	B	E	C	L	E	C	N	I	R	P	I
T	E	L	M	A	H	C	I	T	B	L	O	H	K
T	G	I	N	O	I	T	A	M	I	N	A	P	I
A	I	F	B	S	L	Z	A	O	A	D	D	E	F
M	L	M	S	A	D	K	N	F	V	F	W	L	A
S	L	A	O	F	R	S	I	E	X	O	A	G	R
A	L	Y	N	N	E	A	N	N	H	L	Y	N	C
C	A	J	G	X	N	T	S	S	G	S	E	U	C
I	C	G	S	O	U	T	L	A	N	D	S	J	Y
R	I	W	A	R	T	H	O	G	E	V	O	L	R
F	S	Y	E	N	S	I	D	P	L	Y	O	M	O
A	U	I	E	I	V	O	M	E	E	R	K	A	T
Z	M	X	M	S	C	A	R	T	O	O	N	I	S
Z	A	Z	U	B	T	H	E	A	T	E	R	U	T
M	U	F	A	S	A	A	B	M	U	P	L	A	Y

The Lion King

K	E	L	B	U	O	D	U	M	M	Y	C	V	F
H	T	R	O	N	S	O	U	T	H	A	N	D	S
F	A	T	R	I	C	K	S	C	O	R	I	N	G
L	C	L	O	C	K	W	I	S	E	A	A	U	K
L	I	Y	S	T	I	U	S	P	M	U	R	T	S
A	L	G	G	U	K	R	X	O	A	C	Z	N	B
C	P	I	L	E	E	U	N	H	G	T	P	E	U
N	U	M	K	N	T	D	R	E	D	I	D	M	L
C	D	S	T	S	S	A	E	A	R	O	E	A	C
O	Q	R	A	E	E	W	R	R	A	N	A	N	H
M	A	E	B	G	D	E	A	T	C	T	L	R	A
P	W	Y	L	D	A	S	L	S	S	E	I	U	N
A	N	A	E	I	P	T	C	A	R	T	N	O	C
S	K	L	W	R	S	L	E	V	E	L	G	T	E
S	E	P	K	B	I	D	D	I	N	G	J	M	K
I	Y	M	I	R	E	B	B	U	R	U	O	F	D

Contract Bridge

J	L	E	G	A	L	X	E	L	P	M	O	C	H
U	N	I	T	S	A	T	N	A	N	E	T	W	S
B	T	A	R	O	T	A	V	E	L	E	N	E	E
E	U	A	P	F	N	R	B	G	S	C	E	I	L
G	Y	I	L	A	E	L	U	E	O	O	D	V	L
A	N	T	L	F	R	E	I	C	P	M	I	Z	O
G	H	I	I	D	Q	T	S	S	T	M	S	W	O
T	A	I	L	C	I	S	M	R	O	U	E	S	P
R	L	D	B	L	O	N	O	E	W	N	R	N	R
O	L	I	I	O	E	N	G	N	N	I	A	E	O
M	W	C	S	R	A	W	D	W	H	T	H	I	P
L	A	N	D	L	O	R	D	O	O	Y	S	G	E
F	Y	E	S	A	E	L	D	E	U	L	E	H	R
M	S	W	A	L	Y	B	F	M	S	O	M	B	T
P	I	H	S	R	E	N	W	O	E	F	I	O	Y
O	V	G	N	I	S	U	O	H	B	T	T	R	S

Condominium

L	R	Y	P	H	Y	S	I	C	S	C	H	B	F
I	W	O	R	K	D	I	R	E	C	T	I	O	N
Q	I	S	N	O	I	T	A	U	Q	E	R	D	L
U	S	N	G	D	E	E	P	S	L	C	Z	I	A
I	E	V	A	Y	O	H	W	I	E	H	S	E	W
D	L	K	L	I	G	H	T	S	V	N	C	S	S
S	C	E	I	R	N	C	P	C	M	O	I	Y	C
H	I	P	L	Y	E	O	A	U	S	L	N	T	I
A	T	L	E	J	S	L	T	S	V	O	A	I	M
I	R	E	O	I	C	N	A	W	I	G	H	V	A
T	A	R	T	U	E	M	I	T	E	Y	C	A	N
R	P	I	L	M	M	A	C	H	I	N	E	R	Y
E	O	U	O	X	M	A	T	H	U	V	M	G	D
N	S	M	O	T	A	G	A	L	A	X	I	E	S
I	S	T	U	D	Y	V	E	L	O	C	I	T	Y
A	C	I	T	E	N	I	K	E	N	E	R	G	Y

Classical Mechanics

T	S	P	E	L	T	N	V	T	E	L	L	I	M
I	W	D	E	T	U	N	T	S	E	H	C	A	R
T	E	I	E	A	T	U	N	L	A	W	C	F	E
E	H	B	L	E	N	T	I	L	S	A	O	R	W
S	S	J	R	D	S	U	S	E	D	C	W	U	O
N	A	B	A	A	R	Z	T	A	Z	F	P	I	L
A	C	E	C	H	Z	I	M	S	N	I	E	T	F
E	R	F	O	C	H	I	C	K	P	E	A	S	N
B	S	L	R	P	A	G	L	E	I	H	S	M	U
Y	N	A	N	N	M	P	I	N	E	N	U	T	S
O	I	X	H	A	Z	E	L	N	U	T	K	D	E
S	A	B	U	C	K	W	H	E	A	T	N	N	M
N	R	T	E	Y	E	Q	U	I	N	O	A	S	U
R	G	B	S	Y	N	I	K	P	M	U	P	D	G
J	K	B	C	E	R	E	A	L	S	Q	Q	S	E
T	F	D	K	S	N	B	A	R	L	E	Y	N	L

Edible Seeds

Y	H	D	I	G	I	T	A	L	E	V	A	R	T
D	A	N	N	P	Y	A	L	P	S	I	D	A	O
N	N	U	V	B	M	D	C	L	F	U	T	L	W
I	D	O	E	I	O	G	I	K	E	O	K	A	E
W	S	R	N	G	N	O	R	C	M	B	E	R	R
A	E	T	T	B	O	L	T	I	O	M	S	M	A
L	T	I	I	E	R	A	C	T	N	U	E	S	L
L	U	M	O	N	T	N	E	L	O	L	C	E	O
R	N	E	N	S	S	A	L	G	R	U	O	H	S
A	I	P	X	L	A	T	E	Z	T	D	N	C	Z
E	M	I	L	I	T	A	R	Y	E	N	D	T	F
Y	R	E	T	T	A	B	A	U	M	E	S	A	N
C	U	C	K	O	O	D	M	C	M	P	C	W	O
U	N	E	V	I	T	A	R	O	C	E	D	H	O
L	A	I	D	N	U	S	E	T	T	I	N	G	N
M	O	N	T	H	S	Q	R	Q	U	A	R	T	Z

Telling Time

N	X	D	E	S	K	T	O	P	S	T	M	G	T
C	O	P	I	E	R	A	W	D	R	A	H	A	R
J	M	O	N	I	T	O	R	S	E	S	H	R	O
S	J	G	N	I	K	R	O	W	T	E	N	A	P
R	I	N	K	J	E	T	T	D	U	R	W	G	P
E	E	C	P	O	L	K	I	S	P	V	B	E	U
T	P	N	A	A	L	G	T	A	M	E	U	G	S
N	E	D	O	L	I	X	E	L	O	R	S	D	T
I	R	L	R	T	I	A	P	E	C	S	I	I	O
R	A	N	A	A	N	F	M	S	I	D	N	R	R
P	W	L	Y	G	O	L	O	N	H	C	E	T	A
A	T	D	N	A	R	B	C	R	R	D	S	R	G
O	F	F	I	C	E	O	Y	I	N	E	S	A	E
S	O	N	S	C	A	N	N	E	R	I	P	C	B
M	S	A	R	E	M	A	C	D	K	S	A	A	C
S	P	O	T	P	A	L	A	B	O	L	G	X	P

Hewlett-Packard

W	R	T	L	G	N	I	I	K	S	S	S	L	M
C	R	E	E	K	N	M	D	N	O	P	P	L	V
E	P	R	W	C	O	I	I	E	K	L	I	E	W
D	C	U	O	O	U	W	T	N	L	O	G	W	H
I	R	N	D	S	H	A	A	A	E	T	O	Y	T
T	F	O	M	D	P	S	F	V	O	R	T	R	A
W	C	F	P	W	L	R	R	B	E	B	A	O	B
T	T	F	A	S	E	E	I	G	H	S	I	L	B
G	N	T	L	T	S	F	N	N	N	E	C	T	T
B	E	L	A	N	P	I	I	I	K	A	E	N	S
R	R	W	O	A	K	U	A	H	Z	L	B	E	R
I	R	C	X	N	J	Q	R	S	T	I	E	R	I
D	O	M	I	G	D	A	M	I	X	O	R	R	H
G	T	R	N	A	E	L	C	F	F	B	G	U	T
E	D	P	O	T	A	B	L	E	R	Y	S	C	V
S	B	A	Y	S	T	R	E	A	M	A	E	T	S

Here's Some Water

F	Y	C	Z	S	B	M	B	Q	B	P	U	O	S
A	O	O	N	N	H	O	M	E	T	R	A	U	Q
W	U	O	G	N	I	V	R	E	S	E	R	P	G
R	A	K	D	L	W	T	V	H	E	S	A	I	D
A	I	T	I	S	T	A	E	M	V	S	J	C	F
A	O	N	E	T	E	L	G	D	A	U	N	K	I
Q	G	Y	G	R	F	O	E	E	C	R	O	H	S
S	X	P	N	L	N	D	T	L	U	E	S	N	H
T	H	G	I	T	R	I	A	A	U	J	A	R	S
I	R	F	G	N	K	W	B	E	M	E	M	N	A
U	E	R	A	S	D	I	L	S	B	O	A	D	R
R	N	E	K	C	Y	U	E	K	M	E	T	A	L
F	N	S	C	D	E	S	S	E	C	O	R	P	H
H	A	H	A	G	F	A	C	T	O	R	Y	F	P
A	C	P	P	G	L	E	G	A	R	O	T	S	G
F	A	N	U	T	R	J	E	L	L	Y	L	S	U

Canning

M	U	L	T	I	B	A	L	L	D	R	A	I	N
I	P	L	A	Y	F	I	E	L	D	M	M	T	P
L	M	A	G	I	C	P	O	S	T	P	O	A	S
I	T	B	R	E	V	O	L	L	O	R	D	R	X
G	S	E	A	U	T	O	S	A	V	E	E	G	O
H	T	E	M	B	O	P	D	M	S	P	S	E	B
T	O	R	B	A	I	L	A	T	P	P	T	T	K
S	P	F	O	N	C	T	O	I	M	G	N	S	C
E	P	R	N	K	C	H	L	L	A	I	I	N	A
H	E	E	U	H	S	F	I	T	R	N	O	P	B
C	R	K	S	G	R	E	G	N	U	L	P	O	U
T	E	C	N	G	E	G	A	M	E	A	U	P	T
I	P	I	T	O	P	K	C	A	J	N	C	P	T
W	L	K	O	B	M	O	C	Y	C	E	O	E	O
S	A	H	C	N	U	A	L	E	F	J	I	R	N
Q	Y	J	O	R	B	I	T	S	O	U	N	D	S

Pinball

S	T	L	N	S	Y	V	Y	O	T	I	L	A	K
T	N	A	O	E	R	F	D	N	B	E	N	C	H
N	E	I	I	C	U	E	E	R	U	N	E	T	W
E	D	R	S	I	J	D	N	O	I	N	I	P	O
M	E	T	I	T	I	E	N	F	E	I	H	C	L
U	C	O	C	S	T	R	E	B	O	R	G	Y	A
G	E	Y	E	U	S	A	K	Y	I	O	I	E	W
R	R	R	D	J	I	L	R	Y	V	M	N	A	Y
A	P	P	E	L	L	A	T	E	S	I	S	P	E
S	E	S	A	C	I	I	R	G	N	H	B	P	R
E	C	C	X	C	R	N	N	D	I	Y	U	O	S
G	S	N	I	O	M	I	T	N	O	V	R	I	A
D	P	D	J	E	L	E	G	A	L	C	G	N	M
U	U	A	N	U	E	T	A	N	E	S	K	T	O
J	M	T	R	U	O	C	H	G	I	H	W	E	H
P	L	A	I	N	T	I	F	F	Q	M	C	D	T

The Supreme Court

E	S	O	N	O	O	T	R	A	C	O	R	A	L
I	S	F	E	E	R	X	Q	Y	E	N	D	Y	S
V	K	Y	E	N	R	U	O	J	R	J	S	E	N
O	R	E	H	T	A	F	E	N	O	M	E	N	A
M	A	B	A	R	R	A	C	U	D	A	R	S	C
H	H	G	I	L	L	S	C	C	I	L	U	I	I
Y	S	U	K	R	D	H	U	L	N	O	T	D	L
P	M	U	A	N	I	M	A	T	I	O	N	L	E
T	I	D	R	L	A	R	U	W	L	H	E	L	P
S	Y	X	D	C	T	T	I	K	R	C	V	U	J
I	D	R	A	S	M	U	H	C	A	S	D	G	A
T	E	T	U	R	T	L	E	S	M	F	A	A	N
N	M	A	S	S	W	I	M	M	I	N	G	E	C
E	O	G	M	O	J	E	L	L	Y	F	I	S	H
D	C	W	H	A	L	E	M	X	N	A	E	C	O
F	W	A	T	E	R	Y	R	O	D	I	V	E	R

Finding Nemo

W	Y	G	O	L	O	C	E	C	N	E	I	C	S
A	G	E	N	E	T	I	C	S	P	U	O	R	G
I	R	E	L	I	G	I	O	N	T	O	O	L	S
W	S	N	N	S	E	G	A	U	G	N	A	L	A
C	E	O	P	E	T	H	N	I	C	I	T	Y	K
A	I	I	C	H	A	C	U	L	T	U	R	E	S
H	R	T	P	I	I	L	A	C	I	S	Y	H	P
U	T	U	S	E	O	L	O	F	A	M	I	L	Y
M	N	L	B	I	O	L	O	G	I	C	A	L	D
A	U	O	C	O	U	P	O	S	Y	T	H	G	U
N	O	V	Q	D	I	G	L	G	O	I	R	L	T
I	C	E	R	U	T	A	N	E	Y	P	R	A	S
T	S	N	I	G	I	R	O	I	V	A	H	E	B
Y	R	A	C	E	T	H	N	O	L	O	G	Y	P
R	E	S	E	A	R	C	H	I	S	T	O	R	Y
D	P	I	H	S	N	I	K	F	O	S	S	I	L

Anthropology

F	E	V	O	T	S	C	I	E	N	T	I	S	T
O	B	P	G	N	I	T	N	I	R	P	G	U	A
U	I	R	L	M	L	S	V	S	O	A	O	I	L
N	F	E	I	J	I	I	E	P	H	T	V	N	M
D	O	S	G	A	G	R	N	O	T	R	E	E	A
I	C	I	H	I	D	I	T	S	U	I	R	G	N
N	A	D	T	D	I	T	I	T	A	O	N	A	A
G	L	E	N	U	P	A	O	M	D	T	M	J	C
P	S	N	I	Y	L	S	N	A	W	S	E	L	I
O	E	T	N	R	O	O	S	S	E	F	N	M	R
L	I	R	G	A	M	S	V	T	F	Y	T	I	E
Y	N	E	G	R	A	E	A	E	Y	E	N	O	M
M	O	H	L	B	T	T	R	R	R	K	B	C	A
A	L	T	M	I	S	S	C	I	T	I	L	O	P
T	O	A	K	L	O	A	C	T	I	V	I	S	T
H	C	F	B	N	E	W	S	P	A	P	E	R	W

Benjamin Franklin

M	O	I	B	L	H	Z	V	E	N	E	E	R	D
E	T	U	L	F	P	W	T	F	D	R	A	O	B
B	R	I	A	U	E	M	A	R	F	L	T	U	X
L	R	W	D	Q	D	C	C	S	G	E	N	T	H
D	L	G	E	O	E	O	F	X	G	S	I	E	A
R	K	E	G	U	O	G	O	E	I	I	O	R	E
E	C	R	R	D	E	W	R	W	N	H	J	E	Z
B	A	T	A	G	L	R	T	I	D	C	G	M	I
M	R	I	I	B	N	N	A	F	T	R	E	M	S
U	V	M	N	D	R	I	M	U	O	O	A	A	L
L	I	A	T	E	V	O	D	O	Q	S	H	H	I
R	N	R	T	I	R	E	V	L	L	S	C	M	N
A	G	T	D	T	B	E	K	A	I	C	N	H	B
S	A	H	I	N	G	E	B	N	F	U	E	Y	N
P	E	S	I	V	Q	D	A	D	O	T	B	B	H
R	E	P	A	R	C	S	T	D	H	T	V	D	F

Woodworking

T	Y	P	B	R	A	Z	I	L	B	L	A	C	K
N	D	E	C	A	F	H	W	F	R	E	N	C	H
A	B	S	O	T	N	A	S	T	L	J	A	V	A
T	A	R	O	M	A	R	R	U	T	A	C	N	R
S	K	C	U	B	R	A	T	S	R	M	V	O	S
N	N	A	I	P	O	I	H	T	E	A	M	O	V
I	R	P	W	S	C	A	F	F	E	I	N	E	R
A	O	P	W	U	O	F	A	O	T	C	A	S	O
D	E	U	F	M	L	R	C	V	A	A	I	P	A
N	R	C	T	A	O	I	I	O	Y	N	I	R	S
A	O	C	M	T	M	C	P	N	N	D	A	E	T
G	B	I	O	R	B	A	Y	O	E	R	W	S	E
U	U	N	C	A	I	P	T	D	K	I	A	S	D
R	S	O	H	X	A	M	A	N	A	P	H	O	A
E	T	T	A	L	N	B	O	U	R	B	O	N	R
P	A	C	I	B	A	R	A	M	A	C	A	P	K

Coffee Varieties

G	I	N	I	T	R	A	M	O	V	I	E	S	C
U	I	I	D	F	L	E	M	I	N	G	I	P	N
N	E	K	A	H	S	I	T	I	R	B	O	I	S
S	C	M	L	I	F	S	V	C	A	S	J	E	N
G	C	H	T	H	T	N	E	G	A	L	I	S	L
R	O	M	O	O	N	R	A	K	E	R	R	O	G
L	C	S	N	E	M	O	W	S	K	I	A	O	M
O	E	E	Y	E	N	E	D	L	O	G	L	H	O
H	W	Q	E	R	U	T	N	E	V	D	A	F	C
C	A	R	S	F	U	G	B	O	F	N	N	O	T
Y	O	S	N	I	A	L	L	I	V	O	O	N	O
M	O	N	E	Y	P	E	N	N	Y	B	I	I	P
D	N	V	N	H	R	G	A	D	G	E	T	S	U
K	R	V	E	E	E	Y	Z	J	E	M	C	A	S
O	D	R	M	R	R	R	U	S	S	I	A	C	S
A	O	D	Y	S	S	Y	S	G	X	R	K	D	Y

Bond Movies

W	K	Y	E	N	I	L	N	O	T	S	Y	O	T
S	S	E	C	C	U	S	H	I	Y	R	F	G	V
D	R	N	I	A	H	C	D	S	L	A	E	D	F
O	Y	S	V	I	M	E	Y	E	S	L	L	U	B
O	P	T	R	A	R	R	W	C	E	W	R	D	S
F	R	O	E	C	L	E	A	R	A	N	C	E	A
T	O	R	S	I	J	U	A	H	I	W	R	P	L
N	D	E	O	L	R	P	E	T	P	A	G	A	E
U	U	S	N	G	P	A	U	R	W	T	N	R	S
O	C	P	A	A	O	R	V	E	M	O	I	T	H
C	T	H	S	I	E	L	S	L	O	S	H	M	O
S	S	E	N	I	S	U	B	I	N	E	T	E	P
I	D	A	B	O	O	K	S	A	E	N	O	N	P
D	O	L	C	H	E	A	P	T	Y	N	L	T	I
R	O	T	U	L	L	A	M	E	R	I	C	A	N
M	G	H	Y	R	E	C	O	R	G	M	J	Z	G

Target Corporation

F	N	X	D	O	L	L	S	A	A	S	N	B	Z
R	I	Y	Z	G	D	L	N	U	I	E	Z	F	U
I	S	R	Y	D	L	W	Y	A	R	R	N	O	G
S	E	R	L	A	A	N	T	F	A	R	M	N	J
B	L	A	B	S	E	R	U	G	I	F	S	W	P
E	B	E	M	T	O	Y	C	A	R	S	T	H	V
E	R	B	E	R	N	K	K	Z	C	B	U	I	K
L	A	Y	S	H	E	C	N	X	R	L	F	S	F
Z	M	D	S	F	W	I	X	L	A	O	F	T	S
Z	D	D	A	M	K	T	F	H	F	C	E	L	K
U	K	E	N	B	J	S	O	X	T	K	D	E	C
P	S	T	E	A	B	O	M	H	D	S	V	S	U
N	S	W	C	R	P	G	F	L	H	E	W	C	R
U	P	K	A	B	Y	O	T	R	E	K	N	I	T
M	S	T	T	I	C	P	O	T	J	G	T	T	N
B	Z	N	F	E	M	A	G	B	F	X	O	N	I

Fun for Kids

S	P	A	C	E	R	E	H	C	N	U	A	L	P
N	N	P	I	N	Y	J	S	E	T	S	E	M	J
F	R	O	T	K	V	E	N	S	R	O	T	O	M
L	E	G	S	R	E	C	O	V	E	R	Y	D	I
I	D	E	A	E	T	T	I	Y	M	O	T	E	A
G	U	E	L	V	C	I	T	L	A	C	E	L	Q
H	T	E	P	I	U	O	I	B	E	K	F	F	I
T	I	N	H	S	R	N	N	M	R	E	A	I	G
H	T	G	S	O	T	V	G	E	T	T	S	N	F
R	L	I	H	L	S	S	I	S	S	R	I	S	U
U	A	N	O	P	N	A	C	S	D	Y	G	T	N
S	S	E	O	X	O	S	M	A	L	L	I	I	H
T	P	S	T	E	C	W	E	F	L	I	I	K	O
D	E	P	L	O	Y	M	E	N	T	E	D	U	B
C	E	E	T	U	H	C	A	R	A	P	E	G	B
P	D	O	O	W	U	F	I	R	E	P	A	P	Y

Model Rocket

Y	T	E	X	T	B	O	O	K	S	G	Y	M	H
O	Y	E	L	S	T	U	D	E	N	T	S	U	S
P	T	C	O	L	L	E	G	E	M	V	C	S	I
E	I	N	O	I	T	A	C	U	D	E	O	I	L
N	S	E	H	T	A	M	L	S	S	Y	M	C	G
E	R	I	C	G	S	U	A	D	E	R	P	A	N
R	E	C	S	N	C	P	S	Y	I	A	U	F	E
D	V	S	E	I	B	L	S	R	T	D	T	E	T
L	I	G	R	N	U	A	R	A	I	N	E	T	E
I	N	R	P	R	I	Y	O	T	V	O	R	E	A
H	U	A	A	A	L	G	O	N	I	C	S	R	C
C	T	D	P	E	D	R	M	E	T	E	T	I	H
E	E	U	E	L	I	O	S	M	C	S	X	A	E
X	S	A	R	U	N	U	G	E	A	A	M	G	R
A	T	T	M	Y	G	N	E	L	D	D	I	M	S
M	S	E	S	U	B	D	R	E	A	D	I	N	G

Going to School

H	T	N	A	Y	O	U	B	O	A	R	D	S	R
Q	N	A	T	U	R	A	L	R	F	B	A	R	K
R	C	L	S	S	S	T	A	O	L	F	F	E	U
N	H	A	N	D	L	E	S	I	B	Z	L	P	F
O	A	E	L	O	L	A	G	U	T	R	O	P	I
F	M	S	L	L	A	W	C	D	D	D	O	O	W
K	P	K	A	O	K	R	O	C	T	N	R	T	T
V	A	B	B	E	N	O	R	X	S	E	I	S	H
E	G	U	E	U	W	A	K	L	C	L	N	U	G
U	N	L	S	S	Y	X	S	Y	A	S	G	B	V
S	E	L	A	S	T	I	C	I	T	Y	O	E	V
Q	N	E	B	I	V	L	R	S	F	T	R	R	P
U	L	T	W	T	I	E	E	E	T	N	P	I	U
M	J	I	P	N	T	E	W	L	E	Z	L	N	L
F	N	N	G	A	E	C	E	I	R	R	Z	A	R
E	S	B	M	V	C	L	L	T	T	L	T	I	R

Cork

S	G	I	N	T	E	R	N	E	T	A	P	E	S
L	D	Y	E	L	E	A	R	N	I	N	G	X	E
S	O	V	R	E	S	R	E	T	U	P	M	O	C
R	C	A	D	A	R	M	E	D	I	A	N	K	R
E	A	H	N	O	N	F	I	C	T	I	O	N	U
A	T	S	O	R	W	O	R	R	O	B	I	O	O
D	A	F	E	O	N	F	I	N	E	S	T	W	S
I	L	V	H	E	L	P	C	T	Y	N	A	L	E
N	O	I	T	C	E	L	L	O	C	A	C	E	R
G	G	N	I	D	N	E	L	Q	Y	I	U	D	M
C	S	E	C	N	E	R	E	F	E	R	D	G	O
H	C	R	A	E	S	E	R	V	I	A	E	E	V
P	U	B	L	I	C	H	I	L	D	R	E	N	I
E	U	D	R	E	V	O	F	E	L	B	A	T	E
B	O	O	K	S	M	A	G	A	Z	I	N	E	S
N	O	V	E	L	S	E	S	S	A	L	C	D	S

At the Library

R	H	G	N	I	H	S	A	W	M	E	A	L	S
E	U	I	T	Y	R	D	N	U	A	L	A	W	N
P	S	B	R	X	J	K	I	T	C	H	E	N	S
A	B	K	R	O	W	E	S	U	O	H	H	O	E
I	A	T	B	O	N	W	O	M	E	N	O	R	C
R	N	G	T	S	O	I	E	P	C	U	U	P	I
S	D	R	N	Y	E	M	N	A	H	T	S	A	V
C	C	O	E	I	A	R	R	G	I	R	E	G	R
L	H	C	M	K	S	P	O	N	L	I	H	N	E
E	I	E	E	E	E	A	R	H	D	T	O	I	S
A	L	R	G	T	S	U	H	O	C	I	L	P	E
N	D	I	A	T	F	T	O	C	A	O	D	E	H
I	R	E	N	W	E	F	I	W	R	N	H	E	T
N	E	S	A	C	G	T	K	C	E	U	K	W	O
G	N	I	M	U	U	C	A	V	F	B	P	S	L
O	D	U	S	T	I	N	G	N	I	K	O	O	C

Homemaking

L	O	N	D	O	N	D	N	A	L	G	N	E	L
G	H	G	R	A	T	I	U	G	I	R	O	C	K
E	S	C	N	S	T	R	E	C	N	O	C	R	H
Y	T	U	I	I	Y	S	C	L	D	I	Y	O	S
M	A	T	C	R	R	A	I	S	A	T	B	V	I
M	R	H	R	C	O	V	D	V	I	D	A	I	T
A	P	V	E	G	E	T	A	R	I	A	N	D	I
R	E	Y	L	R	P	S	B	L	E	T	E	A	R
G	R	R	P	O	M	E	S	D	B	T	C	E	B
S	F	O	P	K	L	E	U	F	H	U	S	A	R
E	O	T	A	E	B	J	F	G	U	O	M	E	Z
L	R	S	C	C	Y	A	I	C	P	L	T	S	Y
T	M	I	G	E	M	N	S	M	O	N	A	I	P
A	E	H	H	O	K	N	O	S	I	R	R	A	H
E	R	M	U	S	I	C	I	A	N	S	O	L	O
B	L	S	G	N	I	W	P	L	E	N	N	O	N

Paul McCartney

S	E	L	L	I	N	G	N	I	P	P	O	H	S
P	R	O	F	I	T	N	U	O	C	S	I	D	T
D	U	Y	R	E	V	I	L	E	D	E	M	B	E
D	E	S	E	S	A	H	C	R	U	P	O	U	L
R	C	P	C	U	S	T	O	M	E	R	S	Y	T
S	R	M	A	K	M	O	N	E	Y	W	W	E	U
G	E	A	V	R	E	L	S	C	W	H	W	R	O
N	M	R	Q	S	T	C	U	D	O	R	P	S	P
I	M	K	V	E	I	M	M	L	Z	H	Y	B	R
Y	O	E	S	I	T	R	E	V	D	A	O	E	I
U	C	T	T	S	C	S	R	N	L	U	G	W	C
B	R	I	O	A	A	E	S	P	T	A	K	A	I
L	E	N	R	L	B	U	S	I	N	E	S	S	N
L	D	G	E	E	R	I	Q	A	S	D	O	O	G
A	I	R	S	S	D	U	M	A	I	L	I	U	L
M	T	A	C	H	E	C	K	O	U	T	K	Q	S

Retailing

D	N	S	E	N	I	L	R	U	L	G	L	J	C
T	N	E	M	P	I	U	Q	E	N	L	E	F	J
U	I	V	G	Q	D	R	A	I	N	A	G	E	Q
B	A	L	C	A	X	D	P	W	R	E	N	C	H
I	M	A	O	F	P	I	R	F	S	L	O	O	T
N	R	V	U	I	P	B	K	I	T	C	H	E	N
G	E	R	P	T	R	S	U	X	N	G	G	P	F
K	T	E	L	T	Q	T	S	T	S	K	I	L	L
Z	A	B	I	I	E	E	P	U	H	C	I	S	A
I	W	M	N	N	G	L	M	R	E	T	Y	N	N
C	R	U	G	G	A	I	U	E	A	S	A	Q	G
I	O	L	Y	S	W	O	P	S	T	R	S	B	E
T	K	P	T	F	E	T	N	E	E	E	K	R	S
P	P	I	P	E	S	B	M	D	R	T	N	A	N
E	C	A	W	E	T	S	A	W	S	E	I	S	E
S	H	O	W	E	R	T	R	A	P	M	S	S	R

Plumbing

G	N	I	N	I	A	R	T	U	O	K	R	O	W
Y	S	E	E	F	B	A	R	B	E	L	L	S	E
M	E	M	B	E	R	S	H	I	P	O	O	C	F
N	N	W	E	L	L	N	E	S	S	E	K	I	B
A	I	E	O	L	G	E	L	C	S	U	M	B	T
S	H	I	I	I	N	S	T	R	U	C	T	O	R
I	C	G	D	P	I	L	A	T	E	S	F	R	E
U	A	H	R	T	M	L	C	O	L	E	F	E	A
M	M	T	A	I	M	E	B	Q	C	S	F	A	D
M	T	S	C	C	I	B	X	L	Y	S	A	F	M
A	G	O	Y	A	W	B	S	E	C	A	C	I	I
E	P	O	O	L	S	M	N	P	R	L	I	T	L
T	N	E	M	P	I	U	Q	E	O	C	L	N	L
S	V	M	Y	G	S	D	L	O	G	R	I	E	S
A	N	U	A	S	R	E	N	I	A	R	T	S	N
D	M	H	E	A	L	T	H	A	C	M	Y	S	E

Health Club

D	H	S	U	G	A	R	E	T	I	L	S	C	V
O	R	A	N	G	E	I	C	E	D	T	E	A	P
W	P	U	R	Y	S	N	R	O	C	G	P	C	U
S	E	B	Y	T	G	P	E	X	A	P	O	T	N
R	P	O	T	E	I	D	R	R	N	K	P	I	E
O	S	T	R	R	N	F	E	I	E	I	A	S	V
V	I	T	E	E	G	V	I	N	T	T	D	O	E
A	Y	L	P	E	E	P	A	C	N	E	O	P	S
L	Z	E	P	B	R	U	D	U	I	A	S	E	E
F	Z	D	E	T	A	N	O	B	R	A	C	D	L
A	I	R	P	O	L	F	S	S	S	A	L	G	B
N	F	I	R	O	E	W	M	J	U	I	C	E	B
T	G	N	D	R	E	D	A	N	O	M	E	L	U
A	H	K	R	E	F	R	E	S	H	I	N	G	B
W	A	R	T	S	E	I	R	O	L	A	C	B	A
E	N	I	E	F	F	A	C	E	P	A	R	G	T

Soft Drinks

R	J	M	A	R	O	T	S	I	S	N	A	R	T
O	R	E	D	L	O	S	C	O	M	P	L	E	X
T	I	U	C	R	I	C	S	W	P	B	R	J	P
C	E	R	O	C	A	M	P	L	I	F	I	E	R
U	E	C	A	P	A	C	I	T	O	R	S	T	O
D	L	L	H	A	N	A	L	O	G	E	T	A	C
N	E	A	E	N	N	W	R	D	M	E	N	R	E
O	M	V	T	C	O	O	O	E	E	N	E	T	S
C	E	L	E	I	T	L	W	S	M	I	N	S	S
I	N	S	A	S	G	R	O	I	O	G	O	B	O
L	T	I	I	Z	A	I	O	G	R	N	P	U	R
I	S	S	B	O	A	R	D	N	Y	E	M	S	E
S	E	P	I	H	C	O	R	C	I	M	O	K	W
R	N	S	R	E	T	U	P	M	O	C	C	T	O
H	A	R	D	W	A	R	E	V	I	S	S	A	P
C	Q	E	C	I	V	E	D	N	R	E	D	O	M

Integrated Circuits

S	P	E	C	I	A	L	X	H	G	S	O	U	S
Y	R	T	N	A	P	R	O	N	N	Y	F	K	G
Y	R	T	S	A	P	E	L	L	I	R	G	B	T
S	O	R	D	E	R	N	V	E	K	A	B	O	M
K	I	T	C	H	E	N	S	E	O	N	P	V	M
I	T	R	F	A	N	I	R	V	O	I	W	E	T
L	E	E	L	T	T	D	E	I	C	L	N	N	M
L	E	S	I	U	I	Y	S	T	B	U	R	N	R
E	R	S	N	N	C	S	T	U	G	C	G	P	C
D	A	E	E	I	E	E	A	C	N	R	C	L	S
I	P	D	C	F	F	V	U	E	I	E	U	A	M
S	E	L	O	O	R	I	R	X	N	A	I	T	B
H	R	R	O	R	E	N	A	E	I	T	S	I	O
E	P	D	K	M	N	K	N	K	A	E	I	N	E
S	A	L	A	D	C	A	T	E	R	I	N	G	H
S	L	E	T	O	H	M	E	A	T	H	E	A	D

Professional Chef

W	D	E	T	N	E	M	G	E	S	L	T	K	T
O	N	E	E	R	G	F	B	R	P	A	G	L	R
L	E	A	V	E	S	R	A	O	R	R	N	I	E
L	P	T	E	Y	I	R	Y	V	I	V	I	S	E
E	F	D	C	G	L	A	M	I	N	A	D	P	K
Y	U	S	H	E	A	F	S	B	G	L	I	U	Y
Q	Z	T	A	S	S	T	R	R	O	N	L	P	P
P	Z	N	I	U	Y	N	S	E	C	O	S	A	D
E	Y	A	R	M	R	E	I	H	T	P	N	A	N
S	J	L	Y	M	H	H	W	U	E	T	M	V	E
T	E	P	W	E	C	O	B	C	E	A	U	A	G
S	Y	Q	G	R	R	U	I	N	G	R	T	B	N
H	E	G	A	M	L	E	N	E	M	O	D	B	A
T	S	N	S	A	S	A	L	L	A	M	S	S	H
O	O	H	R	N	E	D	R	A	G	W	X	H	C
M	U	O	W	N	T	B	Q	J	I	I	V	B	H

Caterpillar

A	S	N	T	F	B	G	C	I	R	C	U	S	V
B	O	O	E	O	O	L	S	P	A	C	E	C	T
R	C	A	P	R	N	A	U	Z	O	O	A	I	A
A	I	F	O	E	O	M	O	P	S	P	W	E	T
I	A	R	R	S	B	I	R	R	T	M	I	N	I
N	L	I	A	T	O	N	O	I	R	I	L	C	B
S	U	C	N	C	M	A	V	M	O	H	D	E	A
T	V	A	G	S	O	I	I	A	N	C	V	L	H
U	S	G	U	R	T	M	N	T	G	O	L	A	Y
D	T	N	T	Y	E	G	M	E	L	I	N	F	E
Y	R	I	A	M	N	A	O	U	R	A	Y	A	K
N	E	B	N	A	M	O	T	O	N	W	B	M	N
N	N	M	H	M	G	I	G	A	D	I	A	I	O
U	G	I	A	N	O	G	B	J	P	A	T	L	M
F	T	L	O	N	G	A	R	M	S	E	L	Y	K
Z	H	C	R	A	E	S	E	R	T	O	O	L	S

Chimpanzees

S	O	E	X	P	E	N	S	I	V	E	L	Z	D
W	K	C	F	G	O	L	A	N	A	L	M	T	Y
I	I	E	O	O	C	I	T	I	Z	E	N	R	J
S	E	I	O	I	S	A	C	P	C	C	E	A	E
S	S	P	R	I	N	G	O	H	H	T	M	U	W
W	K	E	P	L	G	C	A	A	T	R	G	Q	E
A	C	M	R	K	K	N	I	A	A	O	T	H	L
T	O	I	E	E	I	N	B	L	L	N	E	O	S
C	L	T	T	C	E	T	A	D	D	I	L	U	R
H	C	T	A	W	P	O	T	S	I	C	E	R	I
S	I	L	W	R	I	S	T	W	A	T	C	H	A
I	T	A	S	E	T	U	N	I	M	A	A	A	P
L	S	T	D	F	A	S	H	I	O	N	R	N	E
V	A	E	S	R	E	B	M	U	N	W	B	D	R
E	L	M	L	A	T	I	G	I	D	N	A	B	Q
R	P	A	R	T	S	D	N	O	C	E	S	U	B

Watch It

L	D	X	E	L	P	A	M	F	P	A	P	E	R
V	T	D	D	E	L	M	S	U	I	A	X	Z	Y
A	I	M	S	U	Y	R	R	E	H	C	I	E	H
M	M	H	M	O	W	A	G	L	S	T	O	N	K
M	B	B	A	F	O	R	E	S	T	U	Y	I	T
K	E	K	Y	R	O	K	C	I	H	N	O	P	E
R	R	S	C	E	D	A	R	D	A	S	F	H	R
A	T	U	N	L	A	W	T	G	L	L	A	N	Y
B	D	O	O	W	T	F	O	S	O	I	C	O	L
S	T	R	E	E	S	H	H	O	U	G	U	O	G
T	A	B	L	E	A	O	R	H	D	D	T	B	C
A	Q	I	O	M	P	I	S	A	N	D	W	M	L
I	F	F	G	G	N	I	V	R	A	C	P	A	X
N	I	A	R	G	N	K	S	D	R	A	O	B	S
N	R	U	B	I	R	C	H	Q	B	L	H	G	F
G	G	R	F	L	F	M	N	C	N	S	C	E	G

Wood

D	I	U	Q	S	F	G	C	R	A	B	S	N	E
A	D	E	E	W	A	E	S	I	O	P	R	O	P
S	E	A	O	T	T	E	R	S	H	M	A	M	K
E	E	N	I	R	A	M	B	U	S	I	I	L	R
G	G	U	L	L	A	A	A	P	I	R	V	A	A
N	G	T	I	R	C	K	B	O	F	H	A	S	H
O	S	O	L	T	E	C	A	T	D	S	C	N	S
P	N	I	E	C	T	A	L	C	R	O	L	O	M
S	N	R	O	K	A	B	O	O	O	Y	A	E	O
C	I	R	R	L	C	P	N	L	W	S	H	G	L
A	A	I	G	L	E	M	E	G	S	T	W	R	L
L	L	A	A	P	A	U	D	I	V	E	R	U	U
L	E	M	O	C	N	H	S	I	F	R	A	T	S
O	S	D	E	T	R	I	T	U	S	S	N	S	K
P	S	U	L	I	T	U	A	N	E	E	L	A	B
S	M	O	T	A	I	D	O	L	P	H	I	N	N

Marine Wildlife

R	E	E	S	N	E	C	I	L	B	V	G	H	L
P	Q	E	Z	L	O	C	A	T	I	O	N	A	I
B	U	S	I	N	E	S	S	E	B	V	I	G	S
P	I	A	A	W	I	R	W	K	U	A	S	E	T
O	T	E	P	A	S	E	C	R	I	L	U	N	I
S	Y	L	R	L	E	N	O	A	L	U	O	T	N
T	T	P	O	N	X	W	M	M	D	E	H	S	G
C	P	N	P	O	A	O	M	K	I	C	N	E	N
A	T	N	E	M	T	S	E	V	N	I	Y	R	I
R	I	K	R	M	M	O	R	T	G	A	G	E	S
T	O	T	T	O	T	E	C	I	R	P	B	T	O
N	N	T	Y	C	J	R	I	D	H	E	S	N	L
O	B	E	L	S	E	L	A	S	R	O	F	I	C
C	C	A	R	A	X	E	L	P	U	D	M	F	G
G	N	I	L	L	E	S	S	N	A	O	L	E	O
D	B	R	O	K	E	R	G	N	I	Y	U	B	S

Real Estate

Q	Y	D	Y	E	S	E	N	I	R	U	G	I	F
B	R	O	U	H	A	T	S	S	K	O	O	B	J
S	E	L	T	T	O	B	C	L	A	N	I	H	C
D	T	L	E	N	S	D	R	A	C	T	S	O	P
R	T	S	A	E	H	L	W	M	F	B	N	C	A
O	O	S	P	W	P	M	I	I	I	I	O	U	O
C	P	A	O	S	A	J	N	N	L	C	T	R	E
E	L	L	T	P	R	T	E	A	M	P	T	R	M
R	A	G	S	A	G	A	R	W	S	S	U	E	A
O	T	Y	P	P	O	Y	C	A	E	T	B	N	G
C	E	T	M	E	T	J	E	L	I	L	R	C	A
K	S	O	A	R	U	C	B	N	E	N	R	Y	Z
S	N	Y	T	S	A	M	R	S	S	D	S	Y	I
N	I	S	S	N	I	U	V	F	D	I	O	L	N
U	O	E	S	H	F	M	U	S	I	C	D	M	E
G	C	X	T	O	S	E	A	S	H	E	L	L	S

Collectibles